Real Love

Real Love

in pursuit of cultural justice

Andrew Ross

NEW YORK UNIVERSITY PRESS

New York and London

NEW YORK UNIVERSITY PRESS
New York and London

Library of Congress Cataloging-in-Publication Data
Ross, Andrew, 1956–
Real love : in pursuit of cultural justice / Andrew Ross.
p.   cm.
Includes bibliographical references.
ISBN 0-8147-7504-7 (clothbound: acid-free paper). — ISBN
0-8147-7505-5 (paperback: acid-free paper)
1. Social justice.   2. Social justice—United States.   3. Culture—
Social aspects.   4. Culture—Social aspects—United States.
5. Popular culture.   6. Popular culture—United States.   I. Title.
HM216.R65   1998
303.3'72—dc21   97-45241
                        CIP

New York University Press books are printed on acid-free paper,
and their binding materials are chosen for strength and durability.

Manufactured in the United States of America

10 9 8 7 6 5 4 3 2 1

Contents

Acknowledgments

These essays were written during the Clinton years, and several have been substantially revised for this book. They were all written for specific occasions, commissioned as public lectures or for planned publications. Some were penned as public journalism, others were addressed to academic or artworld audiences. A few emerged out of the "Weather Report" column I wrote for *Artforum* from 1992 to 1997. Their common inspiration lies in a mix of personal, political, and scholarly interests—that blended genre of essay writing in which I feel most comfortable, honest, and real.

"Jobs in Cyberspace" was originally written at the invitation of Michiel Schwartz and John Thackara for a conference at the Netherlands Design Institute in Amsterdam. Portions were published in *New Perspectives Quarterly* 12, 1 (Winter 1997) and *Artforum* (December 1996). Many thanks are due to Heather Champ, Stefanie Syman, Vivian Selbo, and Marisa Bowe (and to Nicole Rustin, Rik Treiber, and Mabel Wilson, student fellow travelers on this trail).

"Mr. Reggae DJ, Meet the International Monetary Fund" was originally written at the invitation of Barry Chevannes for a conference at the University of the West Indies in Mona, Jamaica. An earlier version appeared in *Black Renaissance/Renascence Noire* 3 (Fall 1997). Many thanks are due to Norval Edwards for his help and comments. Also thanks to David Scott, Annie Paul, Joe Pereira, Stuart Hall, and Carolyn Cooper for their insights and hospitality.

"The Gangsta and the Diva" was originally written at the invitation of Katrina Vanden Heuvel for publication in the *Nation* (August 1994).

Hilton Als and Isaac Julien both encouraged me to develop the dialogue in different ways.

"The Private Parts of Justice" was written for publication in Toni Morrison, ed., *Race-ing Justice, En-Gendering Power: Essays on Anita Hill, Clarence Thomas, and the Construction of Social Reality* (New York: Pantheon, 1992). Special thanks to Wahneema Lubiano for her input and coordination.

"If the Genes Fit, How Do You Acquit? O.J. and Science" was written for publication in Toni Morrison and Claudia Brodsky Lacour, eds., *Birth of a Nation'Hood: Spectacle and Script in the O. J. Simpson Trial* (New York: Pantheon, 1997). Thanks to Dorothy Nelkin and Christine Harrington for their indispensable comments.

"The Great Un-American Numbers Game" was originally written at the invitation of John Hanhardt and Tom Keenan for a conference at the Fundacio Tapies in Barcelona. An earlier version was published in J. Hanhardt and T. Keenan, eds., *The End(s) of the Museum* (Barcelona: Fundacio Tapies, 1996). Students at the Whitney Independent Studio Program, along with Ron Clark, helped in crystallizing several of the ideas in this essay.

"What the People Want from Art?" was originally written at the invitation of Joseph Bakshtein for a symposium at the Institute for Contemporary Art in Moscow. An earlier version was published in *Artforum* (January 1994). Thanks to Vitaly Komar and Alex Melamid for a series of colorful dialogues and to Steve Fagin for his unabashed skepticism while in Moscow.

"The Lonely Hour of Scarcity" was originally written at the invitation of Sandra Tomc and Michael Zeitlin for a keynote address at the Canadian Association of American Studies in Vancouver. An earlier version was published in *Capitalism, Nature, Socialism* 7, 3 (September 1996). Jim O'Connor and Alan Rudy encouraged helpful revisions.

"Claims for Cultural Justice" was originally written at the invitation of Austin Sarat for a Colloquium in Law, Jurisprudence, and Social Thought at Amherst College. An earlier version was published in A. Sarat, ed., *Law and the Domains of Culture* (Ann Arbor: University of Michigan Press, 1997). Bruce Robbins, Toby Miller, Tom Keenan, and Christine Harrington all tried to keep me on track with this essay, and I am grateful to them.

Thanks are also due to Eric Zinner for taking this book to the next step, and to Alison Redick for her tireless research assistance.

A live dancehall performance in Jamaica can be a full body experience. Folks in the audience are not listening so much as responding at the top of their lungs to the motormouth flow of flirting, calling, and suggestive phrasing tossed out by the performer on stage. When half of the people in the crowd fall silent, inspect their feet, and stand to attention, you can't help but notice the shift in tone. This is the near-universal male response when a popular female performer like Lady Saw steps to the mike. Among female DJs, Saw leads the field in interpreting the lewd style of dancehall reggae. Her frank simulation of sexual acts, in gesture and lyrics, has gotten her banned from performing in other Caribbean island nations and has long attracted the censure of Jamaica's middle-class morality brokers. But when she performs for her fans, the silence of men is a powerful if sullen act of respect, as fiercely stifled as the enthusiasm of the women is unbridled. In this mute appraisal, she is being recognized for her skills, for doing justice to the dancehall genre, for seizing the lyrical prerogative in a field of DJs that is so competitive that performers have to petition their public constantly to stay in contention.

Paying respect with impassivity is a gendered rule of appreciation, although it is not reserved for males alone. In the nightclubs, it is the ultracool indifference of the ruling diva queens that commands the dance floor in the face of male attention from all points of the compass. Reading the rules in such an environment is a complex affair, and it is especially easy to mistake the theatrical conventions of performance for, say, codes of courtship.

In American R&B and hip hop, fans habitually distinguish between performers who "front" and those who "represent" (the real spirit of the genre). Keeping it real—a core watchword for integrity—is not just a

1

gesture of love for the music; it is also an act of faith in the community that the musical genre binds together and, more often than not, a tribute to the concern for social justice that underpins so many black musical traditions. While *realness*, that much-sought-after characteristic of vocalists, registers the authentic quality of a performance, it also records performers' awareness that theatricality has roots in social and economic conditions. Realness is a reminder of where they and their audiences have come from, and it is part of the contract that each genre sustains between performer and audience (and sometimes between different performance genres, as I try to show here in "The Gangsta and the Diva"). The interplay, for example, between Lady Saw's wanton acts and her silent male admirers makes more sense if you see it against the backdrop of social and economic changes that have accompanied the rise of dancehall music over the last fifteen years. In the chapter entitled "Mr. Reggae DJ, Meet the International Monetary Fund," I examine the relationship between these changes—which deeply affected the employment patterns and respective social standing of men and women—and the gendered conventions of the dancehall itself. Even in the party-driven genre of dancehall reggae, Jamaican popular music, long a primary source of information and public opinion, is not an escapist flight from social hardship so much as a stylized dialogue with the impact of economic forces.

The vital connection between economic life and cultural expression is a theme that runs throughout this book. This connection is what keeps culture real by giving meaning to the material conditions in which we find ourselves, and by helping to identify political claims that emerge from our dissatisfaction with these conditions. The strong version of this thesis has led me to dedicate this book to the passionate pursuit of what I call cultural justice—a real love, as I refer to it in the title. This concept takes a number of forms in the essays included here: doing justice to culture, pursuing justice through cultural means, and seeking justice for cultural claims, to name just three. However, readers are warned that they will not find here a compact theory of cultural justice to be commended or rebutted. With the exception of the first chapter, these essays are primarily case studies, and the arguments they offer arise out of the raw materials of a case history rather than from some preconceived explanatory pattern. Each tries to chart where the passions that underpin cultural justice have led us and, since they are always in social motion, where they may lead us yet. When it comes to cultural justice, nothing is very formalized.

For many of us who have been intellectually and politically active in an age bruised and scarred by the Culture Wars, it is second nature to view cultural politics as an inescapable part of any advocacy of social change. A countervailing view suggests that cultural politics is not *real*, or that it diverts our attention from the real issues—predominantly economic in nature—that inspire people's quest for justice. If ever there was a false dichotomy, both disabling and divisive, this is it.

The vast economic forces that take their daily toll on our labor, communities, and natural habitats are the most powerful elements in our social lives. The power with which they work on our world is exercised through cultural forms: legal, educational, political, and religious institutions; valued artifacts and documents; social identities; codes of moral sanctity; prevailing ideas about the good life; and fears of ruination, among many others. Without these forms, economic activity remains a lifeless abstraction in the ledgers and databases of financial record. Without an understanding of them, we impoverish our chances of building on those rights, aspirations, and collective affinities that promise alternatives to the status quo. If the cultural differences between people are a means of generating inequality, then the respectful recognition of these differences can also be a vehicle for the material and ethical improvement of our lives. Resourceful thinkers and activists have shown that it is possible to reverse the channels of official neglect, economic subordination, and cultural denigration and turn them into routes toward pride, empowerment, and equity.

Such observations are often now referred to as the "politics of recognition." I expand on this topic in the final essay in this volume, "Claims for Cultural Justice," which surveys some of the attempts to establish claims for cultural rights as a supplement to human rights. Should the state recognize group rights that arise out of the cultural membership or cultural identity of individuals? Questions like this, arising from the tradition of liberal thought, generally ignore the ways the state is far from neutral, inasmuch as it already favors the cultural rights of majority populations. In a multiethnic, multinational state like the United States, liberal concepts of equity and fairness are corrupt from the get-go, because the proverbial "level playing field" is already heavily defined by default settings that value Anglo-conformity, Christianity, heterosexual family life, and masculine privilege as normative features of the national symbology, curriculum, workweek, and taxation system. The recent ruckus over affirmative action and multiculturalism suggests that it may be best to consider cultural rights a more or less permanent feature of the political landscape rather than a temporary form of restitution for past injustices. In view of the current political climate, it remains to be seen whether such rights can and should be further formalized. Yet the inequities parlayed by the legal system—discussed in part here in the case of the O.J. trial ("If the Genes Fit, How Do You Acquit?") and the Anita Hill–Clarence Thomas hearings ("The Private Parts of Justice")—are too profound for us to evade the challenge.

While culture may be viewed as a vehicle for rights or political claims, part of my purpose is to show that justice must also be done to culture itself. Doing justice to culture, for example, includes respect for the rules and law of a genre. Verdicts passed upon the controversial or prejudicial content of cultural forms are often bereft of any knowledge about the genre—its ruling conventions, its history of formalistic self-consciousness, its particular demands on performers, its shifting contract with audience expectations, its social origins and uses, and so on. Any lay user or fan knows that the conventional rules exercise a kind of quasi-legal sway over what is possible to say and do within the limits of the genre; generically speaking, characters don't suffer gory deaths in TV sitcoms any more than they can be reincarnated without the help of advanced technology in science fiction novels. All too often, however, generic conventions are habitually neglected when charges of sexism, racism, or homophobia are brought to bear against a film, a song, or a custom.

In these hard times, dominated by the cruel, low-wage revolution of neoliberal economics, cultural activity is a major source of income and jobs in its own right. Traditionally, cultural work has been an invitation to underpayment. The new forms of creative labor in the information industries are no exception. There are jobs in cyberspace, but they don't pay much, and they utilize technologies that are often associated with disemployment. The recent emergence of an Internet industry based on digital arts design and Web journalism has promised a brave new future for online content and multimedia creativity. But it is not clear if Net libertarianism, which routinely ignores the labor conditions underpinning the information revolution, can live with the venture capitalists who have come calling in Silicon Alley. "Jobs in Cyberspace" describes the latest attempt to mix culture with commerce, and reviews the odds for and against honest job creation.

"The Lonely Hour of Scarcity," the penultimate essay in the book, scrutinizes the conditions under which a pro-scarcity culture has emerged since the onset of global economic restructuring in the mid-1970s. It disputes the conventional wisdom that austerity is based on a dwindling of resources and a contraction of distributable wealth. Environmentalist appeals based on Malthusian ideas about overpopulation and natural shortages have often been confused in the public imagination with the socially generated scarcity that elites employ to manage the distribution of resources. In a pro-scarcity climate, redistribution, especially to historically marginalized communities, is strictly limited in such a way as to encourage uncivil competition for a share of the public good. Appeals to demographics and population classifications become paramount.

In the census-driven America of statistical communities, the cult of numbers is balanced precariously against the concept of cultural rights. Numbers are democratic, yet their restrictive use as markers of entitlement offends people's sense of individual opportunity. Persistent debates over affirmative action may be the most visible expression of this conflict, but its impact can be found in a broad sector of public life. "The Great Un-American Numbers Game" and "What the People Want from Art?" examine how the cult of numbers, as applied to minority representation, has affected the principles of selection in museum exhibition and the art-world's realm of value judgment.

It is no coincidence that the rise of claims for cultural justice has occurred at a time when a pro-scarcity climate of austerity is also being established. The result is a widely shared perception that this is one form of justice we cannot afford. It is time to debunk this cynical perception, oppose its punitive consequences, and urge that we meet the next challenges of history in the spirit of the culture-and-class coalitions that have too often eluded us.

ONE

Jobs in Cyberspace

Remember all the giddy talk about the "information superhighway"? Well, it never got built—at least not the way Time Warner, Microsoft, and AT&T imagined it. As recently as 1993 the media Goliaths were spinning blue-sky fantasies about delivering five hundred cable channels and personalized pay-per services to your home, while collecting access tolls for the individual use of vast corporate libraries of information and entertainment product. The fantasies are still kicking around; unlike in 1993 when phone-cable mergers like Bell Atlantic-TCI were the model for interactive use, they are currently being traded between cable companies and software giants like Microsoft. Now that Microsoft has acquired WebTV along with the cable operator Comcast in June 1997, its hopes are pinned on consolidating high-speed Internet access via cable as the pipeline for vertical and horizontal integration of all entertainment and information services. Whether this strategy will prove any more financially viable than the earlier attempt at media convergence, there's no doubt that those revisions of the Telecommunications Act in 1996 and the Telecom Competition and Deregulation Act of 1995 that facilitate multimedia corporate mergers have laid the legal groundwork. Our hard-earned paranoia about the growth of monopolies in the world of old media has prepared us for the worst. Yet, as in all matters related to New Media, it seems as if the theory has preceded the practice. Everyone thinks they know what is supposed to happen . . . but it always hasn't happened yet.

The example of WebTV is a case in point. Its main purpose, after all, is to deliver the Internet to middle America. Four years ago, it was unthinkable that the Internet would even figure in this kind of scenario. It was not supposed to be invited to the corporate cyberparty. Once earmarked as a nigh obsolete relic of the pioneer days of digital communication—

reserved primarily for academic communication—it has now truly become the network of networks that was once its faux-grandiose moniker. Practically speaking, the Internet now functions as the information superhighway, and the big corporate players have reluctantly come to accept this fact. Microsoft's wholesale switch to Internet-oriented strategies ("Embrace and Extend" is the company motto) in December 1995 and the spirited entry of its Internet Explorer into the browser wars with Netscape Navigator have been one massive attempt to catch up with what many predicted would have been left sucking dust. Of course, since it entered the open standards environment of the Net, Microsoft has tried its level best to insinuate a proprietary architecture onto the World Wide Web (WWW). The Explorer—and Netscape in response—began to create proprietary HTML tags that the other cannot recognize, making it increasingly difficult to design Web pages that work with both browsers. While the Internet has absorbed the new corporate presence much more easily than anyone might have predicted, overtly proprietary moves like these are perceived as riding roughshod over its resident crypto-anarchist philosophy.

The Internet's physical infrastructure of cables, routers, and switches has proven less than adequate for the massive volume of new traffic. In place of the early projections of the National Information Infrastructure's (NII) Gigabyte Testbed Initiative for huge bandwidth serviced by billion-bit-per-second wires, the reality is more claustrophobic: brownouts plague major intersections on the Internet's regional backbones where waves of data packets converge and often disappear because of insufficient bandwidth. The explosive growth of multimedia applications—real-time audio, shockwave, video, animated gif files—for the graphic-intensive WWW is responsible not only for the traffic jams, but also for the rapid ascendancy of the Internet itself. In April 1997, the one millionth Web site address was registered, by Bonny View Cottage Furniture of Petroskey, Michigan. For those boosters who proclaim that the WWW has ushered in the greatest publishing breakthrough since the printing press, this is perceived as a million new "publications." But for those weaned on old media definitions of public communication, the geography of the Web is a strange landscape to host a new public sphere. After all, it was the Web that brought us the shopping malls and cyberstores, the advertis-

ers, the financial real estate, indeed the entire world of commercial agen
in hot pursuit of good addresses from which to promote and shop their
wares. Once the barbarians were on the Web, there was no looking back.
While distasteful to Net purists, the new commercial presence had little
difficulty, initially at least, in fitting in with the open architectural milieu
of Net culture. Nothing in the house religion of Net libertarianism
seemed at odds with the laissez-faire ideals of the corporations. Except, of
course, when it came to paying for stuff ("information wants to be free" is
a Net mantra). A free market and freedom of speech are one thing; free
products and shareware ethics are another. They are inevitably at odds.

But that little contradiction could be deferred for a while, at least as
long as Wall Street was boosting Netscape (with the largest IPO in financial history in 1995) and other public offerings of Internet stocks through
the roof and the venture capitalists were helping fund start-ups right,
left, and center. Optimists had some reason to believe that, against all
odds, some unholy marriage of cultural content, commerce, and community autonomy might provide a sustainable basis for the brave new
world of self-publishing, remote in ethos and practice from an old media
environment where the press was free only for those who own one. In a
classic example of theorem preceding evidence, Josh Quittner, writing
for *Wired* magazine, had even coined the anticipatory term "Way New
Journalism." If ever there was a technoculture setting itself up to be frustrated, this was it.

Predictably, then, 1996 was the beginning of the great shakedown. New
York's burgeoning Silicon Alley, the locus of the new content-driven revolution, suffered one setback after another. Multimedia mainstays like
Prodigy and Voyager withdrew their operations, the Murdoch group col-
lapsed iGuide and Delphi, Pipeline was sold, Mindvox went under, and
many of the established Webzine indies died off or were gobbled up by
media giants. In California, *Wired*'s failed attempts—twice—at an IPO
tarnished its pretensions to espouse a high-minded kind of Jeffersonian
digital populism. Other indies like American Cybercast and Out (run by
Out magazine) ceased publication. Larger corporate content-oriented
Web sites like Politics Now (a collaboration of the *Washington Post*, ABC,
and National Journal, Inc.) shut down, while Time Warner's Pathfinder
supersite was reputed to be running at a loss of $10 million a year. Indus-

try pundits began to doubt whether any profits could be generated and sustained from media whose users have always taken "freedom of information" at its literal meaning—that is, no billing, please. Currently, none of the business models—banner-based advertising, subscription, pay per use, metered bits, digital cash, microtransactions, consumer branding— used to sustain content-oriented Web sites are working. The current wisdom pronounces that successful Web shops will need 4 to 5 years to show a profit. While this anticommercial outcome could be viewed as some kind of victory for the resident anarchist philosophy of the Net, it does not augur well for those who are willing to equate this new culture industry with the possibility of honest job creation.

The Bad Hand of Government

The Internet, like most modern technologies, is an offspring of military and other government contracts, but its users have long since developed an antipathy to the hand that once fed it. Antifederalist sentiment is as fervent among some Net communities as among the militias. For example, the consciousness event of 1996 in the United States was the fight against the Communications Decency Act's ban on online indecency and offensive speech, overturned in the courts after intensive activity by the Electronic Frontier Foundation (EFF) and other lobby groups from the Internet community (as well as the ACLU and a number of gay/lesbian civil rights groups). If you were a netizen in good standing, you would have received a barrage of e-mail notices circulating about this life-or-death crusade for free speech. By contrast, the fact that Congress threw the welfare state down the toilet that year barely registered at all, except on specialized listserves and Usenet groups. So fierce is the Internet doctrine of untrammeled individualism that it sometimes translates into a general phobia about any government activities, not just those directly affecting the New Media. A portion of this response is well founded: the pro-encryption, pro-censorship crusades of the Clinton-Bush administrations have been klutzy and cynical moves, undercutting the official state rhetoric about the glorious liberties promised by the new information order. But the cyberlibertarian response is often bereft of a sober appreciation of the regulatory frameworks that are necessary to ensure civic freedoms and equities. This is a familiar paradox in liberal theory: forms of regulation prevent corporate monopolies from gobbling up all of public speech. The most extreme illustration of this near-myopia was EFF maven John Perry Barlow's now famous response to the indecency provisions of the Telecom Act, flamboyantly couched as "A Declaration of the Independence of Cyberspace":

> Governments of the Industrial World, you weary giants of flesh and steel, I come from Cyberspace, the new home of Mind. On behalf of the future, I ask you of the past to leave us alone. You are not welcome among us. You have no sovereignty where we gather. . . . Governments derive their just powers from the consent of the governed. You have neither solicited nor received ours. We did not invite you. You do not know us, nor do you know our world. Cyberspace does not lie within your borders. Do not think that you can build it, as though it were a public construction project. You cannot. It is an act of nature and it grows itself through our collective actions. . . . We are forming our own Social Contract. This governance will arise according to the conditions of our world, not yours. Our world is different. . . . We are creating a world that all may enter without privilege or prejudice accorded by race, economic power, military force, or station of birth. We are creating a world where anyone, anywhere may express his or her beliefs, no matter how singular, without fear of being coerced into silence or conformity. Your legal concepts of property, expression, identity, movement, and context do not apply to us. They are based on matter. There is no matter here. . . . Your increasingly obsolete information industries would perpetuate themselves by proposing laws, in America and elsewhere, that claim to own speech itself throughout the world. These laws would declare ideas to be another industrial product, no more noble than pig iron. In our world, whatever the human mind may create can be reproduced and distributed infinitely at no cost. The global conveyance of thought no longer requires your factories to accomplish. These increasingly hostile and colonial measures place us in the same position as those previous lovers of freedom and self-determination who had to reject the authorities of distant, uninformed powers. We

must declare our virtual selves immune to your sovereignty, even as we continue to consent to your rule over our bodies.

You would be hard put to find a more lucid expression of the unfettered individualism at the core of Net libertarianism, California-style. It's all there: the disdain for the obsolete order of industrialism, the desire for self-liberation from the social life of mortals, the retrofitted nostalgia for a Rousseauesque state of nature, and the aspiration to outrun transnational capital in the race to enjoy sovereignty beyond the boundaries of any petty state bureaucracy. Add to this the powerful legacy of countercultural (not to mention anticolonial) rhetoric, and the result is a clean, messianic break with the world most of us inhabit. This is the freedom we have always been falsely promised: let us emancipate ourselves from technical slavery by taking the new tools with us into secessionary exile!

Many critiques have been offered of this kind of hauteur, from both within and without the cyberspace community. The one that concerns me here is the resident blindness to what could be described as the "material conditions of production" of cyberspace. Far from heralding a Tofflerian end to either the age of "factories," equated by Barlow with "pig iron," or the age of government intervention, equated with "public construction projects," the aery layer of cyberspace inhabited by Barlow's self-liberated Netsters is underpinned everywhere by a new industrial economy that is the engine of the emergent information order. Masses of people work in cyberspace or work to make cyberspace possible. It is not simply a medium for free expression and wealth accumulation; it is a labor-intensive workplace. In recognizing this, we do not need to spurn the liberatory impulse that drives the Barlovian worldview. What's more important is to turn Barlow on his head, as Marx once did to Hegel, and see how and where this impulse can be generated within the labor process—the core of social sustainability.

First, it must be acknowledged that the hand of government is not exactly inactive. While the bulk of Net attention has been focused on the issue of censorship and civil liberties, state policies are everywhere more and more oriented to facilitating, if not directly governing, the shape of information industrialism. The massive revisions of the Telecommunications Act were a clear example of the use of the affirmative power of the state to sanction the aspirations of the giant multimedia corporations, legislated at a time when the U.S. state was withdrawing those same powers from its commitment to social welfare. Government sponsorship of the NII, presented as a "creative investment," has been tied to ensuring national competitiveness in the information industries and, under the rubric of the Global Information Infrastructure (GII), to U.S. dominance in the transnational field. Nurtured by U.S. federal investment, the Internet is now perceived as a leading asset in the game of comparative advantage, not to mention a decisive force in the long war over English-language global dominance. Policy initiatives like Clinton-Gore's "Next Generation Internet" agenda in 1996 rebut the prevailing mythology that government finally withdrew from its wardship of the Internet in 1995, when Net traffic was handed over to commercial service providers.

Nor has the military—the original source of the impulse to decentralize communications in the interests of reducing vulnerability to attack—withdrawn its hand. Take the Internet naming system, known as the "domain name system," which has its roots in the U.S. Department of Defense bureaucracy and was designed to identify the purpose of computing locations on the Internet. The ".com" domain was the division given to commercial network addresses, who at the time the system was established were a minority of networks on the Net—the majority being ".mil," ".gov," ".edu," and ".net" In 1995, administration of the name registry system was handed over to the InterNIC (Internet Network Information Center) of Network Solutions, Inc., which has enjoyed a highly profitable monopoly through charging considerable sums for the once gratis name registrations. InterNIC has had effective control over the creation of domain name scarcity, the engine of its profits—since registrants (around fifty thousand new applicants each month) were willing to pay more and more for short, customized addresses. It is also owned by Scientific Applications International Corporation (SAIC), a $2 billion company with very strong ties to the Pentagon and the National Security Agency. Its current board of directors includes former NSA chief Bobby Inman, former defense secretary Melvin Laird, and the former head of research and development for the Pentagon, Donald Hicks. Ex-CIA director Robert Gates, secretary of defense William Perry, and CIA director John Deutsch have been past board members. A vast majority of its annual revenue comes from government contracts, including defense, intelligence, and law enforcement contracts. SAIC is designing new information systems for the Pentagon, is helping to automate the FBI's computerized fingerprint identification system, and in 1996 won a $200 million contract to provide "information support" to the IRS. In brief, independents have no fully functioning way of using the Internet unless their rootservers are sanctioned by InterNIC's Assigned Numbers Authority (IANA). In effect, the administration of top-level domains—the bureaucratic center of the Internet—remained in the grip of the military-industrial complex, with its infamous tangle of interlocking directorates. In April 1997 the self-appointed International Ad Hoc Committee of the International Telecommunications Union recommended a series of new global top-level domain names, such as .firm, .web, .arts, .nom, .store, and others. The IAHC recommendation was killed by almost unanimous international opposition from the ITU's signatories.[1]

None of these examples of government or military involvement invalidate Barlow's case—indeed, they provide fuel for his fire—but to ignore these vested interests is pure self-indulgence. More important, if more abstruse, is the principle Barlow refers to as the social contract between legislators and users. Without a representative public stake in the regulation of the information sector, the commitment to *universal access* implied in decades of political rhetoric, from Hoover's "chicken in every pot" to Gingrich's "PC in every lap," is even more hollow than the rhetoric itself. There is simply no point in talking about people's access to high-capacity information prior to their access to employment, income, health, and environmental safety. Many of us have surely heard, in conversations casual and official, the frothy promise that the Internet will "liberate the Third World." Regulation, then, is not simply a fetter on free expression; it can create the conditions for freedoms and rights, paramount among these being the right to equity among freedoms. Such claims, stakes, and obligations have no moral authority in the commercial marketplace, although they sometimes coincide with the effects of that marketplace.

The most acute problem with Barlovianism lies not with its ultralibertarianism, but with its neglect of material labor conditions. Net intellectuals in Barlow's camp, no less than most information professionals, rarely focus on the labor that produces their computer technologies, nor are they attentive to the industrial uses to which these technologies are put in the workplaces of the world. This blindness is understandable, though not excusable, when these sectors are remote and invisible—on the other side, as it were, of the international division of labor. But it is difficult to exonerate the neglect of working conditions that lie at the heart of the cyberspace community itself. Like all other sectors of the economy, the Internet industries have been penetrated by the low-wage revolution—from the janitors who service Silicon Valley to the part-time programmers and designers who service Silicon Alley. Just as Silicon Valley provided a flexible model for postindustrial employment, Silicon Alley may be poised to deliver an upgrade. The initial indications show that there are indeed jobs in cyberspace, but most of them don't pay that well or offer much job security.

In the brief analysis of Silicon Alley that follows, I will focus on the particular example of cultural labor in an employment market—New York City—that enjoys a surplus of such labor. No less than in the arts and education, creative work in Silicon Alley generally is undercompensated because of the invisible wages that come in the form of psychological rewards for personally satisfying work. At a time when no one seems immune to the plague of low-wage labor, it's important that artists, educators, writers, and designers see this discount arrangement for what it is—exploitation of the prestige of cultural work to drive down wages in a market where the labor supply will always outstrip demand.

The Great Wired Way

Silicon Alley has been hailed as the first new urban industry to emerge in New York in well over a generation. In a city associated as much with its independent culture as with its forced financial meltdown in the 1970s, its decaying infrastructure, and a chronic habit of hemorrhaging jobs, it is notable that the new presence is also a culture industry of sorts. Breathlessly heralded in all the city's media organs as a superrush of adrenaline to the urban economy and culture alike, the Alley is customarily described as running in a thin strip from the Flatiron District above 23rd Street down to lower SoHo, and staffed by creative East Coast hipster geeks (as opposed to Palo Alto techies and Bay Area self-styled supergeeks). Its multimedia Web shops not only provide corporate and public institutions with Internet design, programming services, and entertainment software, they also harbor a neobohemian community of online publishing and graphic art.

Among other things, the much lionized emergence of the New Media's small, independent entrepreneurs drew on the human resources and skills of the downtown artworld, creating some accomplished new art sites like ada'web (http://adaweb.com), Artnetweb (http://www.artnetweb.com), and The Blue Dot (http://www.thebluedot.com) (adding to older, invaluable artworld resources like Echo [http://www.echonyc.com] and The Thing [http://www.thing.net] and newer ones like Rhizome [http://www.rhizome.com]). These sites contributed to the flourishing electronic arts movement, and ada'web's projects by Vivien Selbo, Matthew Ritchie, and General Idea were the first online works to be acquired by a major museum institution, the San Francisco Museum of Modern Art, in February 1997.

By 1996 pioneer Silicon Alley Webzines like *Word* (http://www.word. com), *FEED* (http://www.feedmag.com), *Urban Desires* (http://www. desires.com), *Total New York* (http://www.totalny. com), *Stim* (http:// stim.com), and *NY@work* (a labor-oriented site) had formed an independents sector of original content publishing, distinct in feel and opinion from Microsoft's power-oriented *Slate*, the industry lifestyle-oriented *Hot Wired*, and Time Warner's megasite *Pathfinder*. In the spring and summer of 1995, when half a dozen local would-be publishers had followed *Urban Desires* into the Web publishing arena, the heady expectation was that native New York creativity would steal a march on the West Coast and launch a more independent and sociable sector of the high-tech community, drawing an audience and advertisers to a new medium where no one controlled distribution. The alternative, countercultural ethos of hacker vintage suffused the indies sector and fueled a classic culture clash when venture capitalist groups from the West Coast or from New York City (Flatiron Partners—the VC arm of Chase and Softbank, and the city's own Discovery Fund) came calling all along the Alley.

Today, *FEED* is the only first-generation Web site that still functions *solely* as an online content publisher (helped along by recent deals with

Wired and the New York Times Electronic Media Company). The others have either folded, been sold, or are serving as creative window displays or calling cards to attract clients for their Web developer owners. In the meantime, the potential of the medium remains largely unfulfilled. The graphic scrolldown space is still clunky, slow, and wearisome to read after a few screens, and while feature articles have been developed in ways that are appropriate to the medium, the Webzines have yet to break a big story.[2] The deliciously irreverent and heavily hypertexted daily media commentary from *Suck* (http://www.suck.com) is the only publication in this field to win itself a must-read audience. No one yet believes that "way new journalism," art, and multimedia performance have matured—the scene is often likened to early TV, when radio shows were reissued in new formats—but there is much that is promising and much more to come. While none of the delivery schemes, the ad tracking mechanisms, or the direct marketing plans have been able to support the content boom on Silicon Alley, it's clear that the appeal of online independence is now a formative part of youth culture and that down the line, the second- or third-generation wave is likely to alter the New Media landscape for good. The sense of living within and contributing to a "revolutionary" culture, or at least a new paradigm, may prove powerful enough to propel segments of youth culture through some of the managerial constraints exercised by information bureaucrats and venture capitalists alike.

Silicon Alley was in part the creation of city politicians and real estate investors looking for a way to revive the ailing early 1990s downtown economy with its alarming building vacancy levels (as high as 23 percent); in part, the response to an immediate need for WWW content providers and designers directed at the vast local labor pool of creative workers (many of them would-be artists and journalists); in part, the entrepreneurial outcropping of the self-publishing movement driving the great WWW boom; and in part, the result of a new generation of twenty-something trust fund babies looking for a glamorous outlet, much like the collectors and gallerists who frequented the East Village art scene in the 1980s.

In an age of outsourcing and virtual decentralization, why should such an industry exist at the heart of a core city like New York? The reasons usually cited (and recorded in a Coopers and Lybrand report of 1996)[3] focus on access to editorial and artistic talent, access to clients and strategic partners in advertising, publishing, and entertainment, and access to the cultural prestige of New York City. Ironically, for a digital work culture often oblivious to its physical location, the capacity to maintain face-to-face social contact also ranks high. Contrary to all the Internet hype about the elimination of the centralized workplace through virtual networking from remote terminals, the "schmooze factor" is an important, cohesive part of the social space of Silicon Alley. This is no less the case in New York's garment industry, where buyers, manufacturers, designers, and retailers still like to schmooze on Seventh Avenue in the garment district; this highly social feature of daily industrial life may be just as important as fast turnaround time in production—habitually cited as the main cause of job retention in an age of offshore production.

For those who still worry that postindustrialism is a contradiction in terms, it's not clear that the neobohemian dot.com corridor of Silicon Alley constitutes anything like an industry, in the sense of producing and distributing a product far beyond its borders. Among other things, it is a service developer for corporate Web site promotion, a low-overhead R&D test bed for software tools and applications, a source of multimedia expertise, a subcontractor of low-wage HTML labor (the cliché is that high school kids are willing to labor for cappuccinos because Web site work is cool), and a welcome, if underpaying, nonunion employer of a generational cohort that might otherwise have ended up being "warehoused" in graduate seminars. The 1996 Coopers and Lybrand study of the economic impact of New Media in the New York region showed more employees, in 1,350 companies—over 700 in Silicon Alley alone generating over a billion dollars in gross revenues—working in New Media than in television and books. The figures of 18,000-plus jobs in Silicon Alley, 27,000 in New York City as a whole, and 71,500 in the tristate area, were variously interpreted, since they included a high percentage of part-time and freelance employees. Nonetheless, these numbers were fast approaching the media industry's larger segments (and projected to outrank them all in the next few years) at a growth rate that outstripped any other business in the city. But the average salary of New Media full-time employees, at $31,421, was well below that of every other segment, ranging from book publishing and movie production, at $47,824 and $48,907 respectively, to advertising and TV broadcasting, at $62,559 and $63,261. (While a $31,000 salary may seem luxurious in comparison with national and global wage levels, it does not stretch far in go-go Gotham these days.) Ironically, the report, with its prediction of a 138 percent increase in full-time equivalent jobs over the next three years (120,000 new jobs—doubling the full-time employees, tripling part-timers, and tripling full-time equivalent free-lancers), appeared at a moment when some pioneer companies were beginning to go under. Many of the surviving Web shops were soon to make deals over the course of the year with the likes of Microsoft, Omni-com, Sun, AOL, Time Warner, and Viacom—deals, admittedly, that remain the unwritten goal of most start-ups. When the smoke cleared, the roads to sustainability were more starkly defined, and certainly the prospects for a critical, IndieNet culture were much thinner and more circumscribed. Many of the new battles were being fought, for example, in the hometown listings wars—exactly the same wars being waged over securing the block advertising revenue of the big entertainment con-glomerates by alternative newspapers (the last grassroots attempt to cre-ate an independent publishing medium) in cities all over the country. With the addition to the market of Microsoft's *Sidewalk New York* in May 1997, there now existed several such sites devoted to informing the surfing public whether the latest Batman movie was still playing at the theater down the street.

If Silicon Alley does give birth to a new kind of culture industry, it is not likely to be a mass media industry, nor will its impact necessarily lie in the realm of leisure or entertainment (business-to-business communica-tion is the more obviously profitable sector). Unlike the culture industries of radio, film, TV, recording, fashion, and advertising, which had their start in the Age of the Machine, the work environment of New Media is entirely machine-based and labor-intensive in ways that are now the leg-ends of cyberspace. "Voluntary" overtime—with twelve-hour workdays virtually mandatory—is a way of life for those in the business of digital design, programming, and manipulation. The fact is, New Media tech-nologies have already transformed our work patterns much more radically than they are likely to affect our leisure hours, just as information tech-nologies have already played a massive role in helping to restructure labor and income in the new global economy—effectively reorganizing time, space, and work for mostly everyone in the developed world. It would be more accurate to say that we are seeing the dawn of new forms of leisure time governed by labor-intensive habits tied to information technology. But let's not forget that for every one of us who wants our PCs and software to go faster, there are fifty others who want them to go slower. And in the United States, the hours of work put in by fully employed workers, whichever side of the labor divide they inhabit, has increased steadily for three decades.[4]

The difference in these attitudes to computing speed speaks volumes about how New Media straddle the division of labor, and should remind us why it is necessary to make links between work cultures that are ordinarily kept apart. Silicon Alley has been showcased as an urban enclave for whizzkids, a chunk of some future utopia of cooperative work in the virtual city, and in this respect its work culture is philosophically akin to the creative, hard technology sectors of Northern California and Boston's Route 128 corridor. But to focus only on the creative sector of its contingent workforce is to encourage the assumption that it is wholly disconnected from industrial sites of very cheap labor—electronic chip production and circuit assembly in Asia and the Caribbean, and the armies of word processing and data entry clerks in Ireland and India. So too, the general belief that these "symbolic analysts" constitute the fastest growing and most lucrative middle-class sector of employment is belied by the fact, as Doug Henwood points out, that "jobs with high information account for [only] 15 per cent of total job growth over the next decade," while the real growth areas are all in those categories of low-wage labor—"sales clerks, cashiers, janitors, security guards"—that appear to swell locally in proportion to the growth of select information-intensive industries.[5]

In July 1996 a posting on the WWWAC (World Wide Web Artists' Consortium) list provoked a squall of comments that reflected the onset of labor anxieties in Silicon Alley itself. A New Media publisher announced it was "looking for HTML slaves. Applicants must love grunt work, long hours, fluorescent lights, caffeine and other stimulants, and display grace under pressure." Despite, or because of, the dark humor of the posting, it touched a nerve among Silicon Alleycats, but it was a telling reflection of the economy of low-wage subcontracting that has already worked its way beyond the periphery of the industry. The result is a steady depression of the wage floor, and not just for basic HTML markup. Improved software can—overnight—turn skilled programming, coding, and image manipulation into grunt work, while the recent development of software like Fusion has rendered obsolete an entire temporary cadre of that low-grade work. At the time of the posting, there were public revelations about the garment sweatshops producing Kathie Lee Gifford's clothing line for children. *Suck* cunningly revealed that the *Wired* staff occupied a floor in a building full of garment sweatshops. Suddenly it seemed as if the professional distance between the high-tech HTML and the no-tech garment industries had been reduced to nothing. The original subcontracting industrial shops of the turn of the century were back in business, cheek by jowl with the new postindustrial ones in the retrofitted manufacturing lofts of the cybercity.

Most of the analogies, or jokes, about Silicon Alley sweatshops remain just that, but recently they have been accompanied by growing anxieties about New Media employment patterns, which, in the 1996 Coopers and Lybrand report, already showed up to 33 percent of the workforce composed of freelance and part-time employees. On the upper side of the industrial divide, contingent, or independent, contractors, in the form of relatively well-paid designers (who can afford to eschew benefits, insurance packages, and other forms of job security), move frequently from firm to firm, "pollinating" the culture in the manner pioneered by California's Silicon Valley, the original model for this new, flexible style of corporate organization.[6] This highly mobile, elite cadre is to be distinguished from the army of temporary workers who work when and where an agency dictates at agreed upon rates. Nonetheless, the existence of a number of well-paying positions is habitually cited as evidence that New Media are a boom industry for young career seekers. For at least two years, Silicon Alley did provide this kind of boomlet environment, offering a rapid step-up for those who had more or less taught themselves how to design from the only existing HTML manual of style. In a steadily maturing industry, the days are all but over when entry-level workers could ease into the upper cadre after less than a year of basic designing. While creative content will always remain at the core of New Media activities—48 percent of Silicon Alley labor is creative—as much programming and technical design as can be transferred to low-wage employment will undoubtedly follow that path in the years to come.

There is nothing revelatory about these labor patterns; they are endemic to the business environment of start-ups. But such anxieties are alien to the culture of the Internet world, driven by a resident cybertopian boosterism that lends inflationary zeal to this fledgling industry. A year of high-profile job losses and gloomy industry predictions has all but deflated the bubble, and whatever vestiges of the utopian Barlovian temper had survived the passage from California's blue skies to Gotham's urban grit were all but stripped of their arrogant edge in the weekly struggle to survive. For many owners of small Web shops (for whom maintaining a content-driven site can cost between $300,000 and $1 million a year), the future of their business lies in petitioning the city and state for tax exemptions, especially those sales, utility, and unincorporated business taxes that affect telecommunications unduly. In June 1997, New York City mayor Rudolph Giuliani responded with a $30 million job creation loan fund aimed at emerging high-tech industries. Earlier tax and infrastructure packages were designed to attract New Media companies to the northern tip of the Wall Street area, home of 55 Broad Street, the New York Information Technology Center—the model "wired" building—and its immediate environment, peppered with "plug'n'go" prebuilt, Internet-ready office space. Silicon Alleycats are eager for such incentives, but loath to move so far south. They may not yet be emulating the ways of the Wall Street giants, who threaten to move their office workforce to another state unless they are granted massive tax breaks, but the goal of tax exemption hardly distinguishes New Media developers from the garden-variety corporate tax evader. Others swear that the marketplace alone should make or break Silicon Alley. A third, admittedly more utopian, option is publicly assisted job creation—jobs in the name of culture! Is there any special responsibility on the part of a liberal society to justly reward creative labor? Questions like this open up heady regions of speculation about the costing of labor value and the estimation of hidden wages. Women and minorities have campaigned for equal pay to compensate for the (higher) wages of masculinity and whiteness (some portion of these wages being quite invisible, since they are cashed in the form of social privileges in daily life). In a market-driven economy, some forms of cultural labor may need to be protected, most notably in the areas of arts and education. But these are not propitious times for appealing to state support for artistic or intellectual freedoms. A more effective form of public discourse might be to cost out the disparity in creative work salaries between the undercommercialized sectors and the fully commercialized, profit-driven ones.

Whether or not there will ever be a defensible position from which to demand sustainable assistance, the New Media sector, barely three years old, is already being confronted with basic choices about the nature of cultural work in a business economy. This is not just a quandary for industry insiders. Given the avant-garde industrial location of the Web shops, the outcome may serve as a model for at least the next generation of cultural workers. So before we all hop on the Info Love Boat, let's make sure that everyone is getting paid enough.

Speeding Away

Let me return to my unproven assertion about computing speed. All the readers of this book probably want our computers to go faster, and yet most of the people who work with computers already want them to go slower. Information professionals are used to thinking of ourselves as masters of our work environment and competitors in the market for skills, resources, and rewards. Our tools are viewed as artisanal, and they can help us win comparative advantage in the field if they can access and extract the relevant information and results in a timely fashion. In such a reward environment, it makes sense to respond to the heady promise of velocification in all its forms: the relentless boosting of chip clock speed, magnification of storage density, faster traffic on Internet backbones, higher baud rate modems, hyperefficient database searches, and rapid data-transfer techniques. These tools are rhetorically aimed at the compression of space as well as time. No longer bound by quaint regional customs like traveling by Gophers, popping up whimsically all over our national maps, our vehicles are now oceangoing Navigators and global Explorers, although they are still called "browsers," as if to suggest that we are still in the local bookstore or branch library. If we ourselves are not whizzkid designers of these technical environments, many of us know people who are. A common repertoire of industrial, design, and Internet user lore binds us together and reinforces our (para)professional *esprit de corps.* But that shared culture also tends to disconnect us from the world of work where people want computers to go slower, even though these two worlds often overlap, sometimes in the same office space.

In the other world, the speed controls of technology are routinely used to regulate workers. These forms of regulation are well documented: widespread workplace monitoring and software surveillance, where keyboard quotas and other automated measures are geared to time every operation, from the length of bathroom visits to the output diversions generated by personal e-mail. Occupationally, this world stretches from the high-turnover burger flippers in McDonald's and the offshore data entry sweatshops in Bangalore and the Caribbean to piecework professionals and adjunct brainworkers and all the way to the upper-level white-collar range of front office managers, who complain about their accountability to inflexible productivity schedules. It is characterized by chronic automation, the global outsourcing of low-wage labor, and the wholesale replacement of decision making by expert systems and smart tools; it thrives on undereducation, undermotivation, and underpayment; and it appears to be aimed primarily at controlling workers rather than tapping their potential for efficiency, let alone their native ingenuity.[7]

Some of you will object, quite rightly, to my crude separation of these technological environments. Putting it this way encourages the view that it is technology that determines, rather than simply enables, this division of labor. This objection is surely correct. It is capitalist reason, rather than technical reason, that underpins this division, although technology has proven to be an infinitely ingenious means of guaranteeing and governing the uneven development of labor and resources.

So too, you might protest that many "first worlders" resent the pace of upgrading, enhancement, and boosting; they perceive this fierce tempo as augmenting, not reducing, their labor; and they are self-critical about their addiction to the principle of the accelerated life. Likewise, many "second worlders" see upgrades as the basis of the industrial adjustment that saves their jobs, and information technology skills as their passport to occupational mobility, higher income, and social status. This objection is a little more tricky because it involves a conflict between how people perceive technological speed and how they respond to it. While there is much talk about the widening gulf between information "haves" and "have-nots," the information-rich and the information-poor, it is less easy, though by no means impossible, to say whose work and time are *unequivocally* regulated, and whose are *unequivocally* assisted and enhanced by technology. One of the risks of this game is that you may end up believing that it is the designers, programmers, and developers who are free from surveillance and who are thus personally responsible for the decision making that shapes the regulatory capacity of the technologies. In other words, we end up with the fallacy of designer determinism, which is just as misleading as that of technological determinism.

Let me therefore revise, or qualify, my original assertion. I don't want to reject it because I believe it barely needs to be proven that for a vast percentage of workers, there is nothing to be gained from going faster; it is not in their interests to do so, and so their ingenuity on the job is devoted to ways of slowing down the work regime, beating the system, and sabotaging its automated schedules. It is important, then, to hold on to the observation that complicity with or resistance to acceleration is an important line of demarcation. But equally important is the principle of *speed differential*, because this is the primary means of creating relative scarcity—the engine of uneven development in the world economy.

Commodities, including parcels of time, accrue value only if and when they are rendered scarce. Time scarcity has been a basic principle of industrial life, from the infamous tyranny of the factory clock to the coercive regime of turnaround schedules in the computer-assisted systems of just-in-time production. It is a mistake again to hold the technologies themselves responsible: the invention of the clock no more made industrialists into callous exploiters of labor than it made Europeans into imperialist aggressors. Capitalism, on the other hand, needs to manufacture scarcity; indeed, it must generate scarcity before it can generate wealth.

Ivan Illich pointed this out in his own way in his 1974 collection, *Energy and Equity*, in which he noted that the exchange value of time becomes a major economic component for a society at a point where the mass of people are capable of moving faster than fifteen miles per hour. A high-speed society inevitably becomes a class society, as people begin to be *absent* from their destinations and workers are forced to earn so much to pay to get to work in the first place (in high-density cities where mass transportation is cheap, the costs are transferred onto rent). Anyone moving faster must be justified in assuming that their time is more important than those moving more slowly. "Beyond a critical speed," Illich writes, "no one can save time without forcing another to lose it."[8] If there are no speed limits, then the fastest and most expensive will take its toll in energy and equity on the rest: "the order of magnitude of the top speed which is permitted within a transportation system determines the slice of its time budget that an entire society spends on traffic."[9]

Illich's and others' commentaries on the emergence of speed castes from monospeed societies have progressively refined our commonsense perception that the cult of acceleration takes an undue toll on all of our systems of equity and sustainability: social, environmental, and economic. You don't have to subscribe to the eco-atavistic view that there exists a "natural tempo" for human affairs, in synch with, if not entirely decreed by, the biorhythms of nature to recognize that the temporal scale of modernization may not be sustainable. Faster speeds increase a society's environmental load at an exponential rate. The lightning speed at which financial capital now moves can have a disastrous effect on the material life and landscape of entire societies when regional markets collapse or are put in crisis overnight. The depletion of nature is directly tied to the degree to which the speed of capital's transactions creates shortages and scarcity in its ceaseless pursuit of accumulation. Regulation of social and economic speed in the name of selective slowness is a sound and indisputable path of advocacy. But it is important to bear in mind that state and World Bank economists already practice such regulation when they decide to "grow" economies at a particular speed in order to control the inflation specter and when they impose recessionary measures on populations in order to enforce pro-scarcity regimes. It may be crucial to observe that only those going fastest possess the privilege to decide to go slower, along with the power to make others decelerate.

Arguably, the emergence of Internet communications speed has enabled activist organizing to build a global network that can respond in some measure to the cruel work of these transnational managers. The capacity to organize dissent and resistance on an international scale has been an undeniable asset of the new information landscape. But it has also magnified the gulf between the temporality of activists—based around urgency and instant mobilization—and the temporality of intellectuals—based around the slower momentum of thought and theoretical speculation. Many forms of radical thought require a patient process of germination that is antipathetic to the new speed of information circulation. One traditional function of intellectuals—putting their names on petitions—has come into its own with the new global public sphere of the Internet, but the necessary links between movements of ideas and movements of action have been more difficult to make in a virtual world where everything has to be done yesterday.

The Sophisticated Traveler

Illich's analysis of time scarcity is, of course, drawn from the model of transportation and not communication technologies. In our time this distinction has become less important, because cybercommunications are increasingly a means of near-instant transportation for information commodities of all descriptions, while they have reduced the need for transportation in the case of information homeworkers, and encouraged WWW users to see themselves as casual globe-trotters. It would be a mistake to take this conflation of transport and communication services too literally, although it *is* part of the vision of the corporate sponsors of New Media technologies to embrace many different industrial sectors in a bid to service all our needs through "one-stop communications." The introduction of each new mass technology—telegraph, railway, electrification, radio, telephone, television, automobiles, air travel—has always been accompanied by a spectacular package of promises, guarantees, and assurances that it will fulfill all our democratic ideals, delivering life, liberty, and the pursuit of happiness at a discount price, and restoring our lost community into the bargain. Increasingly, however, the concentration of multiple industries into single, transnational conglomerates has meant that the control over these comprehensive but illusory promises is invested in companies that actually do have the power, in principle, to reach out and touch us in many different aspects and zones of our waking lives.

Perhaps that is why our New Media hardware cannot afford to advertise any single function through its design in the way it used to do. In the Machine Age of high progressive futurism, design observed the principle "form follows function." In the case of art moderne, streamline design conveyed the sense of a world moving fast, even when it was stationary. This design aesthetic applied not just to fast-moving vehicles but also to domestic objects like pencil sharpeners and kettles. The whole world was moving in one direction—forward.[10] This design aesthetic has not been applied generally to technologies in the Information Age. The casing designs for information hardware have retained the chunky, robotic iconography of office equipment, and have not generally sought to simulate the physical sensation of unidirectional speed, opting instead for the comfort-oriented ergonomic designs of recent years. No different are the designs for laptop computers, which emphasize their compact mobility in a circumspect, low-profile way; there is no outward sign of what these sleek dark boxes are actually used for. For those who do not possess them, or who do not live in the world of high-speed communications, they have the sinister look of stealth technologies, aggressively associated with defense, security, and inaccessibility. We are far removed from the blithe, self-promotional impulse of Cadillac tailfin styling. Which is to say that these new machines are not ostentatious billboards for the good life. They appear as status symbols of access, inscrutable gateways to an invisible world of wealth, power, and knowledge, even carnal, that is always just out of reach. Predictably, mass audience ISP salesmanship often employs the voyeuristic rhetoric of the circus peepshow or sexclub barker, promising salacious experiences that lie just beyond the black curtain. Sign up for Internet access and it will all be yours, uncensored, or, as McKenzie Wark has satirized the techno-sublime equivalent: buy more RAM and you will be free!

The selling of the Information Age has rested on many such promises of hidden delights but has also appealed to anxieties about being left behind, without a stake or address on the frontier when the bonanza finally arrives. Three years ago, telephone giant AT&T ran a series of bizarre advertising campaigns, remembered as the "You Will" commercials, informing us that when the information superhighway finally does get built, their company will be the one to serve you. This was blue-sky futurism at its most perverse, and probably betrayed more about corporate anxieties than about those of consumers. Today, it is the TV manufacturers that are banking on the more familiar, domestic architecture of the television set to deliver access in the form of WebTV. Most mass customers still have no idea what it is they are buying into. The benefits of being able to surf around the WWW are much more difficult to conceptualize than were the benefits of watching a football game live on TV or traveling quickly and comfortably from Philadelphia to Cleveland. It is no surprise then that the design inscrutability of the cyberbox—its refusal to communicate any messages about its function, rather like the monolith in *2001*—can be viewed as a commercial asset because it suggests unrestricted though indefinite returns to the consumer, and not as a liability, connoting insufficiency, obsolescence, or inertia. In this sense the cyberbox is the physical embodiment of the flexible, multidirectional global vision of the transnational corporation. It is never out of place because it can be anywhere, it can do anything; nothing in the material world is lost in its translation of space, and what is lost in the way of temporality is gained by always being in more than one place at the same time. The history of corporate logo design can show us in shorthand how we got here. Consider the historical progression of corporate logos, which have moved away from the typographic solidity of block capitals, in the age of incorporation and national capitalism, to the celebration of speed and mobility suggested by sans serif lettering at the dawn of postindustrialism, and finally to the widespread use of globes and orbital pathways in the logos of today's age of transnationalism.

These are smart motifs, indelibly associated with today's smart machines and the competitive SAT scores that are supposed to measure the cognitive speed of our students' mental processing. They also evoke a world of immateriality, which, on the face of it, appears to be cleaner, and less toxic to natural life, than the smokestack age. Consider, however, the sheer volume of nature that has to be moved to produce computer hardware. According to a study by the Wuppertal Institute, the fabrication of each PC requires the consumption of from fifteen to nineteen tons of energy and materials. The high-grade minerals used for PC components can be obtained only through major mining operations and energy-intensive transformation processes. By contrast, an average automobile requires about twenty-five tons.[11] Mass computerization holds little guarantee of an eco-friendly system of production.

The progression from auto to PC has not stood in the way of the widespread, and apparently anachronistic, use of the automobile age metaphor of the information superhighway, or Infobahn, which functioned for a number of crucial years (I don't believe it does any longer) as the most persuasive point of reference for describing the new communications networks. One is tempted to think of the use of this metaphor and all its accoutrements—ramps, regional backbones, testbeds—as an example of what McLuhan called rearview mirrorism, whereby the forms of an older technology are reflected in the content of the new. My instinct is to suggest a less formalistic explanation.

In the United States at least, the metaphor was introduced at a time, in the early 1990s, when government was being petitioned to fund a large portion of the infrastructure. Some legislators, many public interest groups, and most small companies saw this form of sponsorship as the only way of ensuring that the telecom giants would not build and dominate an entirely privatized system of networks from the get-go (as the railroad robber barons had done in the nineteenth century, though not without lavish gifts, from the state, of millions of acres of public lands). A more recent model of state subsidization of private interest was the interstate highway system, a public works project constructed in the name of national defense and General Motors, and powerfully overseen in the Senate by the father of Al Gore, who subsequently became the most vocal proponent of the information superhighway, spouting the rhetoric of the NII and the Global Information Infrastructure (GII) at every available moment in the first term of the Clinton administration. With the ascendancy of the Internet, all these plans have changed. The corporations that had been promised the role of gatekeepers and highway toll collectors have been obliged to reorient and rechannel all their development strategies through the Internet. Talk about the information superhighway is scarce these days.

Webbiness

There is another story to tell, however, about the decline of the information superhighway concept and the rise of more ecologically resonant images and metaphors associated with the Web. It is a story much favored by the Barlovians, in which the biological triumphs over the mechanical, and it is a reboot of the paradigm Leo Marx named the Machine in the Garden, which has been a staple of American philosophical exceptionalism ever since industrialization made its forced entry into the eco-paradise of the New World. According to one version of the paradigm, healthy biotechnics are always on the verge of replacing life-threatening paleo-technologies. In the latest upgrade, popularized by *Wired,* the organic, interconnected world of natural, self-regulating communities and net-worked information technologies is replacing the obsolete, rigid, linear structure of a megamachine civilization built for privatized mobility at the price of hard-energy overconsumption. The bad ecological associations are being discarded, along with the framework of centralized control that had been the hallmark of a Fordist system of production epitomized by the automobile industry. The World Wide Web offers a compact metaphor for the new communitarian ethos, charged with eco-friendly iconography.

Government's green hand was also apparent in the figure of Al Gore, who, contrary to reputation, has been more active in the realm of technol-ogy than in environmental legislation. In the White House, his profile as an environmentalist served him well in instigating the first official trial runs of the Infobahn concept, in November 1992, with the creation of a National Information Infrastructure Testbed, called Earth Data Systems. This testbed project linked computers via telephone lines at nine sites across the country to share twenty years of environmental data on tropical deforestation and ocean pollution. Pursued by a model network of public and private institutions (AT&T, Oregon State University, the Department of Energy's Sandia National Laboratory, the Digital Equipment Corpora-tion, University of California, Berkeley, Ellery Systems Inc., Essential Communications, and Hewlett-Packard), this was intended to be a show-case public interest project—no pornography, no data snooping, no con-sumer marketing, no virtual shopping clubs, no corporate computer crime, in short, none of the embarrassing traffic that has plagued the Internet with bad PR more recently. Ever since then, one of Gore's jobs has been to supervise the Information Infrastructure Task Force, set up to provide legal guidelines on patent and copyright issues (how to break the hacker, share-ware ethic), privacy issues (how to protect corporate property as well as personal data), and technical policies regarding the "compatibility" of net-works (how to arrange marriages in heaven for the telecom giants).

As for the White House itself, its newfound e-mail capacity to transmit government reports, policy plans, and robo-responses presented an opportunity to bypass the editorial filter of the established news organizations. In principle, the voice of government, disinformation and all, could go directly to the people, unselected and uninterpreted by the media's guardians of public knowledge. The capacity of a central information apparatus to construct a one-way, multilane superhighway appeared to refute Gore's own comparison of the decentralized "design advantage" of systems of capitalism and democracy to the architecture of parallel computing systems.[12] Unlike the command-and-control centralism of communism and CPUs, representative democracy, for Gore, operates more efficiently as a decision-making model, while parallel computing distributes processing capacity more advantageously around the memory field.

The strangest and most revealing comparisons, however, arise from the analogies that Gore drew in his book *Earth in the Balance* between information ecology and the ecology of natural resources. There, he elaborates on the cliché that there is a carrying capacity to our human ability to process information, and therefore that information overload is analogous to the exhaustion of natural resources:

> Our current approach to information resembles our old agricultural policy. We used to store mountains of excess grain in silos throughout the Midwest and let it rot, while millions around the world died of starvation. It was easier to subsidize growing more corn than to create a system for feeding those who were hungry. Now we have silos of excess data rotting (sometimes literally) while millions hunger for the solutions to unprecedented problems. . . . Just as we automated the process for converting oxygen into carbon dioxide (CO_2)—with inventions like the steam engine and the automobile—without taking into account the limited ability of the earth to absorb CO_2 we have also automated the process of generating data—with inventions like the printing press and the computer—without taking into account our limited ability to absorb the new knowledge thus created. (*EB*, 200)

Or another example:

Vast amounts of unused information ultimately become a kind of pollution. The Library of Congress for instance receives more than ten
thousand periodicals each year—from India alone! And given that
some of our accumulated information and knowledge is dangerous—
such as the blueprint for an atomic bomb—keeping track of all the
data can become as important as it is difficult. What if this toxic information leaks into the wrong places? (*EB*, 201)

What are the consequences of this kind of nonsense talk that compares
information resources to natural resources? Perhaps not much, but these
kinds of mixed metaphors increasingly became standard fare in corporate discourse about the ecological virtues of information technology.
The boosterism of media executives and advertisers met the discourse of
government bureaucrats on common ground, reconciling the language
of free-market environmentalism with the language of the Infobahn,
playing off information abundance against resource scarcity in the time-
honored fashion.

The purest examples of this seamless boosterism, however, can be
found in the claims of leading Internet philosophers—the organic intellectuals of the Net, often termed the *digerati*. Kevin Kelley is the most
obvious example, not only because his ideas are consonant with the *Wired*
ethos, but also because they carry on their back a rich history of countercultural memories culled from the early heyday of the *Whole Earth Review*
and *Co-Evolution Quarterly*. It is important to read Kelley's influential
book *Out of Control* with one eye on the countercultural past and one on
the corporate present. That way you will see how the anarchist, libertarian
values of 1960s decentralization, communitarian self-regulation, biosocial
engineering, and relative autonomy within organic connectedness have
become integral to the newly greenwashed corporate philosophies of our
day. Kelley's hymns of praise to the biologizing of the machine, to the
death of centralized, top-down control, to webby nonlinear causality, to
the superorganic consciousness of swarmware, and to the evolved distributed intelligence of parallel computing read like a subtle inventory of
public relations jargon for any large telecommunications company.

Nowhere in Kelley's five-hundred-page book is there any mention of the
"second world" that I described earlier—the low-wage world of automated

surveillance, subcontracted piecework, crippling workplace injuries, and the tumors in the livers of chip factory workers.[13] Nowhere is there any recognition of the global labor markets—with their cruel outsourcing economies—that provide the manufacturing base for the new clean machines. Nor is his book an exception. There is a complete and utter gulf between the public philosophizing of the whizzkid New Media designers, artists, and entrepreneurs and the global sourcing of low wage labor enclaves associated with the new information technologies. Boosters like Kelley speak of an ethic of "intelligent control" that is emerging from the use of the New Media. The term is hauntingly accurate, because it evokes a long history of managerial dreams, on the one hand, and automated intelligence on the other. How you feel about this ethic may ultimately depend on which side of the division of labor you find yourself.

Again, the problem lies not with the technologies themselves, nor, ultimately, with the speed at which they operate. I say this because I have to believe that it *is* possible to have an affordable, sustainable media environment—boasting a diverse range of media, from private to publicly supported to the small bohemian independents—without electronic sweatshops just as it is possible to have a sustainable world of fashion without garment sweatshops. But as long as we keep one realm of ideas apart from the experience of the other, people simply will not make the connections between the two.

Mr. Reggae DJ, Meet the International Monetary Fund

The idea that cultural forms often voice resistance to established power has become a cliché in the later part of the twentieth century. Faux rebellion, packaged for ready consumption in the cultural marketplace, is almost as available as Coca-Cola. No wonder there is a good deal of nostalgia for a more clear-cut age of rebel culture, when Opposition and Establishment had quite distinct moral iconographies. Nowhere was this more apparent than in the anticolonial movements of the Third World, where Amilcar Cabral's concept of "culture as resistance" played a crucial role in appraising how colonial rule had maintained itself for centuries by saturating the majority of the world's population with internalized self-contempt. Decolonizing the mind would prove as important as changing the flag flying over Government House. Subsequently, postcolonial life brought its own landscape of cultural power into being, with suppressed majorities and minorities often struggling to win a legitimate voice in many a liberated nation-state. With the onset of neocolonialism under the technocratic rule of the World Bank and the International Monetary Fund, the balance of power and resistance changed yet again as countries in the developing world fell one by one into the suffocating grip of the "debt trap."

To see how struggles for cultural justice have changed over these successive periods—colonial, postcolonial, and neocolonial—one need look no further than the example of Jamaican popular music as it responded to the slow waning of British rule and the sudden ascendancy of the American eagle. Reggae music, in its variants from ska to ragga, emerged from a provincial folk music to the status of a national artform in the period of postcolonial Jamaica's push for economic autonomy. At the high-water mark of its international influence, reggae became *the* sound of cultural justice worldwide, its waxy mix of righteous dissidence and jubilant hope ringing with moral claims for equal rights and justice for all. In the words of Michael Manley, Jamaica's democratic socialist leader from 1972 to 1980 (and broken ex-ideologue in his 1988–92 administration), reggae went beyond "parochial boundaries" and achieved a global reach precisely because it was "the spontaneous sound of a local revolutionary impulse."[1] But the growth and export of Jamaican music also gave rise to new transnational cultural forms, as expressive of the new migrant world order as of those archaic, prenational traditions that were supposed to have been left behind. If the Two-Tone ska revival in England in the late 1970s was the "ghost dance of the British Empire" (in Dick Hebdige's memorable term),[2] the rowdy dialogue between metropolitan U.S. hip hop and the Jamaican yard tradition of the sound system DJ in the 1980s was a full-blown "black cowboy" genre that would upset the smooth prepackaged style of American pluralism, busy re-creating the globe in its own image.

Murder Dem

At the end of 1996, a year when many city mayors in the United States were trumpeting a noticeable drop in homicide rates, the body count in Jamaica reached an all-time high. The number of murders—over 900 (not including the 145 officially killed by police)—far surpassed the infamous mayhem of 1980, when a bloody election year was marked by a near civil war between heavily armed political goon squads. The militarization of civil society has proceeded apace from that year, and the steady evolution of garrison constituencies recently prompted the current People's National Party (PNP) government of P. J. Patterson to order a Committee on Political Tribalism to investigate the problem. At moments like these, self-scrutiny of the state is not enough; popular morality is also put on trial, and the various media of popular culture—with their likely quotient of sexual exuberance and outlaw bravado—are wheeled out as the usual suspects. In the United States, Hollywood and the TV industry have stepped forward with their own codes and promises of self-regulation in order to deflect heated scrutiny from conservative groups and grandstanding politicians.

In Jamaica the music industry has gone even further. Up to ninety-five performers, songwriters, producers, and media leaders formed a "music fraternity" to sign a Bill of Life, which acknowledged that "by omission or commission, we are partially responsible for the present crime wave and general level of criminality by certain elements of the populace, bearing in mind the influence of our music." The signatories pledged to "ensure that our lyrics will create the type of country we want to live in and wish our children to grow up in," and to work "to show the youth another way to succeed without the glorification of crime, violence, and immorality." Pressure was put on radio station managers to comply, there was early talk about a public record burning, and others proposed a peace concert or event at Torrington Bridge, marking the boundary between Uptown and Downtown—all-important in the heavily territorialized geography of Kingston.

The DJ Beenie Man was the only signatory among the performers who wielded real popular influence among Jamaica's armed ghetto warriors, and the agreement itself had no teeth.[3] But its significance cut many ways. The pledge was read by some as a challenge to political leaders to acknowledge the historic role of their own parties in patronizing the rise of gun culture in Jamaica. In particular, the opposition party (JLP) leader Edward Seaga had long been suspected of colluding with the CIA in the late 1970s to destabilize the country's fledgling democratic socialist administration through the introduction of arms into civil society.

From another angle, the Bill of Life may well feed into attempts to clean up an industry that is being prepared for the kind of promotional treatment accorded to Jamaica's other export-oriented industries. Reggae music is probably the country's most famous export, but because of the lack of industry structure (not to mention the unpredictability of its performers and creative content) it has not maintained the stability required for sustained state or corporate investment in its export potential (estimated recently at $2.5 billion). JAMPRO, the country's investment promotion agency, is now actively considering ways of turning reggae into yet another means of boosting foreign exchange earnings, in line, perhaps, with the export-oriented policies laid down by the notorious structural adjustment programs of international lending agencies like the IMF, the World Bank, and the Paris Fund. Indeed, in January 1997, Jamaican performers were the headliners for the opening night of MIDEM, the global music industry's annual festival in Cannes. It was a glorious opportunity to attract foreign investment. The acts, handpicked by JAMPRO—Tony Rebel, Jimmy

Cliff, Chevelle Franklin, Everton Blender, Freddie McGregor, the Mystic Revellers, Chalice, Mykal Rose, Culture, Ken Boothe, and Maxi Priest— all showcased the morally respectable face of reggae. The playfully flirtatious jams of Shaggy and Papa San were the only questionable elements of the show. There were no hardcore dancehall performers on the bill.

More immediately, however, the Bill of Life fed into the latest outbreak of middle-class morality fever. There had been much hand-wringing in the media of opinion and among religious and political leaders about the rise in public incivility and immorality and the parallel growth of American-style cynicism toward all national institutions. As in the United States, irreverent radio talk show hosts were cited as symptoms of the further decline of civil society, but the number one public enemy remained the dancehall DJ, the much maligned and self-styled "voice of the people." Just as strong in their denunciation of dancehall are the Rasta-dominated programs, hosted by the dub poet Mutabaruka and others, on IRIE-FM, the island's twenty-four-hour, massively popular reggae radio station.

In Jamaica it is virtually a cliché to observe that musical performers are the most influential voices among the general population. For a majority, who do not own TV sets and do not regularly read newspapers, DJs and their traveling sound systems have served as an alternate news medium and a source of information and commentary about politics and local affairs for many decades now. Given their influence among the young, there is an element of truth to the suggestion that popular music is a real medium of education for youth. Yet the act of attributing much of the responsibility for civil disorder to musical performers themselves is itself a cynical, not to mention risky, proposition on the part of the state's managers and morality brokers. It might be said that the ruffneck DJs of Jamaica, no less than the gangsta rappers of North America, would have had to be invented if they had not emerged from the social fabric.

But estimating the influence of the DJs or rappers is not simply a matter of public scapegoating. It goes to the heart of concerns about how culture is reproduced and disseminated, by which I mean culture in the broad sense of prevailing values, civic loyalties, and modes of behavior, expression, and respect for authority. Who governs the reproduction of culture among educable youth is a concern for any state, but above all for an effectively recolonized state whose sovereign capacity to direct its own social, cultural, and economic life has been eroded so radically over the last two decades, as it fell into the Third World "debt trap" common to so many postcolonial nations. Unable to rely on the diminished moral authority of the state, elites are more willing to demonize the "straight talk" of the dancehall MC than to blame the economic violence of structural adjustment programs for the fraternal distrust and incivility that emerge from the sustained hardship and impoverishment of Jamaica's popular classes.

What was the response of the dancehall massive to this bout of moralizing? The loudest chorus of gun salutes and firecrackers at Sting '96 (increasingly the most significant of reggae festivals in terms of the "popular vote" for competing performers) was reserved for tougher than tough Bounti Killer, whose G-man intransigence helped him steal DJ of the year award from his arch-rival, Beenie Man. Also greeted royally was newcomer Anthony B, whose fierce denunciations of politicians and businessmen had led to the banning of his song "Fire Pon Rome." In other respects it was the year of Lady Saw, whose salacious acts and lyrics as the queen of slackness showed no sign of abatement or compromise. Her hardcore transgressions matched those of "poor people's governor" Bounti in going far beyond rudeboy and rudegirl posturing. And if the top song of the year—Barrington Levy and Bounti Killer's duet "Living Dangerously"—was actually a morality tale about an unfaithful woman, its high refrain—the song's title emphasized by Levy's bright "canary voice"— could have served as an ironic requiem for the uneasy times.

But if Bounti and Saw stood out, the themes they represented no longer command the entire stage as they did two or three years ago. The "roots and culture" revival has come on strong, with Luciano, Tony Rebel, and Everton Blender taking over the torch last year from a fading Capleton and a surprisingly inactive Buju Banton. The return of roots veterans like Marcia Griffith, Judy Mowatt, and Dennis Brown was notable, as was the upsurge of the Lovers Rock romance tradition in singers like Beres Hammond and Sanchez. In a setting where shifts, however slight, in the popularity of certain performers, themes, and genres are widely interpreted as indicative of the mood of the public, what invites our attention is not so much the persistence of slack DJs as the revival of cultural reggae with spiritual and political convictions, linked in particular to Rastafarian precepts. Why now? And why in a roots format that Jamaican youth had either ignored or been encouraged to ignore for an entire generation?

Tell Dem Culture Come Back

After the deaths of Haile Selassie and Bob Marley and the subsequent "repeal" of roots reggae in the Reaganomic Jamaica of the 1980s, Rastafarianism receded from the world stage as a cultural phenomenon and suffered retrenchment at home as a social and religious force. Early on in that cruel decade, Peter Tosh wryly declared that "consciousness is illegal." Today, Rasta-inspired music is thriving again in the international marketplace and commanding respect in ragga dancehalls from Kingston to Toronto. Moreover, the roots and culture revival of the last two years seems to be more than a passing trend, more than the belated recognition, in a slow cycle, of those performers and communities who kept the Rasta faith all through the lean years.

The intellectual debt to Rastafari, as the grassroots voice of Black Power and Africanist consciousness in the Caribbean, is profound. Indeed, at a large conference on Caribbean culture in Kingston in March 1996 ("the first such occasion in five-hundred years," as one speaker noted), the audience, while treated to renowned intellectuals like George Lamming, Kamau Brathwaite, Stuart Hall, Lloyd Best, Rex Nettleford, and Edna Brodber, reserved some of its most heartfelt applause for the appearance of Mortimer Planno, the legendary, wizened Rasta elder and Marley mentor who had greeted Selassie off the plane on his epochal 1966 visit to Jamaica. To gauge the current relevance of Rastafari, however, you need to listen not to the postcolonial intelligentsia (with whom the elders have always had fractious relations), but to the booming sound systems that rule over every Jamaican village, and to the patter of every budding street corner DJ youth, spinning rhymes as compulsively as do hopeful young rappers in urban America. Many of the heroes of these youth—including leading performers like Buju Banton, Capleton, Everton Blender, Luciano, Tony Rebel, and Cocoa Tea—have been leading the march away from the X-rated, gunslinging arena of dancehall's lyrical lewdness, or "slackness," onto the higher, morally responsible ground of conscious preaching and spiritual teaching that had typified roots reggae in its 1970s heyday. A noticeable portion of the unruly sexual banter and ruffneck swaggering has already been edged out by more sober statements of righteous uplift. Lyrical praise for punany and Glocks have made way for anthems to Jah and Selassie-I. The way forward from sex-besotted "soldering" and "stabbing" and rudeboy rivalry was paved with positivity and rocked by nyabinghi drum rhythms, resonating with ancestral affinities. The most recent convert, Ninjaman, one of the most notorious dancehall gangstas (now named Brother Desmond), is testimony to the widespread impact and reach of the revival.

The ever protean history of Jamaican music is full of disputed boundary markers: When did mento become distinct from calypso? Who invented the famous afterbeat and when? When did rocksteady really begin? Why did the DJs take over from the singers in 1980? By the end of 1994 it was clear that another significant shift had occurred. Buju's censorious "Murderer," written after the DJ Panhead's death in late 1993, could be taken as one origin of the new mood. Accompanied by Capleton's "Cold Blooded Murderer" and Beenie Man's "No Mama," and followed by the deaths of Dirtsman, Early B, and the charismatic Garnett Silk (who, along with Tony Rebel and the Flames crew, was most responsible for initiating the culture revival in the mountain parish of Manchester), these wrathful sermons against violence in the dancehall community were unequivocal. There was no mistaking their heavy moral rebukes for the conventional lyrical wordplay in which a "murderer" could be a lethal loverman boasting of his sexual prowess or a victorious DJ lording it over some rival in the "sound boy killing" of a clash between sound systems.[4] Soaked in biblical dread ("Don't let the curse be upon your children's children / Abednigo, Shadreck, Meshek, Daniel in the den") and aimed at the neck of political corruption ("stop committing dirty acts for high officials"), Buju's call to hold the trigger hand was direct and forceful. It was also quite conventional, since the cut belonged to an antiviolence lyrical tradition that dates at least from the Wailers' first hit, "Simmer Down," in 1963, and is as endemic to reggae performance genres as the gangsta salutes, from gun-toting Prince Buster to Ninjaman, or the apocalyptic Rasta invocations of "blood and fire" to bring down Babylon. Coming from the rough-voice generator of salacious hits like "Batty Rider," "Woman Nuh Threat,"

"Stamina Daddy," "Love How Di Gal Dem Flex," and "Maasa Girl World," Buju's high moral tone was, at first, suspect. After all, his knack for hitting the sore spots of Jamaican cultural politics was well proven. His first hit, "Love Mi Browning," drew criticism for its pronounced preference for light-skinned women, as did "Serious" for its gunsel misogyny, while "Deportees," the biggest hit of his second album, brought its share of death threats his way. The storm of outrage and the media boycotts generated by "Boom Bye Bye," his anti-battyboy anthem, had threatened to put paid to his international crossover career.

Buju had acknowledged his immaturity before ("Browning" was followed by a tribute to dark-skinned women). This time around, he was unable to back down or apologize for fear of losing his hardcore raggamuffin following, and so his turn toward roots and culture on his 1995 album, *'Til Shiloh*, may have been one of the few musical options available to him. That it coincided with a shared momentum among influential DJs with the potential to turn the market away from slackness and rudeboy ragga was certainly providential. At the time, Buju still occupied the hot seat at the top of the DJ pile and, being so crucial to the dancehall circuit, he therefore had enough clout to do some retreading of his own without appearing to cave in to detractors. Shabba Ranks, his predecessor in the kingpin position, looked as if he might be following Buju's lead with the positive lyrics and African-based beats of cuts like "Think You Got It All." Yet it had been the Shabba of "Roots and Culture"—"I'm not a one way DJ"—who observed that culture and slackness are often closely melded:

> Coin! Two side.
> Get that?
>
> Hear Dis!
>
> Shabba Rankin reggae people's callin' out,
> People from east, west, north, and south.
> Say I'm the MC with the nasty mouth,
> Dem feel like is pure slackness alone I can talk about.

I know me roots & culture,
Who is the route Robert Nesta
And Bunny Wailer follow after,
It is music, mi charge for.
Look how deh world noh stop suffer.
What have black people under pressure.

Some talk dis, and some talk dat,
Say everyting from Shabba mouth is slack,
I love roots and reality straight to the max,
Because I'm a article ilabash.

I love mi roots & culture.
To teach all deh youngster,
And all yuh mudda and fader.
So dat yuh days will be longer.

Some talk dat, and some talk dis,
Nuff ah dem ah fight 'gainst slackness lyrics
You have to please, John Public.
When you're dealin' with deh, Reggae music.

. . . .

Some of dem ah bawl how dem want culture,
And some of dem waah people be vulgar,
I rather to stick to I culture.
Than to be, a dirty character.

. . . .

Come now!
Wine up yuh line if yuh love culture.
Tell Shabba to stop being vulgar.
Change up mi style and ah change mi order.

Shabba's invitation to his fans to choose his style for him is in keeping with the pseudo-electoral rules of competition to be the people's DJ of the year, a local title he nonetheless relinquished after his Grammy successes and his international status earlier in the 1990s, when he toured with North American star acts like Bobby Brown, Mary J. Blige, and TLC. Buju's successor, Beenie Man, put the matter more plainly in a *Vibe* interview when he spoke of his ecumenical approach to performance: "make the people know you are for the girls, for the Rastaman, for the Christian, for the rude boy, for the police." "For the police?" quizzes the interviewer. "Yes, mon, you haffi make Babylon love you. If they hate you, you dead."[5] Like Shabba's volunteer rootsman-for-a-day, Beenie's people-pleasing profile appears unprincipled, even as it acknowledges the pragmatic need to stay in contention, not to mention stay alive, on the DJ circuit. The more significant shift in status occurs when a performer moves from *serving* his various constituencies, as indicated in Beenie's comments, to *representing* those constituencies, and ultimately to representing a large sector of the musical culture in general, in the way some hardcore rappers are judged on their ability to "represent" hip hop as a whole. For a while after *Shiloh*, Buju, like the multitalented U.S. rapper Tupac Shakur (whose youthful career had shared some of the same tortured version of young black masculinity as the Jamaican), seemed set on this path. Arguably the greatest obstacle he and others, like Silk or the new superstar, Luciano, face is the "Bob factor"—the legacy of Marley, whose career is the clearest example and benchmark of this process of popular elevation.

Considered in its entirety, Marley's musical repertoire addressed all of Beenie's designated audiences, including the Babylon of the international corporate music industry, in the slick grip of which he became a world-renowned performer. From 1960s rudeboy steeped in R&B to full-fledged Rastaman with a rockist profile in the 1970s, he performed songs ranging from ghetto badman beats to sufferah anthems and one-world spirituals, leaving virtually no genre in Jamaican music untouched, including the pre-slackness (i.e., softcore) sex jams like "Stir It Up," "Guava Jelly," and "Kinky Reggae." Marley became a hero of the nation-building state culture as a result, rising above the party machine politics that had enlisted the Wailers in Michael Manley's seminal 1972 election campaigns, and even transcending the high-water mark of the 1978 Peace Concert, when he brought Manley and arch-rival Seaga together on stage in an attempt to cool off the street violence engendered by their political strife. By 1981 Marley could say, "I am what politics fights against" because he was "higher than politics." Beyond a certain point Babylon began to need Marley more than he needed the approval of Babylon.

This is not to say that Marley ever ceased to "represent" important constituencies. First there were the rudies—lawless, insurgent bad boys from Back O' Wall, Trenchtown, and other West Kingston shantytowns who typified the will of the ghetto sufferahs not to be marginalized. Next there were the Rasta locksmen from the West Kingston dungle—postcolonial subalterns who had spoken for the alienated black majority and would be lionized, under the rubric of Black Power, as Third World culture bearers. Then there was emergent Jamaica itself—a salient voice in the 1970s in the nonaligned movement, with its own foreign policy of support for colonial struggles in Africa and elsewhere. As the Wailers made the move from local ghetto heroes to global superstars, Marley's voice was crucial to each of these communities and their leadership style. Along the way, the sound of his music came to voice many aspirations beyond its Jamaican roots, including white, countercultural Euro-American groups for whom it replaced protest folk music as the ultimate politically correct sound, providing the habitual backdrop at many a rally or demonstration. Ultimately, of course, the Marley sound would become the winter siren song of the Jamaica Tourist Board, calling the baby boomers, black as well as white, in the northern strongholds of Babylon to their spiritual home in the south: "One world, one love / let's get together and feel alright." A light tonic hallelujah to the good life is conveyed by this anemic, posthumous version of a Marley ska classic, stripped of its resonance with the unity ethic in the Rasta liturgy of "I & I," or even in Marcus Garvey's Pan-African UNIA (Universal Negro Improvement Association) motto for all black diasporic peoples, "One God One Aim One Destiny."

The newly revived spirit of conscious reggae tells a different story than the tourist ads, but may not be unrelated. Shifts in the economy of the Caribbean region are as relevant today to the shape of Jamaican music as they were in the heady post-independence years of ska, rocksteady, and natty reggae. While the cultural dialogue between North American R&B

and Jamaican music had always been crucial and, at times, determined by ebbs and surges in the migrant outflow from the island, the influence of North American economic initiatives (among these, a concentration on the regional development of tourism) has been paramount in the last fifteen years. After its brief but courageous bid for autonomy under Manley's democratic socialist PNP governments of the 1970s, Jamaica was effectively integrated into the global economic system supervised by the World Bank group and the superstate to the north. As a result, virtually all political and economic decisions about national policy were increasingly dictated by technocrat cadres in Washington. The consequences of this integration have been immense, amounting to the de facto recolonization of the island state. Any explanation of shifts in the reigning musical paradigm will be incomplete without some consideration of this loss of effective sovereignty for a people whose "forward march" from colonialism lasted a mere fourteen years, until Jamaica became the test case for the new structural adjustment policies of the IMF. The coercive sway of the international lending agencies increasingly had a direct effect on daily life, turning on and off the spigot of "downpression," sufferahs' lingo for social hardship. The social consequences of this massive transformation of the economy have been exhaustively documented.[6] But what kind of effect did it have, if any, on Jamaican culture, where popular music has played a crucial role in shaping daily civil affinities, not just among people, but also in their relation toward the direction of the state? This essay is an attempt to suggest some answers.

The New Reasoning

The conscious revival prompts many possible interpretations, most of them linked to the ethical distance of roots reggae from the moral postures adopted by dancehall. But other interpretations are tied to the transnational development of Jamaican-American culture that has evolved in the last two decades.

   1) First, sustained public criticism of the DJ purveyors of slackness and rudeboy lyrics has taken its toll. Whether or not the acute infl-

uence of DJs is directly tied to the ghetto violence, it is not a good time for any public performer to be honoring, let alone heroizing, armed violence. Although the target of the shantytowners is more likely to be politicians than musicians, the criticism is increasingly coming from the poor neighborhoods themselves, not just from the middle-class opinion leaders who perennially fill the pages of the *Daily Gleaner* with moralistic homilies about the decline of the national character. A similar outcry against U.S. gangsta rap has prompted a major deflection of hip hop energies into the harmonizing swingbeat of R&B and sweet-and-spice soul. Hardcore rap is more and more an industry niche rather than a prevailing pressure zone in the culture at large.

2) In contrast to slack dancehall, spiritual reggae, with its conscious stance against corruption and injustice, is much more appealing to the generational cohort that is increasingly responsible for the social and moral management of the state. In the 1970s a great majority of liberal, middle-class youth were drawn to the sense of moral and political dissent conveyed by roots reggae. This generation, now professional-managerial, is becoming the most influential voice in the media, in education, and in social administration. As a result of their empowered managerial roles, the revival of reggae moralism means something different to this generation than it did in the 1970s. As for the carnivalesque immorality of the dancehall style, the recent importation of Trinidadian carnival to Kingston by wealthy white and brown Uptowners has offered a respectable alternative to the Downtown-oriented sensualism of ragga. Notwithstanding its own roots in marginalized Afro-Caribbean communities, carnival and soca music are now preferable to the uncouth displays of flesh, indecent costumes, and immodest *solo wainin* of the dancehall. Not for the first time is the double standard of middle-class morality nakedly revealed in its attitude toward nakedness. Not for the first time is the carnival tradition itself being used to obscure its origins in racial protest en route to serving as a colorful, exotic showcase for the multiethnic imagery favored by middle-class nationalism.[7]

3) The appeal of conscious reggae to youth must also be explained. One of the enduring lessons of subculture theory is that members of youth cultures often try to re-create the coherence of the culture once enjoyed by their parents but now no longer available in a world that appears to have fragmented and fallen from grace. Elements of the Rasta revival may pose a "magical solution" along these lines. Attempts to reclaim the style and iconography associated with the heyday of Black Power have been marked in recent years. The Malcolm X marketing boom of the early 1990s is unlikely to be matched by a Selassie or a Marcus Garvey equivalent, but there is no question that such revivals carry more than nostalgia value. Rearticulating the vocabulary of their parents' youth is not simply a retro youth style trend. It also carries a tailor-made conscience for today's youth seeking to match their parents' high idealism in response to the new hard times. Combine this with the profile among leading DJs of coming to maturity after their boisterous youth and you have a generational narrative about the return of the wayward children of Seaga to the prophetic life of the fathers.

4) The sustained levels of hardship and suffering among Jamaica's poor majority have taken their toll on the capacity of performers and the industry to maintain a steady diet of party music at the expense of songs of uplift that accompany popular desires for material improvements in daily life. The effects of the rapid penetration of the market economy in the 1980s—including class polarization, social Darwinism, and unalloyed materialism—helped to create a freewheeling culture that appeared to promise mobility and wealth, but that delivered its promise only to those already privileged and propertied. After fifteen years of this laissez-faire pecuniary culture, the socially denied had gotten their fill; as Bounti's popular lyric summarized it, "poor people fed up."

5) In response to the uncertainties of global integration and the migrating career of regional musics in the world beat market, it is no surprise to see resurgent strains of nationalism within the musical culture. The sound and message of conscious reggae carry

intensely nationalistic associations. The checkered international success of pure dancehall has basically been limited to niche markets in New York, Toronto, London, and Miami, where the heavy patois is readily understood and the club scene sufficiently sophisticated and flexible enough to accommodate the hardcore style. Those performers who have earned commercial visibility, like Shaggy, Patra, Maxi Priest, and Diana King, have all mined the crossover possibilities with rap and R&B. From the fathering Kool Herc on, the debt to Jamaica of hip hop has been immense and clearly audible in countless East Coast hardcore and Miami bass recordings. Indeed, ideas like the rap MC chatting on a mic over records and dual-turntable mixing both originate in Jamaica—a debt that is seldom acknowledged in the broader North American musical culture. But the pace at which dancehall artists like Shabba, Supercat, Yellowman, Mad Cobra, Papa San, Mad Lion, and Burru Banton have been producing reggae hip hop has quickened over the years, and has become almost commercially obligatory. Indeed, Bounti's hit 1996 album, *Xperience*, featured a raft of rap performers, including Busta Rhymes, Raekwon, Jeru the Damaja, and the Fugees. Dancehall's status abroad has increasingly come to be tied to its junior partnership in the career of hip hop, and consequently to the whims of important North American producers and market trends among Jamerican audiences. These Jamerican hybrids are increasingly the innovative model for producers in Jamaica itself—an example, if you like, of re-exportation, whereby goods from the periphery are channeled back from the metropolis. In comparison with this transnational product, roots reggae sounds more local, more like pure, unadulterated Jamaica. The irony of this situation is that most successful reggae acts worldwide continue to be roots veterans like Jimmy Cliff, Burning Spear, the Mighty Diamonds, Misty and Roots, Toots and the Maytals, Israel Vibration, Bunny Wailer, Culture, Mykal Rose, and Third World, all of whom are accepted with more enthusiasm than their ragga counterparts in Europe, Japan, Africa, and the non-Caribbean North America. Bob Marley's records continue to be the biggest money spinner of all, solidifying the universal perception that roots reggae is intrinsically the sound of

Jamaica. Thus is the cultural essence of a country fixed and frozen in place, as it often is in the market of world beat, where global consumption of a regional music is firmly identified with a particular sound (just as in global cuisine, where a particular national dish or regional preparation comes to *represent* the country and its people).

6) Last, Rastafari has been the vehicle for different aspirations at different times in the course of its sixty-year evolution and influence on groups in Jamaica, the Caribbean, North America, Britain, and Africa. The current revival is no exception, faced as it is with the conditions of neocolonialism, as opposed to the earlier periods of colonialism and postcolonialism. The "training" of Marley by Trenchtown elders to disseminate the movement's doctrines has bequeathed a legacy of belief in their ability to somehow govern the moral direction of popular music in Jamaica. But the more likely, and less conspiratorial, explanation for their renewed esteem is that Rastafarians have emerged as the single most respected social group in all of Jamaican society—an extraordinary reversal of their position since the 1950s, when they were generally reviled as social pariahs.

The Great Riddim Shift

To better understand the significance of the Rasta revival in music, we may find it instructive to take a closer look at the last great shift, the watershed of the early 1980s that remains a potent social legacy for so many Jamaicans. After all, Marley's cataclysmic death in 1981 coincided with the collapse of a Caribbean-style socialism that had responded to and fostered the black nationalist impetus of high roots reggae (notwithstanding the protests of many Rasta performers against both political parties' adoption of the music as a propaganda vehicle). In the course of a few years, the righteous nation-language of roots reggae, with its dread beats and militant riddims, had been supplanted by the raw body-language of dancehall, with its rowdy voiceplay, digital wizardry, and rollicking stop-go rhythms.

Unavoidably, this new style, playing fast and loose with all forms of morality, came to be associated with the eight-year rule of the Jamaica

Labor Party (JLP) of Edward Seaga (or CIAga, as he came to be known), the enthusiastic agent of Caribbean-style Reaganomics. The established tradition of Jamaican music, pre-dating the birth of reggae in 1968, held that social and political commentary was an integral part of the mix. In the new dancehall style of General Echo, Yellowman, Rongo, and Lone Ranger, political protest seemed to have dropped off the map entirely. Ironically, it had been Seaga himself, scholar of popular evangelical religions like pocomania and kumina, who first had introduced Rastafari, along with revivalist ritual and nyabinghi drumming, onto vinyl through his recording company (West Indies Records Limited), which produced acts like Byron Lee and the Dragonnaires.[8] Even so, the use of overtly political music at political events had been barred from the time of granting of adult suffrage in the People's Act of 1944 (and backed up by the provisions of the 1911 Night Noises Prevention Act), while protest reggae was systematically banned from the radio—the Wailers' "Small Axe," Junior Byles's "Beat Down Babylon," and "Everything Crash" by the Ethiopians, along with a host of others.

Inevitably, the growing moral authority of roots reggae among youth was enlisted in the campaign of the PNP, the party that promised to break with its allegiance to the brown-skinned, or "Afro-Saxon," middle-class elites and reclaim the socialist mantle it had once worn in the 1930s. In the 1972 campaign, then, the PNP's famous bandwagon included Bob Marley, Peter Tosh, Bunny Livingston, Max Romeo, Clancy Eccles, Judy Mowatt, Junior Byles, and Delroy Wilson, whose "Better Must Come" was adopted as the official party slogan. Manley used Rastafari iconography and symbols, including Selassie's gift, the Rod of Correction, as a spectacular stage prop to enlist the new regional sympathy for Black Power, and established for himself a public profile as the sufferahs' man. Protest reggae became the official soundtrack for the next eight years, functioning like a Greek chorus in passing judgment, by no means always favorable, on the progress of Manley's democratic socialist government. There was little compromise in conscious songs like Max Romeo's "War Inna Babylon," the Mighty Diamonds' "Right Time," Niney's "Blood and Fire," Joe Higgs's "Sons of Garvey," Bob Andy's "Fire Burning," Bunny Wailer's "Battering Down Sentence," Alton Ellis's "Lord Deliver Us," Bob Marley's "Get Up Stand Up," and "War," Pablo Moses's "We Should Be in Angola," or the Revolutionaries' "MPLA."

In response, the JLP lost no opportunity to appropriate to its cause the symbology of roots (Seaga's spiritual mentor was Mallica "Kapo" Reynolds, a widely feared pocomania shepherd-priest), including the de-anglicized dialect and protest reggae lyrics like Ernie Smith's "Jah Kingdom Gone to Waste" and "The Message," Neville Martin's song about law and order. But while JLP campaign slogans like "Equal Rights and Justice" sounded like militant Rasta demands, Seaga's party was much more effective at scaring up the communist threat and utilizing the tactics of destabilization. The latter, which involved the militarization of sectors of ghetto life through organized gang warfare and political intimidation on a national scale, was aided and abetted by a barely covert U.S. policy supervised by the CIA. This policy had been pioneered in Allende's Chile and would have an effective role in destabilizing the politics of other Latin and Central American countries.[9]

By the time of the ultraviolent 1980 campaign, the ethical gravity of Rastafarian culture had lost much of its coherence. Adding to the rivalry between the several Rasta camps, there were doctrinal differences over the meaning of Selassie's death in 1975 and the policy of repatriation. Leading reggae musicians had been either driven overseas by death threats or seduced by lucrative contracts in the transnational music industry. To bring it more into line with the expectations of white rock audiences, reggae performers had adapted the sound (virtuoso guitar additions and less bass) so that, to many, it no longer "felt" entirely Jamaican. Lovers Rock, a smooth pop marriage of reggae and soul, as practiced by crooners like Gregory Isaacs, Sugar Minott, Frankie Paul, or Johnny Osbourne, was seen as another symptom of the expatriation of reggae. The elemental, stripped-down, free-form genre of dub was one response to this situation, favored by the purists and an avant-garde enthusiast audience (the vocals were dropped, it was said, because the downpression was too severe to describe in words). The other response was dancehall, which went off in quite another direction and took the popular Jamaican audience with it. Patois and vernacular earthiness took over. The English language (even in its trickstered, Rasta version) and universal spirituality were pushed aside. Dancehall returned music to the orbit of the local sound systems, away from the stadium rock arenas and concert halls of the world music circuit. Moreover, roots reggae had settled into a sluggish, formulaic mold, akin to trance music, augmented by Sly Dunbar's "rockers" or "militant" drum patterns, which slowed the beat even further. The local recording industry jumped on the challenge of dancehall's dynamic, innovating energy, perceived as more relevant to the restless spirit of the youth massive.

If there was an element of nationalism in this shift, it was not simply Jamaican, but also black. Arguably, this had always been the case, since the birth of distinctively Jamaican popular music in the late 1950s. The fledgling Jamaican recording industry had gotten its real start when the demand for imported American R&B records began to outstrip the supply of these records to the mobile sound systems that played to popular dance crowds. Record companies like Seaga's began to grow out of the sound system circuit. The subsequent establishment of the afterbeat (emphasizing the downbeat on the second and fourth of a 4/4 bar) as the syncopation trademark of Jamaican popular music followed closely upon the incorporation and defusion of black R&B in the United States into the white rock n' roll juggernaut. The persistence of this rhythmic choice (preserved in many dancehall riddims) as an innovation ranks it among the most important in black musical history. The development of an independent industry with an independent sound had immediate resonance for the moment of Jamaican independence in 1962. But the presence of specifically African riddims and meanings had also been registered—*burru* drumming from the famed Rasta drum family of Count Ossie featured in some of the earliest Jamaican recordings, such as the legendary "Oh Carolina." This Africanist frame of reference would take further form in the favorite lyrical theme of "Israelites-in-exile" (as in Ossie's "Babylon Gone" and "Another Moses") and in the emergence of ska, a genre conscious of both its urban ghetto and its rural Afro-Christian roots, and rocksteady, which flaunted and celebrated its menacing ghetto profile. Finally, the high period of reggae is synonymous with both Black Power and Jamaica's bid to forge a political and economic alternative in the Caribbean to the Cuban (command economy) and Puerto Rican (industrialization by invitation) models of development.

Nationalism does not always take the middle-class form of sovereign self-respect. It can also find a subaltern vehicle in licentious popular behavior, which strays from both the middle-class morality of nation building and the fierce asceticism of the militant anticolonial way. While the advent of slackness in the dancehall was partly a result of an unofficial ban on conscious reggae, it was also a parochial expression of popular culture, and raucously vernacular to the degree to which it alienated an entire generation weaned on reggae's push into the international music field. And just as roots reggae lost much of its local urgency when exported through the world beat circuit, so too the sexual carnival of slack dancehall came to mean something else in the raunchy party rap of Luke Skywalker's Miami Bass sound, the T&A slapstick of Sir Mix-A-Lot, and the seamier side of much of gangsta rap. It was as remote in tone from black nationalist rapper-preaching in the United States as from the conscious rights and justice reggae tradition in Jamaica.

Yet the warring duet between the culture and slackness of Jamaica is a variant of ancient tensions within popular culture, where the licentious body-based commentaries of the comic genres are devalued as trivial or decadent in comparison with those genres, like tragedy, that offer commentary about morals and government. Ribaldry is well nigh universal in all folk cultures, but the public showcasing of bawdy behavior and wordplay is a familiar component of black diasporic music that is at other times channeled into overt forms of protest. The history of calypso and R&B displays this seesaw effect, alternating between the tactics of the bedroom and the confrontationalism of the street; with niche marketing, these tensions have become increasingly separated into different genres with different audiences. Intimations of guilt on the part of the sexual boasters are often matched by complaints about the abolition of "consciousness" from the musicians who ply the more political genres.

The emergence of bawdy dancehall in the early 1980s has been interpreted, most notably by British cultural studies scholar Paul Gilroy, as a symptom, or consequence, of Seaga's ascendancy and the climate of intimidation created by his goon squads. In assessing the implications of this displacement of protest reggae by lewd dancehall, Gilroy resists the "simple polarity in which all toasters were agents of reaction and all singers troubadours of revolution."[10] Nonetheless, the tendency of his analysis suggests that there is little to redeem the new style, and it is indeed a view that quickly became common currency among roots singers themselves. The iconoclastic Jamaican critic Carolyn Cooper has presented the most sustained disagreement with this tendency, arguing that slack dancehall's focus on sexuality is also a riposte to the patriarchal moral righteousness espoused in biblically inspired Rasta doctrine.[11] Needless to say, dancehall was reviled by official guardians of middle-class morality, such as the *Gleaner*, Jamaica's influential conservative daily paper of record, and sometime defamer of reggae itself before it was accepted by the middle class in the 1970s.[12] For Cooper, dancehall's earthiness and intimate attention to the female body make it a transgressive genre, as political in its own way as the masculinist, spiritual militancy of conscious reggae. Although it varies from community to community (and is most liberal, and middle-class, in the Twelve Tribes of Israel, to which Marley himself belonged), Rasta doctrine profoundly subordinates women, either through elevation to the status of the noble African queen or through relegation to impure, Babylonian carnality. Women are often assigned to the rank of a defiled and contaminating element of the social body, avoided during menstruation, and generally excluded from cooking and other ritual aspects of the righteous lifestyle.

While dancehall lyrics are often summarily dismissed as disrespectful to women, the dancehall scene has fostered a more complex dialogue about gender and sexuality—noisy, disobedient, and morally awkward—than had roots reggae, traditionally focused on race and class. Subordinated for so long in the Rasta hierarchy, with its rural and biblical moral orientation, women have had a much more participatory role to play in the musical culture of an urban, market economy. In dancehall lyrics, women may be "wicked," in the sexually suggestive sense of the term, but they are not a source of evil. Their sexuality is subject to analysis and devaluation, but in a less fundamentalist scenario in which the male DJ challenges and is often challenged in backchat and body language by the female body he is addressing. The musical performance is frankly addressed to women in a way that roots reggae was not. New York music critic Frank Owen supports this interpretation, against the prevailing view that dancehall "sold out" the militant Marley tradition. For Owen, antipuritanical dancehall pays tribute to the erotic power of women, and its playful sexism is far removed in spirit from the misogyny of so much gangsta rap, which displays a "paranoid fear" of women as "ball breakers" and "gold diggers."[13] Owen's distinction may be a difference in degree rather than a difference in kind. After all, neither gangsta rap nor ragga is a "positive" genre, devoted to racial uplift or utopian images of a better world. As "reality" or "raunch" genres, their mode of confronting the world is no less conventional—it is the result of a long history in black popular music—but they generate a range of emotions and responses that cannot be taken for granted, nor can they be easily contained. Instead, these are sentiments that can be magnified, exploited, mismanaged, and overindulged as they spill over from the constraints of the genre's conventions into the highly personalized complex of daily resentments, desires, and aspirations. Ethical rules of thumb are less certain in the all too human world of Shabba's "Love Punany Bad" or Lady Saw's "Stab Up Mih Meat" than in the ritually cleansed realm of Jah. Babylon is not only the corrupt, commercial order of "politricks" that must be swept away, it is also part of us.

Cooper gives a full treatment to the slackness/culture dialectic. The interplay between the two is obviously not the invention of a cultural critic; it is explicitly played upon in dancehall lyrics, and increasingly so, given the recent challenge to slackness by the culture revival. While the gun lyric is usually placed on the side of slackness, it often straddles the divide on account of its associations with ghetto militancy or insurgency. A thin line, moreover, separates the rules of competition between performers and rival crews and the heroization of gang-style aggression. Gun glorification has been in style in Jamaica since Duke Reid, Coxsone Dodd, Prince Buster, and others ruled over the sound system wars with the iconography of the gangster gun, "murdering" rivals by the dozen. In time, the Johnny Too-Bads of the rudeboy period (like the French New Wave film directors) took the American gangster movie as an existential model for ghetto militancy. Whether as cultural rebels ("posing" for effect), radical youth, political goons, or small-time criminals, many rudies began to adopt a Rasta warrior profile in order to augment their fearsome appearance. Dreadlocks were now the style of choice not only for the dissident youth but also for the badman posses who were recruited and organized into the political machines of the JLP and PNP in the 1970s. Jamaican working-class politics had long been run through gang patronage. It's common mythology that if a party loses an election, the neighborhood it ruled would starve, and so gang godfathers in each electoral district were tight with high party officials in control of constituencies like Rema and Tivoli Gardens in West Kingston, and Nannytown in

East Kingston. While the aggression had initially been more symbolic threat than real violence, Seaga's emergence in the 1970s brought to reality the ethic of "fire for fire, blood for blood" between rival "don-gaddas" and their rankings. The PNP responded with a campaign of discipline called "Heavy Manners." Guns flowed into the country (through U.S.-sponsored channels in the ganja trade, it was widely believed), and the violent transformation of civil society ensued as part of an orchestrated attempt to destabilize a country forging an independent path toward Caribbean socialism. When the smoke cleared after the killings of the 1980 elections, many of the gangsta posses moved north to the United States in the wake of a law-and-order crackdown widely perceived as a PR move by the new government to suggest that the gangs' local political utility to the JLP had been terminated. Subsequently, the North American media sensationalized or embellished the activities of the gangs.[14] The Spanglers, the Renklers, the Shower, the Dunkirk, the Tel Aviv, the Waterhouse, the Forties, and the McGregor Gully posses of Miami and Brooklyn would not only become part of the folklore of gangsta rap and U.S. dancehall, they would also challenge the status of the Caribbean immigrant as a model minority—hardworking, family-oriented, and education-conscious. Not long after the Bureau of Alcohol, Tobacco and Firearms (ATF) launched its Operation Rum Punch against the Jamaican posses in October 1987, the established tabloid wisdom proclaimed that the Jamaican posses had been primarily responsible for introducing Colombian cocaine into America's cities in the form of crack.[15]

In the course of the decade, hardcore rap absorbed ragga rhythms and the rudeboy profiling of the lyrical gangsta. This combination made gangsta rap a prime candidate for the role of public enemy or folk devil in a classic outbreak of moral panic. For more liberal critics, gangsta lyricists, in both the United States and Jamaica, reflected the gangsterization of society from the top down, as the newly deregulated market forces penetrated both the civic fabric and the sensual life of the individual. Once the mental weaponry of social Darwinism was unleashed, gunmetal would surely rule over the new informal economies carved out of the shadowy underbelly of deregulated capitalism, whose own folk heroes were the aggressive corporate raiders of the 1980s—much more powerful public enemies than the street corner hood. Increasingly, Jamaica became inte-

grated into this economy, and the corruption of its businessmen and public officials, and the organized crime of the don-gaddas and ganja lords
mimicked the deformation of civil society in the metropole to the north.
Elites began to complain of an overall "coarsening" of the Jamaican character, or Butooism, as Rex Nettleford described it, in reference to a term
for the unrefined.

On the other hand, the gunman lyrics and the swaggering attitude of
ragga and gangsta rap preserved the formal core of militancy in an age
when conscious music had been pushed to the periphery of commercial
and public culture. In the United States, urban blacks were being radically
marginalized through economic attrition and penal discipline, and so the
musical culture of hip hop became unavoidably confrontational, whether
in its nationalist or ghetto-centric form—the high point being the flap
around Ice-T's "Cop Killer" (not a rap, but a metal, song). Of course,
none of this was bad for sales. Outlaw songs are not only a genre favorite
but also a perennial money spinner in all sectors of popular culture
(Bounti Killer, for example, did not hit pay dirt until he recorded "Coppa
Shot" at about the same time Ice-T's song ran into trouble). Sales depend
on the outlaw genres being periodically taken up and publicly castigated
as an immoral example of civil decline and national decay. Thus, the rude
artillery of dancehall music met with the same public defamation as the
Glocks, blunts, and bitches of gangsta rap.

The ensuing defense ran the gamut from the civil libertarian position
to the traditional realist position that artists simply hold up a mirror to
society. Other familiar arguments included the following: art is often
required to be socially transgressive; lyrical exuberance, bodily excess, and
warrior pride have an ancient role in African or diasporic black music;
symbolic violence in culture is good social therapy for averting actual
strife; the legacy of violence done to black people under slavery and colonialism has been internalized and is never far from the surface of black
expression; black people have only ever achieved rights and justice
through arming themselves, whether in colonial insurrection and slave
uprising or in symbolic confrontation (Black Panthers) with, or as agents
and defenders (soldiers or policemen) of, the state; without the armed
gangs and violent threats posed in ghetto culture, inner cities would more
closely resemble a police state than they already do.

A more complex offshoot of the debate about violence emerged in the 1992 public flap in the United States and Britain over Buju Banton's "Boom Bye Bye," a song that was typical of the anti-battyboy genre that had produced the likes of Tippa Irie's "Battylero," General Degree's "Shot a Faggot," Fragga Ranks's "Girls Highway," Capleton's "Lotion Man," Cobra's "Crucifixion," and countless others. The lyrical attack on homosexuality had become such an obsessive element of the slackness scene and so highly conventional that one couldn't help wondering what lay behind the DJs' devotion to this public ritual of homophobia. In many of the Jamaican dancehalls I have attended, DJs still call out for the crowd to vocally affirm their opposition to homosexuals: "all battyboy fi dead." Enough of the crowd responds for a sense of consensus to emerge. From the perspective of an outsider, this ritual call-and-response can be spine-chilling. Yet the DJ toast is one of the many rhetorical techniques (including the recent emergence of an antipapist call) used to rouse the crowd to a cacophonous vocal pitch. To respond is to affirm your loyalty to the institution of the dancehall itself. Meanwhile, in New Kingston or up in the Blue Mountains beyond Kingston, clientele at a gay club (often viewed as a postmodern form of the maronnage that once thrived in the same mountains) may be dancing, with great irony, to the same battyboy anthems.

Most middle-class Jamaicans will say that since its gestural form is more important than its content, the battyman rant lies beyond or to the side of *real* homophobia, and that it is essentially a lower-class prejudice. Gays and lesbians lead a relatively undisturbed life in middle-class society, provided they do not assert their identity publicly, while working-class queers are often street higglers or vendors, giving back as good as they get in the way of verbal banter and abuse.[16] Whether the battyman obsession is just a cheap crowd-puller or whether, as I shall suggest later, it is linked to more fundamental tenets of state morality, it has proven the least portable aspect of the Jamaican music scene, in the wake of the immensely successful protests over the release of "Boom Bye Bye" on the part of U.S. gay groups like GLAAD, GMAD, and OUTRAGE, and the subsequent highly publicized exclusion of Buju and Shabba Ranks from U.K. and U.S. television talk shows. Many commentators who had explained away rappers' lyrical flights about killing cops as an escapist or therapeutic fantasy of the oppressed regarded the song's targeting of gays

as an oppressor's fantasy and thus as an abhorrent incitement to real violence. Even when such songs were perceived as a desperate attempt on the
part of the downpressed black male to retain power, any kind of power,
over his immediate environment, the condemnation of battyboy-bashing
was as sharply pronounced as the censure of misogyny, its structural counterpart in hip hop. In the rush to condemn there was a tendency to stigma-
tize all of ragga music and Jamaican culture as a whole, just as hip hop had
come to bear the burden of the hardcore gangsta genre's misogyny. The
charges of homophobia generated a heated debate in Jamaica itself. Plans
to organize gay people in a demonstration for civil rights brought down an
avalanche of threats from within this strongly religious society.[17] In the
meantime, the North American press produced a medieval picture of
Jamaican backwardness. In a major *Village Voice* article, the Trinidadian
American Peter Noel wrote, "In Jamaica, hunting batty bwoys is as instinc-
tive as craving for fry fish an bammy, a national dish. The mere sight of
them can trigger the bedlam of a witch hunt" or a "stoning."[18]

Some Jamaican intellectuals saw it differently. In an important article
that showed how the inflammatory English translation of Buju's patois
went out of its way to highlight prejudice, Carolyn Cooper argues that "to
Jamaican ears," "Boom Bye Bye" was as much a salute to heterosexuality—
and a tribute to "the sweetness between women's legs" in particular—as an
assault on homosexuality. "Indeed," she argues, "the implied dancehall
audience in Buju's song is not gun-toting homophobic men but heterosexual women who have a vested interest in the DJ's peg." In this form of dialogue, she sees diasporic "remnants of West African female fertility cults."
Going on to chide the "heterophobia" of northern gay groups, she compares the "cultural arrogance of the new politically correct liberals" with
that of "old world imperialists," and concludes with a warning: "given the
historical context of a dislocating politics of Euro-American imperialism in
the region, 'hard-core' Jamaican cultural nationalists will resist any re-
examination of indigenous values that is perceived as imposed upon them
by their imperial neighbor in the North. In the rhetoric of the lyrical gun,
this heterophobic, neo-imperialist offensive may back-fire."[19]

Cooper's response to "the devaluation of misunderstood local traditions" illustrates the chronic conflict between the universal assumptions of
northern liberal conceptions of human rights and the culturally specific

assumptions of southern countries. This is not the first time that a local song has taken on a different meaning in an international arena, nor is it the first time northern liberalism has been challenged by Third World cultural nationalists. But Cooper's argument that "politically correct" northern liberalism is continuous with classic colonialist patterns is worth examining further, especially in light of the new cultural patterns produced by a globalizing economy.

Cooper's recognition of the strict opposition between local and foreign values does not necessarily do justice to competing forms of nationalism within the postcolonial state, nor does it address the complex moral geography that links Caribbean states with the immigrant-busy metropoles.[20] The spread of economic liberalization and the regional impact of global restructuring have created a migrant geography that bears less and less resemblance to the older core-periphery colonial relationship.[21] In the Caribbean, a dynamic bipolar culture, underpinned by a remittance economy, now links migrant communities in the old metropoles of Paris, London, and New York with the island communities. As this kind of culture has assumed the status of political transnationality (many Caribbean nationals retain citizenship rights even if they take up metropolitan citizenship), the older ideology of return has eroded. So, too, the codes of assimilation have altered significantly. While prewar West Indian immigrants to the United States became black Americans for the most part, West Indian ethnicity has become a distinct form of identity in recent decades, often subsuming all island cultures into a pan-Caribbean formation that makes little sense in the Caribbean itself. (Ironically, the historical movement for such a formation in the Caribbean, peaking in the lapsed plans for a West Indian Federation, had been inspired by hopes for regional autonomy from U.S. influence.) Holding on to an island dialect and emphasizing other island traits carry distinct economic advantages in the U.S. employment market, where West Indians are perceived as better-educated and harder-working than African Americans. West Indian identity is beginning to play a role in local and even national American politics (with the presidential speculations about Colin Powell)—a role somewhat distinct from black American political life and more akin to the organized groupings of white ethnics.[22] For most West Indians in the United States, crossing the ethnicity line into black America is a choice with consequences. In the case of gays it is quite common, affording a safer, slightly less homophobic haven.

For those who retain a West Indian identity, there are many areas of daily metropolitan life where Caribbean moral and religious traditions are seen to be compromised. While this is a familiar immigrant story—the old country (rural) morality giving way eventually in the second and third generation to urban, secular, and cosmopolitan values—its dimensions are less clear cut in the new global city or in cities like Kingston and Montego Bay, where access to massively imported American consumer culture is difficult to avoid.

Above all, the new migrant economy has had a special impact on women as the traditional custodians and bearers of cultural values and morality. In contrast with pre-1965 West Indian migration to Britain, where males had found jobs in the booming postwar economy, women led the subsequent migration to the United States, where employment opportunities in domestic labor, nursing, and the burgeoning postindustrial service sector were less favorable to men. Many women also went "a'foreign" in order to separate or divorce, and were able to pursue a greater degree of economic and social independence in the metropolis.[23] The impact of this independence afforded women a more prominent role in the social forefront of West Indian communities. At home, the impact on women of economic restructuring in the region was even more significant. In Jamaica, up to a third of all households are headed by women, and over 60 percent of the female labor force was employed full-time prior to the IMF restructuring in the late 1970s, constituting over 45 percent of the employed labor force.[24] With their uncommonly high rate of labor participation, women were particularly susceptible to economic shifts, but the IMF policies were designed to exploit their labor in low-wage, export-oriented jobs while reducing their participation in traditional sectors of the economy geared to production for local needs.

Beginning in the late 1970s, the IMF pioneered its structural adjustment policies in the Caribbean, using Jamaica as a test case for its deferral of the southern debt crisis. The terms of IMF loans dictated that resources hitherto allocated to local food production, social security, education, and health services were shifted to export promotion, fiscal austerity, and deflationary adjustment of the dollar. When Seaga declared Jamaica open to free enterprise and foreign investment in 1980, Reaganomics saw its best opening in the region, and international loans poured in. Declaring the region a security priority, on account of the threat of Caribbean socialism, Reagan launched the Caribbean Basin Initiative (CBI) in the guise of a mini Marshall Plan. Loans were secured as part of the security policy agenda—the prototype for NAFTA and the future Free Trade Area of the Americas—and U.S. firms were encouraged to move domestic jobs to the region. An economic and political disaster for countries like Jamaica, the CBI was a tremendous success for the United States, ensuring regional penetration of its exports, limited access to its domestic markets for Caribbean producers, cheaper than cheap labor for U.S. manufacturers, an expanded military presence, and the eradication of any nationalistic ideas about autonomous development. Above all, the exploitation of a low-wage labor pool in its backyard helped U.S. producers compete with Asian imports to its own domestic markets.[25]

The subsequent economic revolution, ushered in by USAID, the World Bank group, and other international debt agencies, was based on the feminization of cheap labor, especially in the new offshore female-intensive industries: garment, textiles, light assembly, tourism, data processing, and electronics. The availability of cheap, low-skill, high-turnover female labor was the key to attracting foreign investment and multinational production to the region, aided and abetted by World Bank/USAID loans, legislation, and policies that brought into being the infamous Export Processing Zones (EPZ) and Free Trade Zones (FTZ), where goods are assembled for export. (The IMF is not known as the International Mother Fucker for nothing.) In some respect, this brought advantages to women, allowing them, as Linda Lim has argued,

> to leave the confines of the home, delay marriage and childbearing, increase their incomes and consumption levels, improve mobility, expand individual choice and exercise personal independence. Working for a local or foreign factory is for many women at least marginally preferable to the alternatives of staying at home, early marriage and childbearing, farm or construction labor, domestic service, prostitution or unemployment, to which they were previously restricted. Factory work, despite the social, economic, and physical costs it often entails,

provides women in developing countries with one of the very few channels they have of at least partial liberation from the confines and dictates of traditional patriarchal social relations.[26]

On the other hand, women, if they had children, now had to bear a double burden—not only functioning as breadwinners, but also compensat-
ing for the retrenchments in health, education, and social services with
their own unpaid overtime work. And if they became unemployed, as has
happened to many since the NAFTA accord sucked their jobs into Mexico,
the only recourse was the informal economy, where concealed wage work
in an unstable environment provided cheap goods and services as a subsidy
to the corporate export-oriented sector.[27] Nonetheless, the informal economy also fostered the one unequivocal gain for women in the flourishing
of higglers (or Informal Commercial Importers, as designated by the government), the famous hustling traders who linked local and foreign produce and goods made scarce by the new export economy to the urban
consumer market, thereby earning their own foreign exchange.[28] The IMF
and CBI policies pulled Jamaica further and further into the "debt trap"
(with one of the largest per capita debts in the world by the late 1980s), and
the austerity measures forced on the nation's people caused immense social
hardship. The traditional "downpression" on the poor locked into a brutal
spiral, reinforced by the post-NAFTA loss of jobs, markets, and income.
Collective action and protest on the part of women, in particular, became
a significant feature of the political landscape from the late 1970s on, just
as the offshore sweatshops became part of the physical landscape, ranged
along Kingston's newly union-free waterfront.

At a time when male employment had been drastically cut by these
same economic forces, the female body became an excessively charged
object of contention. Ever more conspicuous as an economic force in
society, women drew down male anxiety on several fronts. Violence
against women increased as the identity of the male breadwinner was further undermined, and the state's redoubled reliance on women both to
produce and reproduce added more impetus to the moral regulation of
their sexual behavior. Morality became a high pressure zone.

Jacqui Alexander has argued that the campaign of postcolonial nation
building involved the triumph of the conjugal nuclear family over the

extended family. The middle-class markers of a nation fit to govern itself with moral rectitude were upright, manly bearing and normalized sexuality for men and the defense of the family for women. Respectability had to displace the colonial mythologies woven around black males as "hypersexualized stalkers" and black women as wenches or Jezebels.[29] As the postcolonial Caribbean state loses its economic and political autonomy, policing the internal threat of sexual decadence, especially homosexuality, becomes one of its legislative anchors. Making a show of this policing affirms that the state managers can (a) uphold the morality demanded of ranking participants in the global order of nations; (b) enforce a culturally submissive value system on female workers; and (c) reassure male citizens, religious authorities, and tourists about the stability of the realm of sexuality, whether in the conjugal bed or in the for-export sphere advertised by the sensual native body.

As Alexander notes, the latter constitutes a paradox. The state must police sexuality through the morality of the black family—however thin on the ground—while ensuring that the island and its people are represented as sexually inviting and female, in order to fuel the all-important tourist trade. Here, the outlawing of homosexuality offers a bridge, announcing the protection of conjugal heterosexuality and issuing a clean bill of health for the nation's bodies—AIDS-free for the comfort of foreign visitors. Alexander's analysis is of Trinidad and Tobago and the Bahamas (both of which recriminalized homosexuality under recent revisions of the colonial Offences against the Person Act of 1864), but her arguments have much relevance for the Jamaican situation, where rumors about the government relaxing the laws against homosexuality provoked a storm of protest. Subsequently, the PNP administration in Jamaica has been referred to as a "battyman government," a popular interpretation that also refers to the excessively private nature of the prime minister's personal life and the compliant record of his cabinet in its dealings with foreign capital.

Given this agenda of national concerns about morality, it's no surprise that the carnivalesque world depicted in the dancehall provoked sustained opposition from Uptown morality. The dancehall, after all, appeared to revive many of the repressed, hypersexualized colonial stereotypes and give them full, fleshly life in clubs that provided an erotic sanctuary for dirty dancing and exhibition dressing. Here were the oversexed male buck, often a buccaneer, and, above all, the lascivious female skettel, gussied up in batty riders, poom-poom shorts, and punny printers that showcased the buttocks and genitalia, and sporting the kind of shiny, synthetic club outfits and multicolored hair extensions that won some dancehall queens the term "chemical duppies." Many of the women were higglers, the intercultural brokers of the informal economy, who profited enough from their bartering to purchase the often extravagant clothing. As in most subcultures, the flamboyance of a minority defines the whole: most dancehall fans do not choose to, or cannot afford to, participate in the full exhibitionistic drama. Nor is the dancehall world a unified expression of popular feeling or taste.

Some women were among those doing the toasting—DJs like Lady Saw, Patra, Lady G, Lady Apache, Worl-A-Girl, and Shelly Thunder—matching boast for boast, taunt for taunt. In addition, women began to work as producers and managers, and the dance floor certainly provided a more receptive social space for women to enter and for the famous dancehall queens to rule over. The sexualized theater of the dancehall could be seen in general to recognize women's newfound centrality in the economy. But the geography of the dance floor also dramatized the contest over who controlled access to their prized bodies. Acknowledging that they are representing the homosocial majority of the male onlookers or accomplices, the predominantly male DJs address themselves to the women in the dancehall as much in the spirit of competition as from a position of domination. If anything, their boasts announce, often with self-conscious pathos, that their bodies are more attractive and coveted than those of their rivals, male and female. But the ultracool, unperturbable attitude of the ruling divas on the dance floor tells a different story. Often encircled by men whom they barely acknowledge, they choose when and where they deign to respond. Most often the response is directed to each other in the form of heavy female bonding, or in the form of some autoerotic dance gesture, or else in a busy salute of their derriere to the crowd at large, each act in full awareness of their control over the flow of lyrical addresses and male gazes for as long as they choose to be the object of such attention. As the evening progresses, the "barricade" of men inches closer to the queens, but the women are as likely to maintain their distance as to lock into a routine grind with the men. A strong female DJ like Lady Saw alters the whole structure of response. The men in the crowd are mute, the women vocally engaged.

The dangers of abstracting the slack lyrics of the dancehall from this highly structured context should be obvious, and yet radio and recordings make it inevitable. The same might be said of the battyman toasts; in context, they help to underpin the delicate balance of sexual exchange between men and women in the dancehall. A consensus about the exclusion of homosexuality is one of the fundamental rules of play, setting limits to the lengths to which slackness can go. Not all forms of sexual exchange are permitted here, and the rule of heteronormativity serves as a stabilizing feature for the zone of sexuality encompassed by the dancehall. It is not such a great leap to see how this anxious ruling responds in kind to the state's and the churches' concerns about the protection of heterosexual morality, but the dancehall appears to embody these concerns at the same time as it transgresses the degree and quality of middle-class respect for decency. It may be no more accurate to see the music as dirty ghetto talk that undermines middle-class respectability than to see the dancehall as a regulatory safety valve for class conflict or an escapist haven from the hardships of economic adjustment. Like all forms of popular culture, the dancehall is compromised, multivocal, and as likely to serve its faithful with a taste of liberation as with a reminder of society's limitations.

Jah Is Standing by My Side

While reggae had initially sprung from the "ragged" (a favored etymology) social fabric of urban slums, its roots and Rasta substyles often claimed alternative, rural loyalties and were aimed in protest at urban corruptions. Dancehall was entirely urban from the first, and it evolved in the newly privatized world of the marketplace, where goods and services were valued as pure commodities. In this milieu, name brand or designer clothing and material possessions were worn and flaunted like personal spoils, rather than as shared tribal emblems of communal identity (as in Rasta tams, colors, and lion insignia). A DJ might, for example, take the name Spragga Benz, and his clone would be Spragga Lexus, in a wry tribute to materialism. As in hip hop, the music subculture transformed these commodity items into totems of urban folklore, but the comparative advantage of the individual, whether it was measured in pecuniary, sexual, or militaristic terms, became the criterion most valued by the massive.

By the early 1990s the individualizing culture of neoliberal economics had impacted virtually every domain of social habit and popular expression in Jamaican society. So it was hardly surprising that when the born-again bad boys of slackness turned to conscious preaching and teaching, their voices of redemption would sound different from those of Rastafari's recruits in the 1970s. The new return to the fold often sounded more like an intimate version of Christian revival than a full-throated resurgence of the apocalyptic Rasta voice calling on "antique moderns" to fulfill its prophecies of fire and blood in Babylon. The exceptions include Capleton ("the Prophet"), the Flames crew, Tony Rebel, and Anthony B, whose fierce "Fire Pon Rome" was a huge hit in 1996. These voices are a vital link in the dialogue with an older generation. But the dominant mood is characterized less by dread-soaked visions of collective overthrow in the future than by a search for relief from the present and a bright yearning for the past. Luciano's hit songs "It's Me Again Jah" and "He Is My Friend" catch the mix of bashful boy penitence and self-affirmation just right; Jah resembles a personal Jesus more than a messianic vehicle of change.

This new Jah was not quite the same one that had struck a Garveyist chord with the dirtpoor of the shantytowns. This Jah was familiar with the culture of self-help, New Age, and Oprah Winfrey. Of course, he also had his moralistic side, directed as much against the carnal high jinks of the dancehall as against corruption in high places. But what seems unmistakable is the clear strain of confessional self-conviction and the individual pursuit of spiritual growth.

While the liberation theology has not ceased its innovations, Rastafari was now respectfully established in major institutions—in museums as a historical actor in social events, and even on the stage of world politics as an NGO recognized by the United Nations, a status granted in November 1996. The new Rastafari had the feel of an old-time religion, rediscovered by youthful adherents, rather than a climax religion reaching its mature peak. Like all socially acute religious movements, Rastafarianism is a flexible theology, and has meant different things at different times.[30] As it grew in the 1960s and 1970s from a small millennialist cult into the vanguard of black liberation in the Caribbean and beyond, it became an alternative, communal way of life at home and a resonant vehicle for the Third World movement and the counterculture abroad. The 1990s version, at least in its music, is something else again. This is not the anticolonial Rastafarianism that had preferred a black African king to a white English one, nor the postcolonial Rastafarianism that demanded equal rights and justice for the black masses. The new Rastafarianism emerged from the neocolonial order of the IMF, where the redemptive future would not be cruelly denied, only deferred forever, like the lonely hour of the last debt-service payments. The new Time of Reasoning took its spiritual cue as much from the new debt bondage of the Caribbean's foreign masters as from older Rasta lessons about the history of slavery's chains.

THREE

The Gangsta and the Diva

In 1994 Daytona Beach city elders refused to play host to MTV's "Spring Break," a weeklong televised spree of lascivious beach games organized around live musical interludes. A year earlier, in its customary Florida venue, they had taken offense to the hedonistic goings-on, including the now-famous drag queen performer RuPaul's fierce debut at this event. There, at the forefront of commercial youth culture, in the midst of all the dating games involving cross-dressing, suddenly, whoomp! RuPaul was the real thing on the runway. The mostly white college jock audience in Daytona that spring responded with seriously muted applause—a reaction that was probably part embarrassment, part homophobia, and part jaw-dropped amazement at just how damned good she was. This was the same crowd that had bayed with cosexual appreciation for the other black men on the bill—Shabba Ranks, the sexed-up Jamaican toaster, and Naughty by Nature, featuring Treach, with masculinity to spare in his minimalist moves.

Treach's street-bad machete and RuPaul's supermodel sashay represent two polarities of "fierceness" in black popular culture. The first attitude is a reduced, deadpan burlesque of menace-to-society rap, the second a camp alchemist's transmutation of black female assertiveness into diva-rich parody. Either way—whether in the ghetto street or in the nightclub version—being fierce is a theatrical response to the phenomenal social pressure exerted on black males in the waning years of the twentieth century. Blaine and Antoine, those over-the-top queens from "Men on Film" on Fox TV's *In Living Color*, may have been crude, even offensive caricatures, but it's probably fair to say that the figure of the black snap queen rules over camp sectors of queer culture and holds uncontested sway over club nightlife, where RuPaul's dance floor injunction, "You Bettuh Work!"

was one of the wittiest inflections of the puritan work ethic to have pene-trated weekend leisure time. As for the gangsta rapper, whether he was kicking back the day with smooth, laconic beats, Cali-style, or "wrecking the mic" with motormouth rhymes, East Coast–style, he likewise estab-lished his dominion over male youth culture in a field where competition runs high.

The dialogue between these two figures is not supposed to be acknowl-edged publicly, and their relation to each other has been entirely ignored in the recent flap about gangsta rap, attended by so much moralizing. But it is worth examining. RuPaul's song "Back to My Roots"—a wickedly funny tribute to black hair culture—was reportedly suggested, and then rejected, as soundtrack for hardcore rapper Tupac Shakur's beauty salon scenes with Janet Jackson in John Singleton's film *Poetic Justice*—a symp-tom of the homophobic response to any combination of this kind. Nonetheless, voguers—those ghetto performance queens, popularized by Jennie Livingston's documentary *Paris Is Burning*, whose spectacular dance floor competitions were based on dressy impersonations of "real" social types quite removed from their own lives—subtly honored the gangsta with a drag category of bhanjee realness all their own. Voguers belonged to "houses," whose mode of affiliation and social rivalry are not at all dissimilar to the loyalty structure of gangs. Ice-T described Los Angeles gangland as "ghetto male love being pushed to its limit," and there is no shortage of testimony within hip hop culture to the intense homosociality of the crews, posses, and clans (Wu Tang Clan is the supreme embodiment) that dominate the scene with their all-boyz blood-oath families, sworn to the cult of ultramasculinity. While there is no lack of cutthroat spirit to the voguer's one-upping art of "throwing shade" on the dance floor, there's more than a little fussy styling to the ghetto-centric iconography of swagger and scowl associated the world over with hard-core rap. As for the black pop mainstream, now that transvestism has become American apple pie à la mode, it's time to ask where the likes of Little Richard, Michael Jackson, Jimi Hendrix, Eddie Murphy, Prince, Martin, and Arsenio would be if they had not had a showbiz repertoire of draggy gestures to feed off in shaping their own personal style. With the mercurial rise of the cross-dressing Dennis Rodman at the very core of sports celebrity culture, all bets are off.

The profile of the reality rapper, scaled down to the ultimate, low-metabolism vibe of Dr. Dre (who had pursued an earlier glam-with-eyeliner singing career) and Snoop Doggy Dogg, evokes an affectless masculinity, conceived under siege and resonating with the long history of presenting a neutral face as a mask of inscrutability to the white gaze. (Snoop's video retreat into the harmless poses of the playful, late-adolescent prankster or the retro soulboy could similarly be seen as a tactical response to white disapproval of the gangsta as public enemy.) Alternately, when the voguer uses an imaginary compact to "put on a face," or when the snap queen feigns the composed hauteur of the style aristocrat or hams the high-eyed shock of bourgeois outrage, the extravagant use of "face" is plain to see. Whether underplayed or overplayed, these theatrical versions of black masculinity are as much methods of deflecting or neutralizing white disapproval as modes of expressing black traditions. White culture has always compelled black males to perform, usually as entertainers or as athletes. Performance has typically been the obverse of black invisibility in a society of white privilege. Today, however, the underlying trend points beyond invisibility, toward disappearance.

Efforts to evacuate young black men from the public sphere have proceeded on every front. As dropouts from the educational system, as victims of suicides, homicides, and the penal system, as casualties of the incredible shrinking welfare state, as fatalities of the crack economy and the AIDS emergency, and as targets of new and more virulent forms of racism, black male youth are quite systematically being driven toward social obsolescence. It is from this context—the absence of an entire social cohort—that the brouhaha about gangsta rap took its political significance. Those who reduced rap to a discussion of its most disturbing misogynistic or antisocial lyrics ignore how this context merely exacerbates, rather than creates, forms of social prejudice long rife in white, patriarchal America. Those politicians and black preachers who took the high ground against gangsta rap have profited, as their professional status dictates, from media grandstanding. The broad Left (black and white) has no excuse for indulging in this lazy moralizing, least of all when it chooses rap as a vehicle to bash the cause of cultural politics in general.

In these apocalyptic years, before the first batch of the crack-baby generation came of age, hardcore rap was just about the only medium in which ghetto life attained something approaching authentic recognition. Hence the distinction hotly debated among hip hop audiences between rappers who "front" and those who "represent." The distinction separates the pretenders from those who exemplify the true hardcore spirit of hip hop (rather like an athlete who represents a nation in competition) or the ethos of a community: Brooklyn, Compton. But, above all, "representing" involves a demonstrated loyalty to the storytelling genre itself. In rap, genre justice, earned at the microphone, determines how respect is distributed. The rapper's aim is to convince an audience that his "shit is real," but this is a much more complex task than simply proving that the events he describes actually happened to him. For middle-class performers, this is a form of downwardly mobile "passing," no less performative than the upward aspirations of the voguer's role playing. The rap debate in the public media entirely missed such evolved and highly competitive aspects of the genre and instead revolved simply around whether gangsta lyrics represent reality or shape reality—in other words, induce criminal behavior. In the long run both debates may be pretty inconsequential, but they do demonstrate the level of desperation among poor black youth and the sad lack of understanding among the larger public about the political nature of cultural events.

Links have to be made. At the very least, we ought to temper the moral panic about drugs with the knowledge that marijuana is now overwhelmingly the hip hop drug of choice, and that its advocacy among rappers not only challenged the chokehold of the crack economy but also reinforced the arguments for legalizing hemp as a versatile industrial crop—arguments hitherto associated only with white, countercultural voices. Second, we ought to connect the moral panic about guns with demands to demilitarize police divisions up and down the country. The fact that Los Angeles gangstas are armed was quite possibly one of the few obstacles to the partial realization of a police state in Southern California. Just as the Black Panthers made theatrical appearances with guns in public, rap's romance with the gangsta consciously contested the official taboo against images of armed black males (with the exception of black policemen). Of course, much of this was the politics of symbolism, but it also relates to a reality in which the streetcleaning of the gangsta guns would be seen as near-genocidal if it were actually being executed by police weapons. If the recent East Coast–West Coast wars between the Death Row and Bad Boy companies (allegedly linked to the Tupac and Biggie Small killings) proved anything, it was not about how lyrical violence inevitably overflows into real homicides, but rather about the aggressive outcome of cut-throat commercial competition.

The gangs I grew up around in the industrial Scottish lowlands were, by comparison, low-tech in their cult of the flick knife. The gang in my own hometown was called Young Bowery, a parochial imitation of the notorious Glasgow gangs, and, I suppose, the result of some long lost tribute to the first Irish gangs of lower Manhattan. In its Scottish form, the dominant gangster pose of the "hard man" tapped a deep vein in industrial working-class culture, where the strongest manifestations of this personality were often reserved for anticolonial flights of animus against the English. As an outlawed collectivity, the gang had its place then as a minor vehicle for the virility-testing Scottish proletarianism that was losing its muscle, even in my youth. Its more warlike sensibility fed the romance of precapitalist, clannish resistance to the English while at the same time providing fresh fuel to the London media for racist stereotypes of the barbarous Scottish male. As models of masculinity, the small-time thugs I knew had few qualities that would be thought of as "progressive" by the standards of modern sexual politics. Their pathologies did not belong to them, however, but were the cultural frames that defined how, where, and when they were permitted to announce their anger.

Whereas in North America, social divisions are most sharply determined by race, in the West of Scotland they were almost entirely the result of Protestant-Catholic antagonisms, almost as hate-bound as in Northern Ireland and much more meaningful than the weak socioeconomic segmentation that existed within a broadly working-class culture. Actual religious belief had almost nothing to do with this, of course. For the most part, Protestant and Catholic were banners to fight under, marking pseudo-ethnicities that retained their popularity *because they were not* defined wholly by economic conditions, and consequently were regarded as if they were properties belonging to "the people." By contrast, then, when Pakistani families formed the first substantial community of color in the 1980s, their perceived otherness was as much socioeconomic and religious—a petty-bourgeois shopkeeper class that did not observe Sunday closing hours—as it was ethnic.

The point here is that while socially denied people do not express rage just as they please, or under circumstances of their choosing, they do tend to opt for vehicles that are the least likely to be culturally influenced by the powerful. That is why, incongruous as it often seems, gangsta rap came to provide the most articulate frame for black anger available for its young devotees. After a quarter century of sellout black politicians and almost ceaseless economic warfare, it's no surprise that youth believed they could locate sincerity only in a musical genre, top-heavy with humor and creativity, that delivers fantasies much closer to home than the often-distant middle-class dreamworld of affirmative action politics.

As for the white youth who affiliated themselves with the hip hop nation, their identification might not be the ephemeral, and thus comfortable, choice it was for their forebears in the bohemian tradition of the white Negro. The emergence of legions of white hip hop junkies— termed "wiggers" by the tabloid press—may well testify to a significant reversal in the politics of integration. The shoe is now on the other foot, as white kids seek to integrate into black-and-brown culture in ways that their civil rights–generation parents find difficult to understand. Sure, there is a sizable proportion of suburbanites in this movement, bent, as always, on driving their parents crazy, but just as many are youth propelled by the prospect of their economic redundancy, the ultimate desertion of a white parental culture that can't even offer them the certainty of employment at a living wage. When they are not making some kind of common sense of these conditions with black and brown youth (often by wearing "infantile" fashion as if to defer the future), all they have to fall back on is a parody of white trash; how to look awful and still look good is still the favorite style pursuit of the post-grunge crowd.

Outside its persistence in Levi's ads, where does the injunction "Got to Be Real" come to rest? The hardcore rapper's steady loyalty to ghetto realism (the appearance of being totally determined by one's social environment) finds its counterpoint in the vogue queen's "realness" (the ability to impersonate anything but that which you are). The gangsta MC needs the ghetto to justify his every move and rhyme; without that constant appeal, he falls off, his career is over, he becomes a tired studio gangsta. By contrast, the snap queen only refers to elsewhere; his utopia is to be entirely free of the constraints of class, race, and gender that define ghetto life. Along the way, he will become fodder for the talk shows, just as the gangsta's career trajectory leads him to flirt perilously with the penal system. For both, the ultimate aim is to "get paid," in terms of wealth or glamour, all the while retaining respect from their respective marginal undergrounds: the street and the after-hours nightclub.

These are not positive NAACP role models, nor are they meant to be. Bill Cosby and Michael Jordan have that field covered. Neither are they militant advocates of the sort desired by radicals. We look to the preach-and-teach rapper and the gay black activist for that. Rather, they are semi-outlawed, institutional archetypes, each carrying a rich history of meanings, some ugly, some exquisite, for communities for whom poverty and performance have been daily horizons of existence since slavery days. Like barometric pressure systems, separate but equal, in a prevailing weather front, the gangsta and the diva both command center stage in black popular culture, even if they rarely appear on the same stage. Perhaps this is the latest version of what Amiri Baraka, in a famous and relentlessly homophobic essay, referred to as "the changing same," when he proposed a unity vibe between street R&B and free, avant-garde jazz in the 1960s. Just as that fusion was never realized, it is unlikely that the gangsta and the diva will ever make common cause, despite the remarkable capacity of hip hop and drag to reinvent themselves almost every year. It is no more likely that the beauty, anger, intelligence, prejudice, compassion, and pain of young black men will be found in any one individual type. Why should they be? The full range of masculinity is not individual, it is cultural. A major part of the women's movement has been devoted to arguing this much about femininity. This is not to say that sexism and homophobia should be accepted as part of the "diversity" of masculine culture. But we cannot expect these powerful masculine legacies to disappear simply by denouncing their most powerless manifestations (as in rap lyrics) in the name of moral hygiene, least of all when the offenders in question are drawn from or represent some of the most economically denied sectors of the population. The flowering of fully fashioned types like the gangsta and the diva, with their respective mimicry of extremes of "masculine" and "feminine" behavior, is evidence of the complex challenges faced by proponents of sexual politics today. *Listening* to the incomplete dialogue between these figures might serve as one starting point, and not a conclusion, for a cultural politics of masculinity that is willing to view sexual justice as a radical struggle, not simply as a liberal, consensual limit to intolerance. Perhaps Isaac Julien had it right in his film *The Darker Side of Black*, when he imagined the following scenario:

Saturday night in downtown Manhattan. A bhanji boy and his boyfriend give a homeboy face. "We're here, we're black, and we're queer, get over it," they tell him. The homeboy turns to them, makes his hand into the shape of a gun, and fires it at them. The bhanji boy replies, "It's not me you want to kill, but yourself that you see in me." Somewhere behind every homie exterior lies a homo interior.

FOUR

The Private Parts of Justice

Before the Thomas-Hill hearings came to a close, the Cable News Network ran a feature on how the spectacle had been playing in other countries. Two British citizens, both white, were interviewed on London streets. The first, a rather proper middle-aged woman of means, walking her dog in a Belgravia-type square, told the interviewer that she just couldn't see what all the fuss was about. The second, a younger, more bohemian man, standing on a less posh street, said that the hearings demonstrated that the British had a good deal of catching up to do in the area of women's rights. The CNN double play reinforced some obvious British stereotypes. But its real purpose was to reinforce the perception of U.S. culture as both democratic in its public exposure of political corruption (no doubt quite "vulgar" from the perspective of the middle-class Englishwoman) and pioneering in the advancements of its civil society ("progressive" from the perspective of the would-be male feminist). Among other things, this dual perception of the national culture is the primary shaping principle behind CNN's own house style for editing and broadcasting world news across the major league of nations. Performing the global function once served by the BBC in the age of radio, CNN's decentered corporate populism has effectively replaced the voice of paternal imperialism that used to issue from Europe's metropolitan centers.

To underline the contrast, consider the other sex-and-power scandals that were in the news that week. The British public was still ritually recovering from the latest scandal in the grand national tradition of "kinky barrister sex." Sir Allan Green, the director of public prosecutions no less, resigned after his detainment for "kerb crawling" under the Sexual Offenses Act (a bill that criminalizes the persistent male solicitation of women for sex, and that had been widely used by police on the street to harass immigrant men on a range of unrelated issues). The class dimensions of the barrister sex scandal are such an integral part of the national culture that such instances function discreetly in the manner of a familiar institutional farce with Pythonesque overtones. Every so often a case like Green's is thrown up to resolve the otherwise persistent contradiction perceived by the general public that the upper class can have its own separate morality while at the same time enjoying the authority of policing and judging the morality of all other classes.

In the States the revelations of that week were less discreet and more, as it were, republican. The Kennedy dynasty saga was loudly spinning its umpteenth true-life yarn, televangelist Jimmy Swaggart's tryst with yet another prostitute was being rudely exposed on national TV, a whole slew of celebrities like La Toya Jackson, Roseanne (Barr) Arnold (and her husband), Brian Wilson, and Sinead O'Connor were confessing in the national press to having been abused as children, and, in a small Texas grill, George Hennard, Jr., was blowing a fuse while watching Anita Hill's first televised press conference: "You dumb bitch! You bastards opened the door for all women." This was the man who would slaughter twenty-three people the very next day, ostensibly as an act of revenge against women—"Those mostly white tremendously female vipers," as he put it—who had wronged him in his life.

These were the bizarre ingredients of a media celebrity culture, where the express elevator from obscurity to fame, wealth, and power is often shared by the most unlikely occupants. On Capitol Hill another episode of the great exceptionalist national soap opera called "Only in America" was being telecast, and if at times it resembled what Senator Charles Grassley (R-Iowa) called "a soap opera about the elite, and aspiring power brokers here in Washington, D.C. [where] there was plenty of talk about Yale law school, establishment law firms, and moving up the political ladder," no one involved needed a populist cue card to know when to evoke the lowly social origins of the chief witnesses or when to address the people of America as a jury in attendance. As a media event, the hearings, to use Marshall McLuhan's terms, were both "hot" and "cool" by turns, stage-managed to quench the mini prairie fire of women's spontaneous anger that had precipitated the need for this gathering. In the course of the hearings, women's anger was redefined as a shadowy conspiratorial impulse, ruthlessly conjured up in the form of the slick legal tactics of equally shadowy fifth-column interest groups; the "real women of America," the female equivalents of John Q. Public, were ventriloquized as speaking out against a star witness who had been cast as delusional and repressed; and the sentiments of African Americans, whom none of the white senators felt comfortable about ventriloquizing, were represented by the anemic statistic of a poll percentile.

So much for the populist elements. As for the elite soap opera, the glamour had been written out of the script, revealing an awkward and pathetic underside—a full ethnographic exposure of the style and manners of powerful white males stretched out for three days on the prime-time rack, exhibiting classic confessional types, from the shambling, guilt-tripped liberal on the left to the unregenerate misogynist pit bull on the right. It is difficult to imagine a more effective way of dramatizing the crisis in legitimacy of the country's ruling elite than this pitiful comedy of manners in which distinctions between sexual harassment, date rape, seduction tactic, flirting, and erotic fantasy (not to mention the distinction between public questioning and lynching) were all quite deliriously jumbled up in the minds of the nation's lawmakers. It wasn't just one bad guy being exposed, as had been the case, say, with the televised Army-McCarthy hearings forty years earlier; what was on trial here was a whole class. All that was salvaged on the elite side was the reputation of the TV network news division, for whom the hearings were a no-lose option offered on a plate, guaranteed to wash away the stain of warmongering left over from the Gulf War and to win back some of the news clout lost to CNN during that war.

In the print media, voices partial to Anita Hill's claims were also hoisted on the populist petard. In its Monday edition, the *Wall Street Journal* rolled up its sleeves and set about disparaging "the state of political correctness in the nation's elite newsrooms." Rich as it was to hear the editors of this people's organ proclaim that "the media live in a different reality plane from the people who do things like believing Clarence Thomas and giving landslide victories to a Ronald Reagan," their anti-intellectual line reappeared in many other forms in the wake of polls depicting widespread support for Thomas (three out of five) and not least in the suggestion that feminists were also hopelessly out of touch with the real women of America. Editors wheeled out public opinion, that old ghost in the machine of statistical surveillance, to stick it to the nattering nabobs and protesting prudes. Worse yet, the polls, like those conducted during the Gulf War, were given widespread credence as indicators of popular conviction and provoked much soul-searching, especially among feminists and the African American left. If nothing else, this response proved that, given the lack of anything remotely close to a majority of voters at election time, the capacity of the selectively polled to say yes or no to a set of bluntly diagnostic questions increasingly serves as one of the primary institutions for manufacturing and regulating consent in the modern American technocracy. As a medium, polling tells us no more about what and how people think about politics than does the TV news convention of sound-biting moving bodies on the street. As a medium, polls rarely carry a message; they are the message, to cite McLuhan's consistently misunderstood dictum.

To further illustrate this point, consider that the conduct of the politicians and witnesses involved in the Thomas-Hill hearings was widely interpreted at the time as yet another example of how successful the right wing has been in winning the war of images over the last decade. Conservatives, it is often argued, have come to understand that better than liberals. This argument, which is by now a commonplace, assumes that the language of images is a neutral medium that is simply maximized by those who have the best command of the language. It ignores the fact that the media industries are owned by certain corporate interests, and that they are structurally organized in such a way as to generate consent for the political and economic interests of business and government elites. To put it more bluntly, the spin doctors get it the wrong way round when they say that conservatives understand media better. It's much more accurate to say the currently existing media, both popular and elite, understand conservatives and conservatism better, and that they work to preserve established interests, their own included. This was all too apparent during the Gulf War, when the phrase "military-industrial-media complex" took on a highly visible dimension on nightly TV.

The Thomas-Hill hearings bore out this point in a number of ways. Above all, the hearings were not broadcast, C-Span style, as an unedited event. The sessions were surrounded with, and were stitched together by, commentary from a small battalion of anchorpeople, reporters, lawyers, media managers, and expert opinion makers. It was in the recaps, updates, and summarized reports that a narrative plot was created out of the story's raw materials, accompanied by selected footage to illustrate the plot. Much of this commentary turned on speculation about the apparently weak role of Thomas's White House handlers. By way of compensation, the network news teams habitually framed their commentary to fit the perspective of the White House as it tried to make profitable sense out of the proceedings. While the White House worked around the clock to contain and limit the agenda of the hearings, the editing job performed by the network news teams anticipated, if it did not entirely mimic, the administration's concerns. As they addressed the problem of how to manage such an "unregulated" media event, a shared logic prevailed—the preservation of authority and privilege on the part of news commentators as well as the senatorial oligarchy and the Bush administration. When the rules of the game are so widely agreed on and so faithfully observed by the major players, then the populist wild card—throw 'em all out—turns out to be one of the safest in the pack.

On the face of it, however, there weren't supposed to be any rules. From the very beginning no one on the hearings committee seemed to be able to agree about the rules, except to pay lip service to the bromide that legal rules of evidence did not apply. As for the rules of broadcast TV, it took only a few minutes of Anita Hill's testimony to breach network "family standards" (George Bush averred that her revelations were "deeply offensive to American families") and to open up a floodgate of speech that was all too free by anyone's standards. The result had little to do with the drama of the *personal* that is telejournalism's stock-in-trade. Instead, we saw a hypervisible account of experiences customarily sealed off within the genre of the private, things not seen even in the land of tabloid TV. This is why TV viewers sat openmouthed all weekend; the prosaic shock effect of Hill's plain-style description of everyday sexist behavior broke the viewer's first law of mainstream news reporting—your own politics, if it returns, always returns to you in an alienated form. That was how it felt, at least until the spin people broke the trance at the end of each session of the hearings. Without their contextualizing, the feel of the testimony announced that the rules were being challenged, especially the separation between private and public that is as rigorously observed in TV land as it is regulated in the law of the land.

The Thomas-Hill hearings were nothing if not a media event, a milestone in TV history, as they say. More important, however, they were also a legal event. The letter of the law may have been absent, but the spirit of the law, with all its ideological trappings, was all too present. Although the analogy was often made, the hearings felt nothing like TV courtroom drama, a genre punctuated by a series of tried and true emotional hooks. Nor was there much in common with the new *vérité* courtroom shows, although throughout the hearings that weekend the advertising moment was seized in a timely fashion by Court TV, a new cable channel wholly devoted to "live" trial coverage, which subsequently scored its first big scoop with the William Kennedy Smith trial. On the networks' programming schedule, liberally stuffed with law enforcement shows and yuppie lawyer-lifestyle dramas, the Thomas-Hill show could have been just another popular genre segment to add to the vastly disproportionate attention that broadcast TV devotes to legal culture (disproportionate, that is, in relation to the infrequency of legal interventions in most of our daily lives).

But the hearings were also telling another story about the nation founded on law, and Clarence Thomas, ironically, was the first to sound the alarm, in a prepared statement that lashed out against the "invasion" of his privacy: "This is not America. This is Kafkaesque. It has got to stop. It must stop for the benefit of future nominees and our country. Enough is enough. . . . This is not what America is all about." Notwithstanding that his own conception of "natural law" sounded Kafkaesque to almost everyone to whom it was explained, Thomas was appealing here to the popular ideology of constitutionalism. America, unlike other, more Kafkaesque countries, is supposed to be the place where the legal process is not an instrument of state repression, where it makes sense to its citizens, and where everyone is entitled to a fair shake. "What America is all about" has more to do with the law than is the case in any other national culture. This is why Thomas's complaint carried the rhetorical weight that it did. It is also why his appeal for privacy, served up with lashings of corny pathos, nauseated those who knew that, as a Supreme Court judge, he was likely to legislate against the protection of their own "private" rights.

Aside from Thomas's mock self-presentation as a victim, there were other reasons the hearings questioned "what America is all about." More than any other political event since Watergate, the televised hearings overtly challenged the legitimacy of government by law in a nation that, according to a recent *Harper's Index*, produces fifty law school graduates for every engineering graduate (as against Japan's ten-to-one ratio of engineers to lawyers, a figure that explains, among other things, the rank, unchecked corruption of Japanese politicians). In a society where a great majority of problems and decisions are turned over to the law without any semblance of a prior public debate, how is popular consent obtained for nondemocratic government by law, as interpreted by *unelected* officials in the judiciary, rather than by democratic government by the people, as interpreted by *elected* officials in the legislature? It would be too facile to reply that much of this consent is obtained through TV and filmic representations of the law, and yet without today's barrage of cop shows and courtroom docudramas, people would be less willing to grant officers of the law the kind of powers that they exercise in civil and juridical life. In recent years the need to obtain consent has required the television industry to become a junior partner in the business of law. In a 1981 case, *Chandler v. Florida*, the Supreme Court recognized that states may need to grant direct media access to their courts in order to affirm the legitimacy of their judicial systems. It therefore upheld the Florida court's view that "because of the significant effects of the courts on the day-to-day lives of the citizenry, it was essential that the people have confidence in the process . . . broadcast coverage of the trials would contribute to wider public acceptance and understanding of decisions." Most states today utilize this practice, and Florida itself went to town with the Kennedy trial, the first to be broadcast nationally in its entirety. While Thomas and his senatorial supporters objected histrionically to the close scrutiny of the hearings, it is nonetheless true that the legitimacy of the legal system today is increasingly dependent on some such media scrutiny. Indeed, it is precisely through the integral assistance of a media presence that the legal system is able to continue performing "high-tech lynchings" of the sort that Thomas so dishonestly evoked at the hearings.

No matter how shamelessly lawyers and professional politicians play their cases to the fourth estate, the official presumption is that ultimately the rules of law, being rational, are immune to everything the media represent as an arena of social and political opinion. Consider the following remarks made by Senator Alan Simpson (R-Wyoming), who distinguished himself by the most Neanderthal performance of all the committee's members. In his infamous McCarthyist attack on Hill—"Now I really am getting stuff over the transom about Professor Hill. I've got letters hanging out my pockets, I've got faxes, letters from her former law professors, statements from Tulsa, saying 'Watch out for this woman'"—Simpson unleashed his impatience with "this sexual harassment crap" by reminding us that the truth, in the case of hearings such as these, would always be elusive. The question of "who ate the cabbages, as we say out in the wild west," could not be determined outside a court of law: "I'll tell you how you find the truth. You get into an adversarial courtroom, and everybody raises their hand once more, and you go at it with the rules of evidence and you really push around in it, and we can't do that. It's impossible to do that in this place." Simpson may have been presenting a cowboy version of legal process (among the good, the bad, and the ugly on TV that weekend, he was surely the ugliest, in all senses), but his version was nonetheless an orthodox statement of the liberal view of the rules of law shared by all the lawyers on the committee, regardless of their positions on the political spectrum. According to this view, the rules of law alone can determine the rectitude of judgments because these rules are founded on neutral and objective legal reasoning rather than social and political reasoning. The authority of the law rests entirely on the supposition that legal and evidentiary reasoning is a higher realm of scientific logic. The "correct" judgment will be reached, inevitably, if only sufficiently qualified people—technical experts who alone understand the obfuscatory rhetoric of legal language and culture—have the opportunity, as he put it, to "punch around" in the rule-ordered system of an "adversarial court." Subservience to precedents and prior decisions—state decisions—reinforces the perception that legal reasoning is subject to its own history of ruling, and is in no way bound to political pressures of the moment.

While the senators were not structurally empowered to ascertain who "ate the cabbage," their loud disagreements over the conduct of the hearings fully dramatized the political significance of the rules of redress that were established at the rocky outset and subsequently wrangled over throughout the proceedings. What this debate exposed to view were the actual political decisions that go into creating a consensus about internal rules. As a result, the crucial distinction between internally accepted rules—formally neutral—and externally imposed rules—politically motivated—was inoperative from the get-go. Nor were matters helped by the committee members' repeated caveat that "this is not a trial" and that "this is not a courtroom." Such warnings cast as much disquieting doubt on the procedural logic of the hearings as Magritte's painting *This Is Not a Pipe* had cast upon the rules for representing a pipe.

Of course, it will be said that there is a difference between the rules of order in hearings of this sort and rules of law in a courtroom. It will be said that the political disputes arose only because the rationally proven rules of law were not, and could not be, observed. But this response only begs the question of the social and political underpinnings of all such "neutral" rules. In the course of the hearings what we saw was a dress rehearsal (finally, very little was improvised) of the conditions of expediency under which rules for any such legal proceeding would be debated and agreed on. Deprived of an authentic context for the corrosion-proof discourse of legal reasoning, the senators constructed a makeshift setting from as much of the legal furniture as could be permitted. The architecture of this setting was governed by the rhetoric of disavowal: "although this is not a trial . . ." or "we know this is not a trial, but nonetheless . . ." On the one hand, this could include the familiar methodological structure of persecutorial questioning employed by Arlen Specter (R-Pennsylvania) during Anita Hill's testimony, or Joseph Biden's (D-Delaware) reminder to Thomas that, just as in a court of law, "the presumption is with you" (a presumption that happened to be at odds with the sexual harassment policy drawn up at Thomas's own Equal Employment Opportunity Commission [EEOC], which allowed for the charging party to prevail in cases that lacked third-party evidence). On the other hand, it could also include confessional reminders that the nation's lawmakers are not in the Senate to judge people but to make policy in the name of the people. The combined result looked something like the Janus face of the state, exercising power in a way that is usually not exposed to public view, because the state is supposed to be composed of separated powers, just as the legitimacy of the law depends on its claim to be independent of state power. The effect of its exposé was to trigger a wave of public disgust with the committee, feeding off the kind of social disrespect that habitually makes lawyers and politicians the most frequent butts of antiprofessional humor in our society.

But it would be all too easy to conclude that the hearings vividly demonstrated how law, and everything pertaining to the law, is simply politics by other means. Those devoted to demystifying the authority of the law might well have applauded the whole farce as a job well done: the emperor's clothes were undone, revealing long dong and all. To my mind, this would be a dangerous conclusion. First of all, the decade-long movement for judicial restraint, which is only now beginning to exert its pervasive influence on the entire system, has rested its claims precisely on the argument that the law has been used too expediently for activist purposes in creating new rights and freedoms in the postwar period. It is the conservatives who are now on the Supreme Court who have argued that law should not be in the business of politics. It is in their interests that the law, as we have understood it until recently, should be delegitimized, thereby reining in the power of the courts. Clarence Thomas himself was practicing this philosophy during the hearings when he questioned the legitimacy of the entire process. Playing the Black Panther card—I will not recognize the "white justice" of this "court"—he culled a good deal of sympathy, and helped save his nomination, by assailing the authority of his questioning posse of white patrician lawmakers. Over a decade earlier he (along with Hill, another career Reaganite) had been appointed at the EEOC, like most of Reagan's wrecker appointees at similar agencies, explicitly to gut the agency and to trash its laws and guidelines.

It may not be enough to say, then, that the Court today has lost its legitimacy and is operating as a kind of rogue agency for conservative opinion. This argument makes little headway against conservative claims that the authority of the current Rehnquist court has been earned by a movement righteously aimed at purging politics from the law. That judicial restraint is now defined as apolitical, at least in relation to judicial activism, is a sign of the times, reflecting current conservative power to rule definitions. In the earlier part of the century it was judicial restraint as preached and practiced by liberals that was seen as the political option. So, too, in the early days of the Republic, theories of natural law (even of the sort espoused, however nebulously, by Clarence Thomas) could be invoked on the one hand as a Lockean guarantee of the sanctity of private property and on the other as a populist hedge against the elitist expertise of a lawyer class hired to protect the property interests of the aristocracy. My point here in appealing to legal history, however briefly, is not to demonstrate the utter relativism of claims made by legal theory, but rather to suggest that arguments made about the legitimacy of the law are only as strong as the political forces mobilized behind them. There may be little to be gained, and much to be lost, by analytically reducing the law to a realm of barely tenable language propositions, sustained only by the myth of legal reasoning, on the one hand, and the need to maintain a hierarchical social order, on the other. However alienating its form as an institutional system, the medium of the law also remains of paramount importance to those who have used it as a means of achieving democratic freedoms and rights, and who need it today to preserve and extend those freedoms and rights. Unlike almost anything else, only the law can change itself.

Consequently, what was striking about the Thomas-Hill hearings was not simply their merciless exposé of the political chicanery underlying every aspect of the nomination and confirmation process. What was also on dramatic display was the crucial process by which the law is called on to distinguish between public and private spheres, a distinction between virtually separated spheres that is indeed fundamental to the business of modern law. The law itself may have been on trial during these hearings, but the hearings themselves were important only because it was the law's definition of public and private spheres, challenged at every level by the charge of sexual harassment, that was at stake and under scrutiny.

Anita Hill may have put it best when, in the course of intense questioning about details of her statement by Arlen Specter, she suggested that this seasoned trial lawyer from Pennsylvania could not see the forest for the trees:

> If you start to look at each individual problem with this statement, then you are not going to be satisfied that it is true, but I think that the statement needs to be taken as a whole . . . there is nothing in my background, no motivation that would show I would make up something like this. I guess one does really have to understand something about the nature of sexual harassment, it is very difficult for people to come forward with these kinds of things. It wasn't as if I rushed forward with

this information. I can only tell you what happened, and, to the best of my recollection, what occurred, and ask you to take that into account. Now, you have to make your own judgment about it from there on, but I do want you to take into account the whole thing.

In drawing everyone's attention to the big picture ("the whole thing"), Hill delivered a blow to the fetishizing of detail that was Specter's first-strike weapon in the stockpile of legal reasoning. To dwell, she was suggesting, with hairsplitting precision on specific details would be to miss the much wider social significance of her statement. This wider significance included not only the nature of sexual harassment but also the state of gender relations and race relations in society at the present time. From an evidentiary perspective, legal reasoning has a prior obligation to attend to the logical consistency of claims, statements, and arguments, often at the cost of disregarding the social implications of the law. The spirit of Hill's entreaty was one in which the law, as a socially attuned body of interpretive codes and enabling powers, does have an obligation "to take into account the whole thing." Indeed, it is only from the latter perspective that issues related to gender and race make any sense at all. It would not otherwise be possible to see how, in the course of the hearings, the public import of sexual harassment was consistently privatized, in Hill's case, or, by contrast, to see how Thomas's attempt to protect his privacy was consistently respected.

This contrast was, perhaps, most evident in the attention focused on private bodily parts during the hearings. Here surely was a very literal (even anatomical) example of how the sphere of privacy relates to boundary definitions of the public sphere. As the questioning of senator after senator homed in on discussion of genitalia and other discrete bodily parts, it also provided a dramatic illustration of the methodology of "male" fetishism. Again Hill countered this follow-the-parts strategy by insisting that it was the context of her unequal relations with Thomas in the workplace that gave significance to what would have been otherwise inconsequential to her—the isolated description by Thomas of sexual acts and sexual parts. In other words, it was the relationship of the private part to the public whole that made these descriptions objectionable to her. Arguably, the Republicans' fetishistic strategy of isolating the parts won the day, because they succeeded, partly through their own mock embarrassment, and partly through the systematic character destruction of Hill, to define her as an essentially private individual with private motives. As remote as could be from the stereotype of the public actor who may desire to be "a hero in the Civil Rights Movement," she was portrayed as either overtaken by private erotomaniac fantasies or prudishly incapable of decoding boisterous male social banter. Hill was defined by a private characterology that determined all her responses, rather than as someone whose public identities as a professional, a government employee, a lawyer, an African American, a woman, a Republican, among others, all had a heavy sociohistorical bearing on her treatment in the workplace. In contrast to the kind of private person who might have been influenced by *The Exorcist*, Thomas was allowed to cast himself as the kind of private person who might have read Kafka's *Trial* and understood the Kafkaesque significance of his being the accused in a pseudotrial. In contrast to Hill's fantasy-filled mind, Thomas was accused only of having a "closed mind," a public deficiency in his capacity as a judge that could be easily construed as a virtue when it came to protecting his own privacy, as any self-respecting man would want to do, and would be expected to do, in a context such as these hearings.

The contrast in treatment of privacy in the case of Hill and Thomas was also marked by racial elements. This was particularly evident in the discussion by Senator Orrin Hatch (R-Utah) of the significance of the size of Thomas's penis, a discussion that centered on the public mythologies historically associated with the penis size of black men. In this instance the distinction between the stereotypical phallus and the anatomical penis more or less corresponded to the division between public and private spheres. In the course of the discussions, it was established that the size of Thomas's penis was not, and perhaps could not ever be, a private affair. Thomas's supporters, like Hatch, were trying to show that his privacy in this matter was being violated, and that this was a consequence of racial history. But no one who watched the interchange between Hatch and Thomas could avoid the impression that here was a white man publicly taunting a black man about his sexuality. By suspiciously prolonging the discussion by simulating his own sexual innocence, Hatch was also demonstrating how he still had the authority, as a powerful white man, to exploit Thomas's discomfort. At that moment in the hearings Thomas was being refused his privacy in ways he could not control. If Anita Hill's sexual characterology was defined as nothing but private, Clarence Thomas's sexual profile was defined as anything but private, as equally unreal because it belonged to the realm of racist mythology. This protected his nomination, but it also exploited his identity as a black man, leaving the Republicans laughing all the way to the electoral-race bank. In Hill's case the injustices of race and gender were served up in double helpings (triple, if you count Simpson's homophobic innuendo about her "proclivities"). The message, as they say, was clear enough. How it was received remains to be seen.

TV Watcher's Postscript

Two weeks after the Senate vote on Thomas, CBS's *Designing Women* aired a hastily produced episode called "The Strange Case of Clarence and Anita," which included, in twenty minutes of tight sitcom polemics, some of the most direct critiques of the hearings I saw on TV (*Murphy Brown* pitched in when it aired an episode in February that featured Murphy's appearance before a ruthlessly caricatured Senate subcommittee composed of Hatch, Kennedy, et al.). Playing to wild applause from the studio audience, Mary Jo and Julia, in full Bette and Joan drag from an amateur production of *Whatever Happened to Baby Jane?* channeled their anger through a series of hilarious set-piece dismissals of the hearings' male protagonists: casting Danforth as delusional, Thomas as a ham actor, Doggett as a dog, Simpson as a pig, Kennedy as another dog ("putting Ted Kennedy in charge of sexual harassment is like asking Dom DeLuise to guard the dessert bar"), and Specter as a perjurer. As for Bush, the show ended with the president's words at Thomas's nomination ceremony — "America is the first nation in history founded on an idea, on the unshakable certainty, that all men are created equal" — being played over a poignant shot of Anita Hill, looking weary and defeated, at the end of her testimony. But the most telling moment lay in Mary Jo's dismissal of polls suggesting that most women had believed Thomas. Noting that polls also suggest that most women aren't feminists, she took the opportunity to point out that most women who don't want to call themselves feminists nonetheless agree on all the individual feminist issues: "I am a single parent, and a working mother, and if believing in things like equal pay and mandated child care makes me a feminist, then I'm proud to be one."

This was populism, going out on a corporate medium, but it wasn't the voice of corporate populism speaking.

As for the Supreme Court, let's be mischievous and leave the last word to Charles Manson, who had granted a TV interview with CBS's *Hard Copy* a couple of months earlier, and who, in a choice moment of hillbilly rage, had this to say about the legal system:

> Wake up, [*bleep*]! dammit, ain't you got enough sense to look at it? The Supreme Court was started when there was 13 million people in this country. You had nine judges with 13 million people. You got 250 million people now. How the hell you gonna take a Supreme Court with nine [*bleeps*] and make a court out of it for 250 million people? It's impossible, man. Your government's a shell of madness that you're preachin' off in schools. It's not real, guy, it's a game.

FIVE

If the Genes Fit, How Do You Acquit?
O.J. and Science

I was in Los Angeles only once during the whole O.J. circus, but the memory of a brief encounter in the cocktail lounge of a Santa Monica hotel in August 1994 has stayed with me. A bar bore was getting cranked up, and soon he was broadcasting loud and clear on the topic du jour. He was a white businessman whom the bartender seemed to know all too well and wished she didn't. He was claiming a special knowledge about football players on the basis of having once served on the board of trustees of an East Coast university. Without much egging on from his audience of two, one bluster led to another until he unveiled his theory that, of all football players, the success of running backs on the field depended less on brainpower than on their killer instinct, and that this disposition was probably genetic. In fact, he was sure this was the key to the O. J. Simpson case. When pressed to elaborate, he ventured that the scientists could prove this kind of genetic theory in the courts but they would not be allowed to do so in the upcoming trial. At this point I had to leave to meet a friend. I discreetly expressed my sympathies to the bartender, who would now bear the brunt of these pronouncements alone. What I thought I had encountered in the bar was a new kind of concoction—of half-truths about the links between genetics, law, and crime—that may be more potent and widely consumed than anyone would like to believe.

Back home in New York, two weeks later, a friend—an O.J. trial junkie—who shares some of my interest in genetics sent me a clipping of a *New York Post* headline that read "Murder in O.J.'s Blood." The clipping confirmed my impressions in that throat-grabbing way tabloid headlines have when they tell us, "this is where you live, here and now." The headline—no surprise—bore only an oblique relation to the newspaper story, which soberly recounted that preliminary results of two different DNA tests had matched O.J.'s blood with blood found leading from the crime scene. But the headline's telegraphic announcement suggested something else, much closer to my bar bore's woozy story about the genetic basis of criminality.

What was happening in August 1994 to explain this kind of nonsense?

In "the Simpson matter" (as Judge Lance Ito would famously come to refer to the trial, day after day), the prosecution and the defense teams were both being assembled, shaped by the case that each was going to present. It looked as though the prosecution's case would rely heavily on DNA profiles of blood left at the crime scene and on various objects— the bloody glove, the Bronco—to identify Simpson as the murderer. It would rely to a much lesser extent on the demonstration of motive provided in his history of domestic violence. It had just been announced that the defense would bring on board Barry Scheck and Peter Neufeld, directors of the Innocence Project, well known for using DNA testing to exonerate over a dozen clients who had previously been convicted and imprisoned. These attorneys would play a crucial and perhaps decisive role in casting reasonable doubt on the DNA evidence in the course of the trial. The prosecution, in turn, would call on the expert testimony of Rockne Harmon, George "Woody" Clarke, and other strong advocates of DNA forensic technology. In August, then, both sides were preparing for what the press was referring to as "the DNA wars," scheduled to begin, and potentially end, in the pretrial hearings that would determine the admissibility of DNA evidence. There was reason to believe that some, if not all, of the forensic techniques would be considered inadmissible in the California courts.[1] This is what I think my bar bore might have had in mind when he speculated that the scientists would not be allowed to prove his theory in court.

To get to the pulpy core of his theory, however, we need to step outside the Simpson matter and look briefly at the profound impact that modern genetics has had on public consciousness in the last fifteen years or so, to the degree that it has become routine fare in barroom conversations. In that time, it has become common to refer to genetic causation for virtually every aspect of human behavior, from medical disorders to ethnic traits and personal conduct. Science reporting has encouraged the view that such genetic links are simple and direct, and in popular culture it is currently acceptable to say there is a gene for almost everything, including the urge to make generalizations of this sort. Much of this attribution is droll, and therefore it mocks even as it reflects the exalted status of the Holy Gene. Even so, the popular allure of biological explanations for social behavior is encouraged not only by biotech companies but also by scientists and policy makers who have helped, directly or otherwise, to shape the attack on collective social responsibility in general and the welfare state in particular. Absolving society of all blame or responsibility for problems that can be seen as genetically determined has been a significant element of the conservative crusade to redefine social problems as a matter of individual predisposition.[2] In this view, gene therapy is more cost-efficient than social programs.

Of all the qualities (selfishness, shyness, adventurousness) that have been "linked" to specific genes, the association with criminality is the most notorious. Talk about "natural born killers," a "bad seed," or "tainted blood" is almost universal folklore, but its scientific basis has been consistently explored for over a century, from Dr. Cesare Lombroso's attempted criminal typology on the basis of physical characteristics in the late nineteenth century to theories of the criminal chromosome (the extra Y chromosome in males that gives rise to their aggressivity) that surfaced in the 1970s. Ever since then, ideas about the genetic basis of criminality have been riding the long wave of resurgent biologism into the institutions of social and legal policy making. The currency of these ideas has been tied to the fortunes of the eugenics movement over that same period, rising with Galton in the late nineteenth century, collapsing in the aftermath of Nazism, and surfacing again in new forms in Britain and the United States through the developing paradigms of sociobiology and evolutionary psychology in the last two decades of the twentieth century.

The concept of genetic criminality has contributed specifically to the social psychology of racialization. Most studies of genetic criminality survey incarcerated populations, and since African Americans are incarcerated at a rate ten times that of Caucasians, it is hardly surprising that U.S. studies draw bogus conclusions about links between race and criminality.[3] Given the high public tolerance of the United States' racially skewed incarceration rates, it is easy to imagine the appeal to racists of such conclusions, casually linked, in turn, to other spurious ideas about genetic causality and race, such as the link between race and intelligence.

By the end of the summer of 1994, there were very few public scandals that could have dislodged O.J. from the forefront of North American public conversation. In some circles the publication of *The Bell Curve*, by Charles Murray and Richard Herrnstein, came very close. The cant about genetic links between race and IQ dredged up by Murray and Herrnstein was designed to feed intravenously the anti-welfare policies of the moment. Their ideas about the decline of the gene pool and the racialization of intelligence in the new cognitive hierarchies of an information society seemed to be borne along by some autonomous principle of social motion, at a time when popular opinion is increasingly receptive to arguments that appeal to genetic authority.

The public debate about *The Bell Curve* lasted for several months, and while it did not make much news in the tabloid press, it occupied many of the same media pages as the O.J. trial. However, my extensive database search for stories that mentioned both O.J. and *The Bell Curve* during the relevant period and shortly thereafter resulted in very few matches and none at all that touch on genetics. This discovery surprised me. Both *The Bell Curve* and the DNA typing in the O.J. trial employed a controversial process of testing, appealed to racial or ethnic categories as classified by genetic scientists, and rested to some degree on assumptions about how genetics can be used to elucidate legal or social quandaries. Why then was discussion of one field of genetics so segregated from the other in the public media? Surely there was some reason other than that *The Bell Curve* appealed to a behavioral, and the O.J. trial to a forensic, field of genetics.

Was it because one had been marked "contaminated" by its racist associations, while the other was seen as clean, at least where race is concerned? Given that DNA forensics have evolved in response to the needs of a national law enforcement system with a systematically racist record, only those immune to skepticism would view this as a credible explanation. Indeed, it was partly on the basis of that racist record that members of the O.J. defense team argued their case for the incompetence of the Los Angeles Police Department's criminologists and the racial biases of one or more of its detectives.

Or was it because *The Bell Curve* was perceived as a soft application of molecular biology, and DNA typing as harder and more incontrovertible? Perhaps, but then one of the big media stories about the DNA wars was that the forensic methods were highly contestable. Ever since the 1989 case of *People v. Castro*,[4] which successfully challenged DNA typing as an infallible source of legal evidence, this complex technology has been fiercely disputed in courts and in scientific and law journals, and it was the object of bitter contention in the O.J. trial.

The reasons for the separation of interest in O.J. and *The Bell Curve* do not lie within molecular biology itself. Instead, they arise from the needs of those institutions—in education, law, medicine, commerce, the military, and government—that serve as clients for customized kinds of scientific knowledge. Specialized scientific fields are habitually made to order by powerful institutions or wealthy contractors or because they respond to prevailing ideological needs. In almost every field, the division of labor within the scientific community is shaped by the managerial needs of social and economic elites. Subfields of scientific knowledge are social arrangements of labor (many in the late twentieth century are spin-offs from the military-industrial system). The division between different fields of genetics corresponds in part to the select interests of clients. Invariably, demand from one field shapes developments in another; DNA forensics, for example, relies on population genetics for its identification of suspects. Division of fields, moreover, does not preclude their independent reinforcement of the powerful philosophy of genetic determinism.

When it is not directly converted into capital, specialized scientific knowledge is habitually sought out to intensify respect for institutions and their policies. Consider some of the outcomes of the O.J. trial and *The Bell Curve*. While very few scholars leapt forward to defend the scientific premises of *The Bell Curve*, few would doubt that its poisonous theses about alleged links between race and intelligence have had considerable impact on the public reception of major changes in social legislation, especially those relating to affirmative action policies. Indeed, it could be said that conservative policy makers are proceeding toward the conclusions favored by the book without relying overtly on the junk science offered by Murray and Herrnstein. By contrast, mainstream media wisdom held that the DNA evidence against O.J., while scientifically sound, was somehow disregarded by the jurors. This perception helped fuel widespread disrespect for the jury system in the months after the trial, and may even have contributed to the zeal with which powerful politicians, from the White House down, took up the old game of judge bashing. In the case of *The Bell Curve* the science, even though it was discredited, still helped in some way to "explain" the policy making directed against social programs. In the Simpson matter, more accredited science was called for to better calibrate the institutional fit between the forensics field and its legal interpretation.

Accordingly, the science establishment played its role in helping restore post–O.J. public confidence in DNA forensics. In July 1996 the NRC (National Research Council, the operating arm of the National Academy of Sciences) published an updated report on DNA evidence that issued a clean bill of health for the forensic process: "The technology for DNA profiling and the methods for estimating frequencies and related statistics have progressed to the point where the reliability and validity of properly collected and analyzed DNA data should not be in doubt."[5] Among its recommendations, the report urged the professionalization and accreditation of all crime labs in accord with upgraded standards of performance and accountability. This resolve is consistent with the history of the development of criminological technologies, from fingerprinting to polygraph testing, voice printing, blood grouping, enzyme typing, and DNA profiling. Each has required its own credentialed field of experts, with a professionalized jargon, a supporting record of approval in peer-reviewed journals, and a bureaucratic system of accreditation with institutional authorities. When doubts are cast on the legal interpretation of such technologies, the response has been to increase scientific funding in pursuit of more accurate data and to beef up the supporting, legitimating network of professionalization.

From the time it was first challenged in U.S. courts in 1989, evidence for the fallibility of DNA profiling had been supported by indications that biotechnology companies had pushed hard for the legal admissibility of the tests, the FBI had intimidated scientists who were critical in print,[6] and the "community of experts" responsible for validating the techniques included many scientists who had themselves established a good deal of their reputation through lengthy and lucrative courtroom testimony about the value of the field to criminal jurisprudence. Aside from these more obvious conflicts of interest, the debate about the increasing use of DNA sampling and profiling involves a host of ethical concerns about the threats to genetic privacy posed by the expansion of the state's DNA identification banks, compiled from compulsory testing of prisoners, soldiers, and patients by the Departments of Defense and Justice and other state agencies; the normalization of genetically defined population differences; the further sanctification of biological explanations of the truth; and the applicability of quantitative reasoning to courtroom procedures designed to respect principles and values other than those acknowledged by science. Despite its public visibility and the unusually generous resources available to both the prosecution and defense, the O.J. trial highlighted very few of these concerns.

The trial involved an enormous amount of scientific testimony (ten thousand references to DNA in the fifty thousand-page transcript), inordinately more than, say, the 1953 Rosenberg case, another great "trial of the century," in which the prosecutors had to argue that the lay defendants understood enough physics to pass on the secret of the atom bomb to the Soviet Union. Predictably, the press found much of this testimony on DNA "boring" and an obstacle to the unfolding drama of the trial. Some commentators like William F. Buckley found the trial itself to be an obstacle to those goals of justice that were clearly aligned, in his view, with the evidence presented by the science. Writing in the *National Review*, Buckley lamented that

> justice is dying. . . . from the creeping immobilizations brought on in the name of civil liberties. . . . The only obstacle to the establishment of the guilt of O. J. Simpson is legal. The whole of the epistemological apparatus of the modern world—psychology, science, logic, reason— establishes that he is guilty. Only the law stands in the way of the application, paradoxically, of justice.[7]

Voicing a standard conservative view, Buckley manifests his impatience with the legal system's overzealous protection of the civil rights and dignity of defendants. He sees the cart going before the horse: the law should be driven by science, not vice versa. In framing the debate over scientific evidence in this way, Buckley was rearticulating an age-old concern that the jury system poses a substantial threat to the rule of law (especially visible in the phenomenon of jury nullification). He was also anticipating the torrent of public impatience with the jurors' verdict in the O.J. case. At issue is the Federal Rules' entrustment in the judgment of jurors, over and above those of experts and professionals in science and the law. DNA evidence has presented the most acute challenge to that principle in recent years because it has stretched the capacity of experts to believe that laypeople can understand advanced science. If complex scientific testimony increasingly becomes a customary presence in the courts, what are the prospects for continuing respect for lay judgment?

The Jury on Trial

The fierce public backlash against the O.J. jurors was immediate, palpable, and sustained long enough to have congealed into a media "fact." The main tenor of the hostility stemmed from the belief that a predominantly black jury had exonerated a wealthy black celebrity with a history of spousal abuse in defiance of Marcia Clark's "mountain of evidence," and had done so in retaliation not just for the racist record of the Los Angeles Police Department but also for centuries of "white justice." The reactionary version of this belief was downright ugly, but the more liberal interpretation of the verdict as a healthy exercise in jury nullification may have been no less insulting to many of the jurors. When such allegations were not being made directly, related charges were often insinuated by questions about the jurors' lack of education in the face of the cold, hard facts of the DNA evidence. On many a talk show, we heard again and again the claim that since smart people can increasingly find ways of evading jury duty, juries are inevitably made up of the dumbest folks in the community. This claim has clearly racist overtones if one considers that the substantial increase in minority voter registration (along with the dismantling of all-white juries who, unlike black juries, are statistically inclined to exonerate defendants of their own race) has brought more and more citizens of color into the jury pool in recent years. For example, a March 31, 1996, segment of *Sixty Minutes* suggested that Francine Florio-Bunten—a white juror removed from the trial after Judge Ito received a letter alleging she was working on a book with a literary agency—had been set up by the defense team. The segment implied that Florio-Bunten was the most educated of the jurors and was therefore capable of understanding the DNA evidence—and swinging the jury against O.J. Similar insinuations and suspicions abound in the massive media archive. The famous Internet list alt.fan.oj-simpson featured a wave of repulsive postings after the verdict; typical sentiments included a posting that read, "Hate to say it, but I think *The Bell Curve* hit the nail on the head," or another that confessed, "I don't know if I can look upon blacks as anything other than a subhuman mob with an average IQ of around 80."[8]

How did this backlash affect the jurors themselves? At least three—Armanda Cooley, Carrie Bess, and Marsha Rubin-Jackson, who published their accounts in *Madam Foreman: A Rush to Judgement?*—have described their persistent discomfort at being under suspicion themselves. Such was their impression that, in addition to their resentment at the cameras monitoring the hotel hallways, these jurors imagined that the smoke detectors and fire alarm units in their bedrooms were audio and video monitors (Rubin-Jackson took appropriate measures: "One day I got up in front of it buck naked . . . and shook my bootie").[9] This paranoia was heightened by the intimidating scene outside the courtroom on the day the verdict was announced. Confronting the jurors as they arrived were hundreds of police officers on horseback and in riot gear, while helicopters seemed to fill the sky above. In downtown Los Angeles, this display of a massed police force is by no means a neutral sight, especially for its citizens of color. With the crowd outside considerably swelled and agitated by the announcement of the verdict, these three jurors had some reason to feel they were not only besieged in the courtroom but also in some physical danger: "Every time I looked there were more and more people and I just kept saying, 'Oh my God, are they going to riot, are they going to get us?'" (*MF*, 176).

In order to throw off the reporters and cameras, bailiffs ushered the jurors out of the courtroom through the route reserved for the transport of prisoners ("It was like running a gauntlet. I felt like I'd committed a crime and I was on my way to being locked up," *MF*, 7). This route involved the use of the elevator ordinarily reserved for convicted felons, surrounded by walls of graffiti, both poignant and defiant, scrawled by men and women en route to detention cells. Once outside, they were transported to a secret drop-off point in a "full-size black-and-white-bus with barred windows." Ordered to keep their heads down, some of the jurors were fearful at the sight of the full extent of the massed police force: "Why do they need so many policemen? Do they really think we're going to be assassinated?" (*MF*, 9). No wonder these jurors felt as if they were at the wrong end of the justice system, not only then but in the months to come.

These stories and impressions are important to recount, because they are a record of how and why jurors feel that their involvement with the justice system can bring a share of its (and the media's) punitive power down on them. Something is clearly wrong if the fulfillment of their civic duties renders them vulnerable in this way. Public bigotry will only intensify if the two chief allegations of the O.J. juror backlash—that they practiced reverse racism and were undereducated—are allowed to subsist. For the record, again, let us note what jurors had to say about these allegations.

Having lived "underground" for the period of sequestration in circumstances more akin to detention (with five-hour conjugal visits and routine searches of their belongings), these jurors seemed genuinely surprised to learn that the verdict was being interpreted as a racial message, especially since Simpson was perceived as living "in a white world" of privilege quite remote from their own black one: "You could say we were shocked . . . or outraged, that people would even think of us sitting there making decisions based on race. And it proved to me that they felt we had no intelligence whatsoever" (*MF*, 82–83). The lengthy DNA testimony elicited a similar impression:

> When I got out [*sic*], I kept hearing more and more people saying there was only one graduate on the jury and so forth, so that indicates to me that they felt everyone else was illiterate. . . . I realize that if you have a Ph.D. and you're talking to someone who does not have training in the field of serology or forensic science, you might assume that they're not going to understand some of the basics. Of course, you're not going to understand the total details of that field, but you don't have to. Unfortunately, there's no way to let people know you got it. You can't just

raise your hand and say, 'Dr. Cotton, I understand what you're talking about. Move on.' (*MF*, 114)

As it happens, jurors rated Dr. Robin Cotton, from Cellmark Diagnostics, the Germantown testing laboratory, lowest among the scientists judged on their ability to communicate technical arguments: "She talked down to us like we were illiterates. . . . She talked down and when you talk down to people you tend to lose them" (*MF*, 114). On the prosecution side, Renee Montgomery and Gary Sims, both from the California Department of Justice, and Dr. Lackshamanan Sathyavagiswaran, from the Los Angeles Police Department, rated highly, as did Henry Lee, from the Connecticut State Forensic Science Laboratory, and Barry Scheck, on the defense side. Collin Yamauchi, from the Los Angeles Police Department, who had cast doubt on Lee's handling of the evidence, was perceived as covering up for the egregious errors in gathering and handling of evidence by LAPD criminalist Dennis Fung and his assistant Andrea Mazzola.

In the final analysis, these jurors reported that they *had* in fact understood the testimony relating to the DNA matches. With the exception of one particularly degraded sample (from the rear gate at the Bundy condo) that had been collected weeks after the crime and found to contain high levels of EDTA, a blood preservative used in labs, the jury, in its deliberations, had not questioned any of the matches of the blood samples with Simpson's DNA type. Instead, it was the evidence of the LAPD mishandling and cross-contamination of the blood evidence that were relevant to establishing reasonable doubt.

Of course, no one is obliged to take the jurors' comments out of court at face value, but to ignore them is to add insult to the perceived injury. As it happens, these comments reveal a good deal about the balance between expert and lay opinion that has been affected by the legal admission of complex scientific evidence.

DNA on Trial

One public perception that emerged from the O.J. trial was that the science was only as good as the police lab that processed the blood evidence—a "cesspool of contamination," in the view of defense witnesses. Barry Scheck argued, in a 1994 article about the *Daubert* decision (see note 1), and unceasingly throughout the trial, that laboratory error is the primary flaw in the DNA typing process, and that a lab's error rate should be considered a matter of admissibility, and not weight, in testimony, as judges have been inclined to rule.[10] In the O.J. case, Scheck could hardly have hoped for a more vivid illustration of his contention that laboratory error rates are substantially higher than the DNA profiling estimates that labs draw from trace evidence. As if in response to the unspoken injunction of the O.J. verdict to put the house of DNA forensics in order, the 1996 NRC report issued strict recommendations about forensic protocols and lab proficiency testing. Convened to resolve the legacy of uncertainties bequeathed by the controversial report of the 1992 NRC commission, this second NRC committee was not charged with the task of assessing the impact of DNA sampling on the criminal trial process, nor with its much wider role in the state's databanking of genetic information from a wide variety of convenience samples: criminal records, law enforcement officers, soldiers, paternity-testing centers, blood banks, hospitals. With respect to the former, the NRC committee confined itself to recommending "behavioral" (i.e., scientific) "research on juror comprehension" of evidence from DNA profiles. As is customary, then, the scientific focus on value-neutral fact was isolated from the legal and social concerns: "that's not our department." But in neither department is it possible, or socially prudent, to isolate facts from values in this way.

In recent years, genetic information has become a tool for decision making in a variety of legal fields—torts, criminal, trust, and estate law—and is increasingly used as a defense on grounds of genetic predisposition. Despite its promise of absolute precision and irrefutable truth— its "aura of infallibility," as a Massachusetts Supreme Court decision put it—DNA evidence is commonly introduced in the form of quantified probability. For example, in the Simpson matter, the odds of some of the blood samples matching any African American or Caucasian other than O.J. were estimated as high as 1 in 170 million, and 1 in 6.8 billion Caucasians in the case of the genetic markers matching Nicole and Ron. These astronomical odds, however much they varied from estimate to estimate (another put the Nicole odds, in the case of a particular blood sample, at 1 in 21 billion), conveyed the message that you "can't argue" with such numbers. How could O.J. possibly be innocent, given these odds? Such statistics carry the patina of irrefutable truth in a manner that tends to outweigh other kinds of evidence, like those supporting the motive in the murder charge by reference to the history of spousal abuse. Indeed, these odds were frequently cited in the courtroom of public opinion as overwhelming confirmation that science had proved O.J.'s guilt and that the jury had disregarded science and, in Buckley's words, the whole of modern epistemology. These are false and perilous assumptions.

In a classic 1971 article, "Trial by Mathematics" (long before DNA evidence became a controversial factor in legal adjudication), Lawrence Tribe summarized the problems raised by the practice of using statistical methods to resolve conflicting claims in lawsuits. Even if it were desirable for the legal system to defer to quantitative reasoning, Tribe asserts that statistical proofs "decrease the likelihood of accurate outcomes" in a trial.[11] The impact of introducing statistical evidence to a jury's prior probability assessment of a defendant's guilt has a distorting effect, rendering an inference of guilt that is much greater than the evidence warrants. The hard, quantitative evidence will dwarf other "soft variables" like impressionistic evidence, according to Tribe, and will indubitably warp the jurors' obligation to weigh all the evidence evenly. If the statistical assessment is introduced early, it is difficult for jurors not to focus on these overimpressive numbers, and hence the presumption of innocence is often thrown out before defendants have had their full say. So, too, the probability values attached to variables, such as estimating the risk of a frame-up or an error in testimony, are something that only individual jurors can assign. So, to give mathematical proofs full credence, each juror would have to be able to compute their own complex equations, involving hard and soft variables, to guarantee the accuracy of outcomes. In addition, the authoritative weight of statistics harms the chances of a peer community accepting a defendant's acquittal (in O.J.'s case, this community would presumably be his white neighbors in Brentwood and not downtown African Americans). Finally, Tribe argues that the use of statistics threatens to alter the entire character of the trial process itself, imposing standards unconvincing to the "untutored contemporary intuition," making the legal system appear "even more alien and inhuman than it already does," and undermining its responsibility to protect the defendant's rights as a person.

Given its "aura of infallibility," many believe that the subsequent introduction of DNA evidence in the courts has only exacerbated these problems and has further eroded defendants' rights, especially when the defendant's resources are too meager to muster counterevidence. O.J.'s privilege in this regard is truly exceptional, but it proved nonetheless, *contra* Tribe, that a successful defense can technically be mounted against an overwhelming array of quantitative evidence. The larger flaw with Tribe's argument, however, is its assumption that quantitative evidence and reasoning arise at the outset from value-free knowledge. It is easy to conclude, then, that methodologies of scientific reasoning and the adversarial procedures of the legal system are difficult to reconcile. The one aims at isolating absolute truths that are irrefutable in any time or place; the other expresses the relationship between the individual and the state as defined by civil principles and rights that pledge respect for defendants as persons. As Marjorie Maguire Schultz puts it, "science deals in particulars in order to determine generalizations, law deals in generalizations in order to determine particularities."[12] The legal process is supposed to resolve conflicts, often involving the full coercive power of the state, in ways that protect individual rights and in accord with normative community values. The quantitative reasoning of science is not well suited to taking these values or rights into account. In times like the present, when civil rights and community values are under siege from social conservatives, scientific diagnoses in the service of law enforcement and legal adjudication have a particularly strong appeal to those swayed by right-wing ideas. Under these coercive circumstances, the trust in lay judgment, underpinned in part by American skepticism regarding the authority of experts, comes under fire.

But this acknowledged conflict between science's truth and the law's social wisdom assumes that the domain of science is indeed value-free, sequestered from the social interests of those institutions in government, law, and commerce that exercise their authority through the use of scientific knowledge or expertise. A large body of scholarly literature in science studies has challenged this view and has demonstrated that science is no less shaped by social interest than any other field of knowledge. The story about DNA profiling is no exception. It shows how the law enforcement system defines goals for researchers to deliver very particular kinds of knowledge. In a field largely created by the FBI, the direction of DNA forensic research has been wholly governed by the cliental needs of the Justice Department, while the vulnerability of its commercial and police laboratory environments has been fully exposed and the infallibility of its scientific claims has been hotly contested. Indeed, the meaning of these claims is sufficiently contingent that the probative value of DNA evidence invariably has to be established in the courtroom through lengthy reviews of, or appeals to, the whole peer-review apparatus of scientific and legal literature, as was the case in the O.J. trial. Scientific knowledge, as Sheila Jasanoff concludes in *Science at the Bar*, is not a simple ancillary to the legal process, waiting to be employed in the pursuit of truth. In many instances it is highly provisional knowledge, while its authority emerges out of the courtroom battle to prove that the claims of one side's experts are more contingent than those of the other side's experts.[13] *People v. Simpson* was a dramatic demonstration of this process.

When the probative value of genetic evidence becomes a norm in courtrooms, defendants are more and more likely to be reduced, as sociologists Rochelle Cooper Dreyfuss and Dorothy Nelkin have suggested, to genetic conceptions of "personhood." Instead of the fully entitled person the legal system is ideally supposed to respect, the defendant is seen as a construct of his or her DNA.[14] One of the grave dangers of this tendency is that people brought before the law are once again defined in part by their biological constitution. For centuries, minorities and women have been defined in precisely this way, and more often than not by loose categories upheld by the law.

In his book *White by Law*, Ian Haney Lopez has shown that courts historically relied on science and "common knowledge" to determine racial categories, and in particular to determine who counted as white and who did not. These categories used to be governed by the five antique anthropological classifications of Caucasian, Negro, Mongoloid, American (Indian), and Malay. Even so, ethnic and national groups have always been subject to reassignment from one race to another, often in response to changes in immigration laws. By the 1920s the Supreme Court's reliance on scientific definitions of race had become untenable; it decided to abandon the use of scientific evidence to adjudicate racial prerequisite cases, and to rely instead on common sense or popular knowledge. This resulted in the 1922 decision of *United States v. Thind*, where Bhagat Singh Thind, an Asian Indian, had argued for naturalization on the basis of the Court's own scientifically refereed equation of "Caucasian" and "white." Haney Lopez suggests that the Court was increasingly frustrated with science's inability to accurately identify and quantify racial differences, and that, beginning with *Thind*, it accepted common knowledge as a more reliable way of policing the boundaries of whiteness, most immediately for the purposes of legislating the 1924 immigration bill.[15]

The judiciary has continued to play a major role in determining entitlements and benefits along racial lines, and in doing so it has actively shaped social beliefs about race. Overtly biological notions of race were put on the back burner for at least fifty years. In the last two decades, however, these biological definitions have hitched a return ride on the coattails of the new molecular genetics. While genetic variation is very slight among humans (and much greater between persons than between population groups), those tiny differences have attained immense cultural significance in a period when biological explanations for social problems are increasingly sought out. The rise of the new genetics has been accompanied by, and to some extent utilized in, a brutal rollback of the U.S. state's affirmative, post–civil rights commitment to closing the racialized gap between the formal equality of its citizens and the material inequalities they face daily. Some social science scholarship has made a direct link between the two, none more explicitly than *The Bell Curve*, whose authors fleshed out their reactionary fantasy of an underclass that was both genetic and cognitive, resistant to all social and educational assistance, and marked by a specific racial profile. More generally, civil libertarians are concerned that the explosion in genetic testing and screening will usher in a social order governed in part by the rule of predictive information about the genetic predisposition of individuals. In this new eugenic dispensation, discrimination is institutionally directed against those genetically designated as risks to society, and thus beyond assistance, along with those profiled as menaces to society, and thus subject to preemptive discipline. This tendency has already been borne out, in the former case, in the realm of medical insurance denied to the "healthy ill," and in the latter case, in programs like the Violence Prevention Initiative—tried out by the Bush administration—which called for the screening of 100,000 inner-city children to identify potential criminals.

American courts have an appalling record when it comes to safeguarding the rights of minorities. In light of the history, noted above, of the law's use of science to categorize race, and with an eye to the scary neo-eugenic future of genetically screened population controls, is there any reason for citizens of color to regard the legal application of genetic evidence with anything approaching equanimity? And what bearing, if any, did these concerns have on the O.J. trial?

Race and Genetics

Despite his initial fame as a "black athlete," it was widely perceived that O. J. Simpson was less socially black than almost any other black man in America. As comfortable in Brentwood as he was schmoozing with his white friends at the Riviera Country Club in Pacific Palisades or at LAPD Christmas parties, he held down his job as a Hertz spokesperson for an astonishing seventeen years, shilling for predominantly white businessmen on tight airport schedules. In an angle already covered in the O.J. joke repertoire (What did Rodney King say to O.J.? "Good thing you didn't get out of the car, Juice"), Sistah Souljah declared that the blackest thing O.J. ever did was get chased by the police, even though it was a stretch to call it a chase. Just about the only place where O.J. could not be colorless was in a U.S. court of justice, where no black man has ever felt that the color of his skin has no relevance. More to the point, O.J. was in a court in Los Angeles in the 1990s, facing a charge investigated by law enforcement officers who had established the most racist reputation of any police force since the heyday of white justice in the South. By the end of the trial, many concluded that Simpson had purchased a role for himself in the game of identity politics he had assiduously avoided for so long, and may have done so in order to beat the rap for a gender crime.

From the moment Los Angeles district attorney Gil Garcetti decided to locate the trial downtown, where the jury pool would be more diverse, and where the likelihood of a repeat scenario of the Rodney King uprisings was diminished, the trial had a racialized dimension. With the Fuhrman exposé and the defense case built around his racism by Johnnie Cochran (the legal profession's crown prince of identity politics), the trial's focus on race deepened and was amplified a thousandfold in the echo chamber of media reportage. The prevailing media account of public responses to the verdict fiercely reaffirmed all the divisive fictions about the bichromatic black and white nation. The most corrosive version suggested that this single, racially weighted verdict had compensated for centuries of white justice, and that the judicial playing field would be newly leveled as a result. In retrospect, the whole trial became a racial Rosetta Stone, endlessly scanned for clues to understanding a society on the brink of abandoning affirmative solutions to its most intractable race problems while turning a blind eye yet again to the glyphs that spelled out its gender problems.

In all of this drama, little public attention was paid to the single feature of the trial—the data from population genetics used in DNA typing—that formally focused the legal process on O.J.'s racial identity. When the DNA profile obtained from a trace evidence is matched with that of a suspect, statistics derived from population data are applied to estimate the likelihood of a random match. The accuracy of the probability estimate depends on the criteria used for determining the relevant population from which data on genetic markers can be drawn. In the early years of DNA typing evidence, the reference population was based on the FBI categories of Caucasians, African Americans, and Hispanics, which are far from genetically homogeneous. Dissenting biologists took issue with the treatment of these categories as random mating populations. In 1991 R. C. Lewontin and D. C. Hartl argued that genetic differentiation among ancestral populations in Europe is very complex; and immigrant history is too recent and endogamous mating within ethnic groups too high for Caucasian categories to be internally homogeneous. For African Americans there exists very little reliable data about African slave populations, notwithstanding the extensive mixing with European and Indian ancestry and the complex genealogical differences between recent Caribbean immigrants and northern urban and southern agrarian blacks. Hispanic is the most vague category, ranging from Guatemalan ancestry that is pure Indian to Argentinean that is pure Caucasian.[16] Lewontin, Hartl, and other critics of these categories insisted that significant differences among allele frequencies in ethnic subgroups had to be empirically accounted for. Defenders of the process maintained that the degree of variance in population substructures would not substantially differ from profile frequencies calculated from population averages, and that the latter were good enough for estimating random-match probabilities with accuracy.[17]

The doubts about the subpopulation problem prompted the 1992 NRC commission to recommend a ceiling principle (or more accurately, an interim ceiling principle, in the absence of significant data on ethnic subgroups) based on conservative assessments of data within the major racial groups.[18] Since the principle appeared to favor the defendant, there were strong criticisms of this report from scientists and lawyers, and, as is common, questions were raised about conflict of interest: several members of the NRC panel were found to have financial links with companies involved in DNA testing.[19] In addition, it was apparent that science in the field was being driven by the urgent needs of the court system, particularly the FBI, which tried to pressure the commission to tone down its reservations on the subpopulation issue. Not surprisingly, the technology's proponents also tried to clear the field's name in eminent journals. Lamenting that adversarial lawyers would soon be spreading confusion about science in the upcoming O.J. trial, Eric Lander and the FBI's Bruce Budowle published their exoneration, "DNA Fingerprinting Dispute Laid to Rest," in *Nature* in 1994, only to be further challenged in the journal by Lewontin, who described their article as a "piece of propaganda," and Hartl, who drew attention to the absurdity of FBI scientists being in a position to determine what constitutes the exact "forensic significance" of statistical differences between racial and ethnic populations.[20] Not for the first time in the history of the field, the cops were seen to be guarding the henhouse.

Many of these doubts and controversies were cited by Neufeld and Scheck in *People v. Simpson*, both in their motion to exclude DNA evidence and in their relentless attempts to cast doubt on the expertise of prosecution witnesses, from lab assistants to leading experts in population genetics. In the meantime, the new NRC commission had been appointed at the request of the FBI director William Sessions in 1993 to stave off a general moratorium and to settle the disputes about population subdivision and its role in calculating random-match probabilities. The 1996 report declared that the interim ceiling principle was no longer necessary, given the advances in knowledge about the frequency of genetic markers in ethnic subgroups and the overall statistical improvements in genetic profiling of populations. There now existed an "appropriate data base" to support calculations about population substructures, and the data had shown that differences between broad racial groups were more significant than within them.[21]

The publication of the 1996 report may put to rest some public and institutional doubts about the scientific evidence presented in the O.J. trial, but it resolves none of the issues regarding how complex scientific evidence should be handled in the courtroom or what uses will be made of the state's databanking of DNA samples. For over a century, the state's criminal agencies have petitioned science with demands for an identifiable self-signature that would serve as a reliable medium of surveillance, classification, and law enforcement. Such signatures, from fingerprints to DNA profiles, have invariably raised and dashed the hopes of those looking for biological clues to social behavior. Paul Rabinow points out that the eugenicist Francis Galton was enthused about the first use of fingerprinting in India, motivated by the need of the colonial authorities to counteract the "'proverbial unveracity' of the Oriental races," but was disappointed to find that fingerprints contained no information about race or temperament, no clues about natural or sexual selection.[22]

The last quarter century's research in molecular biology has again attracted the interest of those who believe that people carry within their biological makeup the causes of their own crime, poverty, and poor health. The institutional contexts for DNA forensics in particular have been the laboratories of commercial biotechnology companies, local law enforcement, and the FBI itself, which has its own professionalized research team at Quantico, Virginia, training forensic specialists in the principles of molecular genetics. These techniques are linked to the FBI's National DNA Identification Index, developed in coordination with forensic databanks in at least thirty-two states, and based on extensive sampling studies of convicted felons and over two million armed personnel. A number of soldiers, in Hawaii notably, have already refused to be tested, citing the protection of their civil liberties. The Defense Department, which court-martialed the soldiers, refuses to guarantee that its databanks will not be used for purposes other than identification of the war dead.[23] Nonconsensual testing is nonetheless becoming a norm, as Philip Bereano notes, "at a time of an unprecedented testing hysteria," when everyone from corporate employees to sex offenders is being subjected to scientific testing.[24]

The controversy over the courtroom use of DNA typing created a demand for population geneticists to research the differences in DNA marker frequencies among racial and ethnic groups. The FBI alone undertook extensive population surveys, resulting in the DNA databasing of racial and ethnic differences.[25] Thus the earlier doubts about population substructure, which were dismissed at the time by the FBI, turned out to be a convenient justification for extending the range of the FBI's DNA identification banks.

The concerns about threats to genetic privacy from this databanking are considerable. For example, who gets to use the results once the original demand for this kind of research has been satisfied and forgotten? However, there are also larger cultural and social ramifications. The potential outcome of such research will be to reinforce assumptions about the biological classification of ethnicity and race in a social and political climate where such classifications invariably have destructive consequences. Inevitably, it seems, people will once again link cultural and social traits to these biological classifications. Efforts at population control will be able to draw on biological taxonomies that had proven elusive for centuries. More specifically, genetic testing may be used to affirm the ethnic authenticity of affirmative action candidates.[26] In the world of identity politics, it may also be used by spokespersons to buttress their claims to be "more black" or "more gay" than others. Anything is possible on this burned-over terrain, which is being cultivated yet again after centuries of overpopulation by destructive scientific and social fictions about race and sexuality.

In the case of DNA typing, there has been no easy separation of the scientific agenda from the social agenda. They have been beset by the same contradiction: Should our identities be analyzed on an individual basis or according to group type? Nothing could be more relevant to liberalism's current agony over racial politics. Genetic research has the choice of focusing its resources on individual variation or group variation. (The former happens to be by far the greater of the two, racial difference accounting for only a small percentage of human genetic diversity.)[27] The legal system is

obliged to assess subjects as individuals, but it does so within a social climate and within the framework of community and group values where
race and ethnicity often have a more powerful significance.

In the O.J. case, this contradiction played an important role. There
was arguably less reason to racialize O.J. than almost any other black
American male. While still a black male before the U.S. legal system, he
was as "individual" as it was possible to be. And yet, just as the genetic
evidence in the trial was based in part on references to his racial identity,
the social and cultural meaning of his trial was pushed and pulled into the
arena of public opinion where race matters—big time. These contradictions between individual and group are nothing new; they lie at the heart
of the liberal political system and are increasingly central to public and
policy debates about the shape of a multiracial, multiethnic society. But
there are many good reasons why appeals to biological authority should
be kept to a minimum in such debates. If the criterion of judgment in
matters legal, social, and political is whether the genes fit or not, then we
are going to be in serious trouble. Consider the outcome in the O.J. trial:
the virtual silencing of the prosecution's establishment of motive in the
murder charge, along with much of the supporting evidence of domestic
violence. The obsessive focus on DNA identification, which monopolized
so much courtroom time, helped to overshadow the systematic evidence
of spousal abuse on O.J.'s part. Along with its group-oriented counterpart—the morality play of race politics that Johnnie Cochran's summa-
tion evoked in religion-soaked terms—this drama about identification
may well have buried the evidence for the gender crime that many believe
lay at the heart of the O.J. case. If so, then the individual/group dualism
of the liberal imagination proved yet again that it is not yet up to the feat
of dealing more than two cards at a time.

SIX

The Great Un-American Numbers Game

For many folks in the New York artworld, the most telling facts you needed to know about the 1995 Biennial Exhibition at the Whitney Museum of American Art were on the Guerrilla Girl statistic sheet distributed around town and to those attending the opening (see fig. 1). These statistics became a serviceable shorthand for public opinion, since they coincided so neatly with the indifferent critical reception of the exhibition. The numbers showed a plunge in the percentage of women and artists of color represented in the show, as compared with the all-time high of 1993. For some, the statistics served as a transparent index of institutional injustice. For others, citing the numbers offered a welcome relief from the tiresome obligation to offer a detailed judgment about the show. For still others, they were crude emblems of the great un-American quota mentality, and therefore an affront to the principle of aesthetic meritocracy. For almost everyone, it seemed as if the Guerrilla Girls' body count had finally become an integral and unavoidable part of the response to the most important periodic survey of contemporary North American art. Of course, there were other components to be accounted for in explaining the tenor of the selections, such as the curator Klaus Kertess's own powerful belief in pure aesthetics, or his predilection for painting and formal sculpture—each seen as regressive elements in a critical climate that had so depreciated the modernist canon of taste and the art media with which it had been most associated. But the numbers were the proverbial last word, serving as some kind of lightning rod to channel and ground the turbulent atmospheric energies that had been released by the North American Culture Wars. This was a strange moment, although in many ways it simply brought to the surface and reduced to a statistical format the shifting undercurrents of anxieties and resentments about exclusion from the pan-

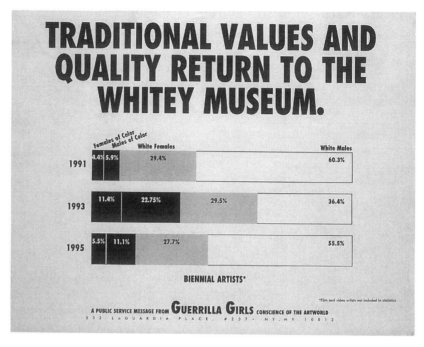

Figure 1   Guerrilla Girls poster.

theon of recognition that biennial surveys have fostered and encouraged in recent decades. Who's in, who's out, what kinds of media are favored, how many dead artists, how many Latin Americans, and so on.

It was also a moment of triumph for the Guerrilla Girls themselves, self-styled "conscience of the art world," after ten years of agitprop badgering of galleries and museums for their underrepresentation of women and minority artists (see fig. 2). The lineage of this activity dates from the first protests against the Whitney's surveys, initiated by Faith Ringgold in November 1968, continued, along with Lucy Lippard, Poppy Johnson, and Brenda Miller, in an organized form as the Ad Hoc Women Artists Committee in 1970 and 1971, and extended under the rubric of Artists Meeting for Cultural Change, formed in 1975 to protest the Whitney's bicentennial offering (see fig. 3). Other groups active during this period were the Women Artists and Students for Black Art Liberation, the Black

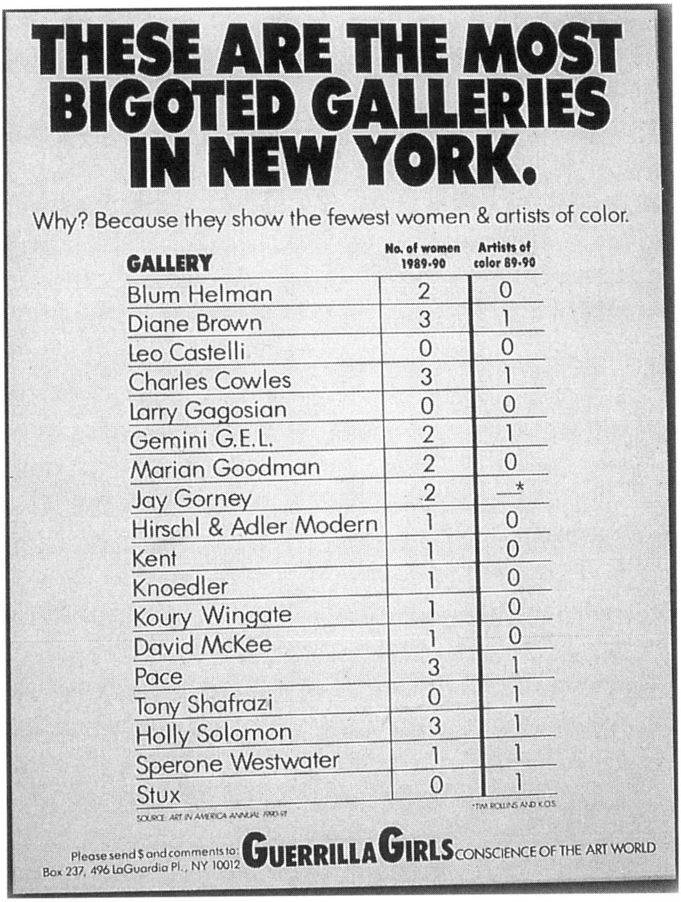

THESE ARE THE MOST
BIGOTED GALLERIES
IN NEW YORK.

Why? Because they show the fewest women & artists of color.

GALLERY	No. of women 1989-90	Artists of color 89-90
Blum Helman	2	0
Diane Brown	3	1
Leo Castelli	0	0
Charles Cowles	3	1
Larry Gagosian	0	0
Gemini G.E.L.	2	1
Marian Goodman	2	0
Jay Gorney	2	*
Hirschl & Adler Modern	1	0
Kent	1	0
Knoedler	1	0
Koury Wingate	1	0
David McKee	1	0
Pace	3	1
Tony Shafrazi	0	1
Holly Solomon	3	1
Sperone Westwater	1	1
Stux	0	1

SOURCE: ART IN AMERICA ANNUAL 1990-91   *TIM ROLLINS AND K.O.S.

Please send $ and comments to: **GUERRILLA GIRLS** CONSCIENCE OF THE ART WORLD
Box 237, 496 LaGuardia Pl., NY 10012

Figure 2   Guerrilla Girls poster.

Emergency Cultural Coalition, and, in California, the Council of Women Artists, who threatened a civil rights suit against Los Angeles County Museum of Art. The original umbrella organization had been the Art Workers' Coalition, founded in 1969, from which emerged the feminist artists group Women Artists in Revolution and the Guerrilla Art Action Group.[1] Today the Guerrilla Girls' allies include Godzilla, the Asian American artists pressure group, and PESTS, a coalition of artists of color.

GUERRILLA GIRLS' 1986 REPORT CARD

GALLERY	No. of women 1985-6	No. of women 1986-7	REMARKS
Blum Helman	1	1	no improvement
Mary Boone	0	0	Boy crazy
Grace Borgenicht	0	0	Lacks initiative
Diane Brown	0	2	could do even better
Leo Castelli	4	3	Not paying attention
Charles Cowles	2	2	needs work
Marisa del Rey	0	0	no progress
Allan Frumkin	1	1	Doesn't follow directions
Marian Goodman	0	1	keep trying
Pat Hearn	0	0	Delinquent
Marlborough	2	1	Failing
Oil & Steel	0	1	underachiever
Pace	2	2	working below capacity
Tony Shafrazi	0	1	still unsatisfactory
Sperone Westwater	0	0	unforgivable
Edward Thorp	1	4	making excellent progress
Washburn	1	1	unacceptable

Source: Art in America Annual 1985-6 and 1986-7.

Box 1056 Cooper Sta. NY, NY 10276 **GUERRILLA GIRLS** CONSCIENCE OF THE ART WORLD

Figure 3   Guerrilla Girls report card.

The Guerrilla Girls have long since established a permanent identity in the artworld, largely through their media-savvy tactics, analogous to the new generation of public and institutional activism forged by ACT UP and its artists' collectives like Gran Fury and DivaTV. Indeed, their use of statistical weaponry was adopted as an activist model by the artworld group WAC (Women's Action Coalition), which left a legacy of chronicled injustices to women in the form of a book, *WAC STATS* (see fig. 4). Alternately, the GG posters have been hung as works of art in the muse-

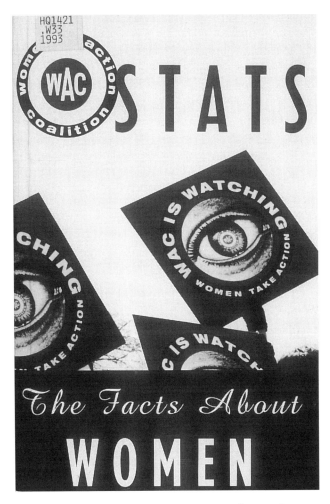

Figure 4   Front cover of *WAC STATS* (New York: New Press, 1993).

ums they have targeted—striking evidence, depending on your point of view, of their success or their failure to combat the ceaseless capacity of postmodern institutional life to absorb all forms of criticism. All the 1970s politically alternative art groupings and spaces—Colab, AIR, JAM, Taller Boricua, Fashion Moda, Group Material, Political Art Documentation/Distribution—wrestled with the dismal paradox that their critiques of institutional art were more likely to become institutionalized than to generate lasting alternatives.[2] This facility to incorporate dissent can be seen even in the formative years of art activism; after the Art Worker's Coalition picketed the Metropolitan Museum of Art in 1967, some of the activists were offered employment by the Met. All the same, it is still disquieting to consider Elizabeth Hess's suggestion that "there are . . . more advantages to being a Guerrilla Girl today than there are to being a woman artist."[3]

There are many lessons to be drawn from the history of artworld activism in the period since the late 1960s. My interest here lies primarily in the use of statistics to organize moral and political dissent in general, and to make arguments about selection and representation in exhibitions in particular. How do we explain the current urgency of this phenomenon in cultural affairs, in that realm of social activity where quantitative reasoning is supposed to have least influence and where aesthetic taste and qualitative value hold most sway? Although it is far from restricted to the hothouse of the North American artworld, it's fair to say that in the example of the Guerrilla Girls we have one of the cleanest, most concise, and most visible displays of this criterion of judging by the numbers. To many eyes, it has produced a standoff between a disinterested principle of selection and one based on accountability to particular group identities. For the most part, this is perceived as a confrontation that has emerged only very recently—the inevitable result of a clash between the upsurge in identity politics, whereby different minority groups demand recognition and parity of representation in the public sphere, and an older, prevailing tradition of assessment that was less conscious of, or intrinsically blind to, its record of exclusions. On the contrary, the discrepancy between these two principles of selection is not simply of recent origin; it can be traced back to the goals articulated in the foundation of the great public museums in the nineteenth century. For the most part, I will focus my discussion on the art museum.

In two recent influential books, Tony Bennett (*The Birth of the Museum*) and Carol Duncan (*Civilizing Rituals*) have documented how the public museums were instituted by bourgeois reformers with the intent of providing a means of self-improvement to the mass of the population.[4] At a time when culture was being drawn into the province of government, museums and other public institutions like parks, libraries, and symphony halls were intended to serve as instruments of peaceable self-reform for urban populations that were becoming increasingly unmanageable. To perform their function in an educative manner, museum collections had to be fully representative of art history: their precursors had been the collections of Renaissance princes, absolute monarchs, and aristocratic gentlemen, which had aimed more at the singular, the exotic, and the wondrous—the Cabinet of Curiosities—rather than at extensive historical coverage. In many instances (in the Met as well as in more provincial institutions) this coverage would be provided initially by plaster-of-paris replicas. Thus was born not only the principle of universal representation, according to the canons of art-historical taste, but also the impossible ideal of the complete collection, as defined, again, by the prevailing aesthetic sense. According to Bennett, this goal of telling the story of Man on the basis of his universality could never be satisfied by any particular display of Man, which would always fall short, as a result of exclusions and bias. So too, there was a contradiction between the use of the museum as a vehicle for universal education and its use as a means of reforming the manners and conduct of its new audiences; one goal addressed its audience as an undifferentiated group, the other actively differentiated its audience according to their level of social and cultural refinement.[5] Despite its universalist intentions, usage of the art museum, then and now, has always been confined to socially upscale populations. Casual visitors to Washington's museum mall soon discover that the big draws are the Air and Space Museum, the most popular in the world, and the Natural History Museum, where the main attraction—the spectacle of the Hope Diamond in a display case—generates the longest line of all. By contrast, one can stroll unimpeded through the miles of uncluttered art gallery corridors and enjoy the relative solitude that art appreciation is supposed to foster and that truly popular art education can only disturb and despoil. The nineteenth-century story was not terribly different. Despite conservatives' fears that the newly admitted masses would desecrate the art on display and generally run riot, the forbidding architectural milieu of the temple-museums and the austere tenor of their educational paternalism were sufficiently off-putting to the majority, while trustee elites privately fostered policies that discouraged popular use. It did not help matters, for example, that the religiously minded trustees of institutions like the Met closed the museum on Sundays, the only day of recreation for the working class. Bending to criticism of this twenty-year policy, the trustees opened the doors in 1891 with the public aim of seducing people away from Coney Island. No doubt they were relieved, but hardly surprised, when the initially large Sunday attendance fell off rather quickly, and the museum resumed its air of an exclusive preserve for urban elites.

Unlike in France, where the king's royal collection had become nationalized in the Louvre, or in England, where bourgeois reformers created national museums *in opposition to* the vast collections of the aristocracy (King Charles's collection had been dispersed by the Puritans), the great American civic museums of New York, Boston, Chicago, and Philadelphia were created by prosperous Protestant elites intent on securing their country's symbolic prestige in the world of industrial nations. The collections were built up through extraordinary gifts from those storied tycoons who effected a massive relocation of art objects from Europe in the later decades of the century. The major museum bequests of the millionaires made front page news and brought them great social status. Thus was the WASP heritage of high European culture established as the American national patrimony.[6]

While the great museums had to retain their public credibility—building on public land, accepting public monies, and advertising their role in public education—they were dependent on the private bequests and were controlled by the interests of their millionaire benefactors. These moguls were accustomed to sit on the self-perpetuating boards of trustees, and many of them maintained their own rooms, with the right to display their own art, in an arrangement that made buildings like the Met appear more like mausoleums to enshrine their benefactors' fame than the people's museums they were supposed to be. The public excesses of the Gilded Age tycoons were eventually curbed in the nation at large. As Duncan notes, one result was the new policy in most museums of discouraging restricted bequests (revived again in recent decades), and, more generally, the advent of professional curatorial control over collections.[7] But there was little decline in the influence of the family names associated with bequests to the nation's blue-chip cultural establishments—Astor, Vanderbilt, Girard, Lowell, Peabody, Rockefeller, Carnegie, Morgan, Stanford, Frick, Corcoran, Gardner, Getty, Mellon, Huntingdon, Widener,

Kress, and Altman. For this class, ties to the elite institutions of the arts and higher education have continued to be an obligatory mark of prestige and social standing. Policing of taste in many of these institutions was preserved through the board of trustees, where, in New York City to this day, the same Social Register names appear on the boards of the likes of MOMA, the Metropolitan, the Juilliard, the New York Philharmonic Orchestra, Lincoln Center, the New York Public Library, and the big-league foundations. They are accustomed to dining regularly, after hours, amid the opulent furniture of palaces like the Met, at fund-raising parties that are as integral to the social season of the wealthy as to the economic health of the high-end arts. It is hardly surprising, then, that the intimate involvement of these institutions with wealthy patrons has sustained the latter's often arbitrary influence over taste and exhibition selection, and that the public mandate of the museums often appears to be a facade.

This historical tradition of sustaining private interest in the name of public enlightenment was extended to the artworld as a whole with the creation of an international art market as early as the 1930s. Under modernism's aesthetic banner of pure formalism, works of art would now work their way from one autonomous sphere to another—from the commerce-free studio through the commodity-saturated marketplace and prestige-rich collection into the canonical museum—without becoming soiled with the taint of dollar value.[8] No doubt this system also depended on the development of advanced security systems. Electronic surveillance has only recently displaced an armed security presence in some galleries and museums. Figure 5 depicts a scene from the Parke-Bernet Galleries, where an armed guard faces down a vicious and unruly mob of Upper East Side matrons.[9] Most of the time, however, security is achieved through self-discipline. Witness the "Oriental gentleman" (as he might have been termed at the time of this image) depicted in figure 6, obviously well versed in the reflexive "Oriental" arts of aesthetic meditation, and therefore an unlikely security risk. Indeed the entire tradition of art appreciation and connoisseurship, as it has evolved, is exemplary of the self-discipline and self-surveillance that are the favored modes of behavioral management in advanced liberal societies.

But security is not there simply to protect art or regulate moral behavior through self-fashioning, it is also there to boost the spectator's estimate

Figure 5   "Unruly mob" inside Parke-Bernet Galleries, New York.

Figure 6   Advertisement for the "Collector's Group" of Cabin Crafts Rugs.

of the value of art. Who hasn't heard the story that the Mona Lisa became a truly valuable work of art only after it had been stolen? In the age of the grand purchase, the huge sums of money raised by museums to acquire art treasures are presented as acts of public service, often attended by a sense of nationalistic urgency if the work is able to augment the nation's cultural capital. This nationalism is ever more pronounced in excolonizing countries, whose patrimony is partly a result of the imperial pillage of other countries' artifacts. (To this day the illicit antiquities trade continues this plunder, particularly of the Third World, and often in the service of providing cultural diversity for Western institutions.) The patrimony principle also supports the tax-evasive habits of the wealthy, for whom their collection of art is often supervised by a lawyer's assessment of the future state of taxation policies and death duties. In this way the principle of accumulation is fully aided and abetted by the state's fiscal recognition of the artworld as a medium for transferring, circulating, and generating capital. At the heart of this process is the use of art institutions to negotiate private investments in the name of public interest. Under these circumstances, it is clear how and why a bullish art market, of the sort sustained in the 1980s, requires an increase in the number of museums. Indeed, the museum-building boom of the last two decades has been matched only by the growth of prisons in certain countries and regions. Almost every North American city and many in Europe initiated a museum-building or -renovation project during the 1980s, usually in the name of civic-mindedness or provincial pride, but also in response to the demands created by the collectors' market. Indeed, the new museum became the prestige building type of the era, identified with a star architect—Meier, Pei, Hollein, Kahn, Sterling, Venturi.[10] In many cases the building opens with virtually no collection and functions as a lavish advertisement for prospective bequests.

One of my reasons for outlining this history of private influence on the development of museums is to remind us that the business of cultural advocacy is not a recent tendency in the history of museums. Cultural claims, in both the public and private interest, have always been strongly promoted and endorsed by and through the museum. Initially, these were presented in the universalist guise of displaying the glories of national or world civilizations. The favored version was an evolutionary, and hence scientific, narrative of aesthetic and technological progress. This presented a linear, affirming genealogy for the currently existing nation-state, with its currently existing racial and class hierarchies.[11] No less disinterested were museum officials' conceptions of their public culture as a mass civilizing medium, in direct competition with other institutions. Some of these rivals were public, in the case of universities, but most were commercial, in the case of palaces of consumption like the grand department store, or spectacles of performance like the popular theater, circus, and fairground. This public mission of the nineteenth-century museum no more stood on its own then than it does today, where the museum's place in the tourist circuit of airport, hotel, restaurant, and shopping is as important as its place at the end of the institutional circuit that runs through the artist's studio, the gallery, the auction house, and the private collection. Nor were the boundaries of public, commercial, and popular so distinct that they constituted entirely separate spheres. With Sears, Bonwit Teller, Filene's, Marshall Field's, Macy's, Montgomery Ward, and Saks on one side and Barnum and Bailey on the other, the competition for mass taste was too attractive for museum administrators to pass up.[12] Nostalgia and spectacle contended with historical aura for the audience's attention. Didacticism made its bed alongside the diorama, integrating what had been separated to some degree, at the great fairs, where the popular genres of burlesque and carnival that flourished on the fringe in the midway often commented parodically on the official exhibits inside the gates.

Above all, the state has always been an interested agent in this process, from the early nineteenth century need for national collections to compete in the league of civilized nations to the most recent flaps over "historical revisionism" in the nation's official institutions of record at the Smithsonian. Bennett argues that the opening of the nineteenth-century museum's doors to the public was a significant administrative move in the modern state's bid to employ culture as a means of social management. The good conduct of the popular classes must come from self-reform, many reformers concurred, and libraries and museums were designated to be as necessary to moral health as good sanitation. Such public facilities would distract the dissolute away from the alehouse and other disorderly sites of free assembly. The museum was to be a "passionless reformer," in the words of George Brown Goode, assistant secretary of the Smithsonian in 1895 at the time he wrote the influential *Principles of Museum Administration*.[13]

Concomitant with the development of liberal society, the vital mission of such institutions was to educate the citizens of popular classes in the habits of self-discipline and self-regulation. This could succeed only if the artifacts of power were on permanent display—nothing could be hidden from view in this transfer of culture from the aristocratic few to the many. In this respect, the museum's commitment to exhibition and display had more in common with the fairs and Great Expositions than with the library or the public park. Bennett's analysis of the function of public exhibition runs parallel with Foucault's discussion of the institutions of punishment and incarceration. For Foucault, the spectacle of trial and sentencing had become newly public at a time when the spectacle of punishment was being withdrawn from public display behind the penitentiary walls. Bennett places the emergence of the museum in the context of public health policy, alongside the state's programs of sanitation. In accord with the administrative principle of "governing at a distance," these programs were designed to harness the concept of the free, self-civilizing individual to a policy of morally reforming the otherwise ungovernable populace. The unruly sphere of popular recreation was vilified in favor of civic instruction, moral uplift, and refinement of taste. Bennett, then, shows how the nineteenth-century museum was introduced as a space where the reform of taste and manners could be presented as a voluntary revision of behavior. Even better, this would take place in environments where costly property would be imbued with new levels of respect.

Thus was the new etiquette of cultural power established. It has not been altered substantially. The significance, for example, of throwing open the doors becomes heightened at moments when the museum is targeted by outsiders or insurgents as an elite fortress. When members of the Art Workers' Coalition were laying siege to the Met in 1971, the director, Thomas Hoving, saw that it was necessary to give the protesters free run of the Great Hall to stage their demonstrations:

We allowed them to do it. And I insisted upon the same type of paraphernalia that groups of that nature demand upon Establishment institutions, which threw them off. . . . And they came, and they had their series of lectures in the Great Hall, and no member of the public really looked or cared, and they closed up shop after two or three hours 'cause it was obviously a fizzle. What they wanted to do was for us to close down the Museum and bar the gates so they could be photographed "locked out," which we decided would be really rather politically unsophisticated. And quite frankly, since that time we haven't really heard anything of them.[14]

In a somewhat less cynical vein, Dillon Ripley, secretary of the Smithsonian, decided that the institute's museums should be opened to the mass of protesters, many of them African American, who arrived to camp out in the Washington Mall as part of the Poor People's Campaign in 1968. In doing so, Ripley rejected patrician concerns about a possible security threat posed by this population of museum novitiates, and correctly interpreted the historical function of his institution's open invitation to self-civilize.[15]

As for the etiquette of behavior within the museum, most of its codes are still extant and have become refined over the years. Let me quote from the opening of a popular manual, entitled *How to Visit a Museum*:

> There is no right or wrong way to visit a museum. The most important rule you should keep in mind as you go through the front door is to follow your own instincts. Be prepared to find what excites you, to enjoy what delights your heart and mind, perhaps to have aesthetic experiences you will never forget. You have a feast in store for you and you should make the most of it. Stay as long or as short a time as you will, but do your best at all times to let the work of art speak directly to you with a minimum of interference or distraction.[16]

The book offers commonsense advice about how to match the conventions of art appreciation with the physical constraints of the museum environment. In general, the tips are about how to manage your time to maximum aesthetic effect by individualizing each available moment, breaking away from the oppressive, mechanistic routines of the tour guide, or avoiding the press of the crowd:

> It is difficult to stand in front of an individual work for longer than a few seconds when people are milling around you, pushing and shoving

to get on with the show. . . . Kandinsky once wrote scornfully of the "vulgar herd" that strolls through museums and pronounces the pictures "nice" or "splendid." Then they go away, he added, "neither richer nor poorer than when they came." Whenever you feel that way, do your best to shut out the sense of being with other people. It takes concentration, but it can be done. It helps when there are breathing spaces in the crowd, and for a minute or two you can be alone. It is wise to take advantage of these "gaps," moving across a room quickly and forgetting about seeing each work in sequence. There are also tricks one can try, like going to a popular exhibition a half-hour before it closes, when audiences will have thinned out.

Enlisting the support of a great artist's disdain for the "vulgar herd," this text illustrates well the principle of the self-maximization of the civilizing effect—the aim being to become "richer" rather than "poorer" as a result. The reader is encouraged to emulate those connoisseurs who shun the museum literature and guides and who are comfortably at home in these vast, templed environments. Less well educated visitors are likely to feel alienated by the sanctimonious atmosphere, tending to stick close to family or friends while their visits, so vital to the museums' attendance figures, are mass processed by guides.[17] Nothing is more clear than that the public's visits are differentiated by cultural class, even in minority or community arts museums. For each social group, a calculus of profit is at play, at once individualizing and massifying, whereby maximum use is extracted from managing quality aesthetic time.

Bennett locates the origins of this principle in the nineteenth-century school of utilitarianism, according to which public institutions were viewed as a means of multiplying the utility of culture. Statistical accounting was paramount in ensuring the maximum distribution of culture among the populace, especially in the provinces, where curators circulated artifacts from metropolitan museum collections in order to spread the effect. In this context, the museum's function ran parallel with the flood of data collecting and numerical analysis that sustained the demographic inquiries of the Victorian period. The United States in particular was undergoing the largest documented population growth of modern times. The warm patriotism associated with surging numbers, seen as the engine of democracy in the first century of the Republic, was joined now by a post-Malthusian suspicion about the burdens and potential dangers posed by population growth, reinforced by a nativist hostility to the new urban working class, swelling with immigrants.

Counting by Numbers

To assess how museums today are responding to claims based on statistics of group representation, we might note, first of all, the many contexts in which "the numbers game" is played out in North American public life in the 1990s. Casual perusal of any daily newspaper will reveal the steady attention to the authority of quantitative analysis, from the blizzard of data breakdowns in the financial pages to the latest cost-benefit analysis from a medical expert showing exactly how many years longer we will live if we run two and a half miles more each week. The current fiscal climate, devotionally bound to the gospel of the balanced budget, is the prevailing pressure system, deeply affecting the treatment of almost every story in the news. The bruises left by the cruel passage across the political land-scape of *The Bell Curve*'s linking of race and IQ are all too apparent. The debate about the role of Scholastic Aptitude Test scores in education sim-mers on. As a legacy of the "regulatory reform" initiatives of the Contract with America, Congress has established statistical risk assessment at the heart of government as the new primary form of administrative rational-ity. We have recently been informed, without too much fanfare, that 1 percent of the U.S. population owns 40 percent of its wealth—a sobering statistic redolent of the days of the robber barons in the late nineteenth century. On the culture front, the much disputed 69 cents a year that tax-payers used to set aside for funding of the arts through the NEA and the NEH has long since attained a bizarre status in public opinion. And on the museum front, the furor about historical revisionism bears the mem-ory of the flap over the *Enola Gay* exhibit at the Smithsonian's Air and Space Museum, which revolved around a revised estimate of the number of Americans allegedly spared by the decision to use the atomic bomb in the war against Japan. Drawing on current historical scholarship, curators of the exhibit had suggested a number of 63,000 instead of the quarter

TOP TEN WAYS TO TELL IF YOU'RE AN ART WORLD TOKEN:

10. Your busiest months are February (Black History Month), March (Women's History), April (Asian-American Awareness), June (Stonewall Anniversary) and September (Latino Heritage).

9. At openings and parties, the only other people of color are serving drinks.

8. Everyone knows your race, gender and sexual preference even when they don't know your work.

7. A museum that won't show your work gives you a prominent place in its lecture series.

6. Your last show got a lot of publicity, but no cash.

5. You're a finalist for a non-tenure-track teaching position at every art school on the east coast.

4. No collector ever buys more than one of your pieces.

3. Whenever you open your mouth, it's assumed that you speak for "your people," not just yourself.

2. People are always telling you their interracial and gay sexual fantasies.

1. A curator who never gave you the time of day before calls you right after a Guerrilla Girls demonstration.

A PUBLIC SERVICE MESSAGE FROM **GUERRILLA GIRLS** CONSCIENCE OF THE ARTWORLD
532 LaGUARDIA PLACE · #237 · NY, NY 10012

Figure 7   Guerrilla Girls poster.

million estimate preferred by the Air Force Association and by veterans in general, in an incident that had incinerated over 140,000 Japanese civilians after the Second World War had ended in all but name. The Smithsonian unconditionally surrendered to pressure from the vets to edit the narrative, and another act of what scholars have labeled "historical cleansing" was accomplished.

The most significant level of attention to numbers, however, has been in the prolonged backlash against affirmative action programs, selected as a "wedge" issue by the New Right to appeal to white voters. Affirmative action, the statistical machinery that emerged from reformed race policy in the 1960s, successfully broke open the occupational caste system but arguably failed, in the abdication of the liberal will to push any further, to break up the de facto segregation of so many sectors of social and economic life. While corporate institutions and businesses have benefited by acquiring a dash of diversity for their statistical profiles, national social

statistics continue to show a marked deterioration in the quality of life—
income, health, housing, educational opportunity—for most minority
communities (see fig. 7). Nonetheless, affirmative action and other claims
for group cultural rights are seen by many as a natural extension of the
representative democratic process, by which the demographics of gender,
race, or ethnic characteristics are more equitably represented in public,
institutional life.

Those of us employed in North American higher education are all too
aware that our own workplace has been established as a front line in some
of the most significant struggles over these claims to cultural justice.
Notwithstanding the initial benefits achieved in education by policies of
affirmative action, it pains to watch the lifeblood of institutional racism
and sexism pulsing on, in tune to the heartbeat of corporate logic, which
increasingly governs the administrative direction of our colleges and universities. All of us also know what a genuine difference it makes to have a
threshold number of students and faculty of color in formerly white class-
rooms and faculty meetings. The conversation *is* different, in ways that
diverge from comparable shifts in gender ratios. In 1997, when the first
decisions against affirmative action went into effect in state university systems in California and Texas, it became clear what a disastrous effect these
legal changes had wrought, not just on minority acceptance rates, but also
on minority applications.

While the principle of group representation and participation has had
some impact on all cultural institutions, those under the aegis of the arts
are predominantly governed by principles of *taste*, and therefore do not
carry quite the same legal (however now besieged) commitment to opportunity associated with public education. Consequently, the Guerrilla
Girls' numbers have been taken as a direct assault on the traditions of
connoisseurship. While numbers cannot speak for themselves, they carry
moral power as a stand-in for some vision of cultural justice that is still
incomplete and ideally would no longer have to respond to number-based
demands for group representation. On the other hand, their proximity to
the quantitative mentality of modern bureaucracy resonates with the history of the state's use of statistics as a medium of social control, stabilizing
disorder, normalizing behavior, rationalizing inequality, and, most relevant here, managing diversity by defining identities and their share of

public resources and representation. In the United States, the exemplary statistical state, the dominion of numbers has come to pervade institutional life, masquerading (like its judicial counterpart, the rule of law) as a neutral arbiter of competing claims on resources and rights. Consequently, such claims are often obliged to appeal to the statistical format in advance of any other moral language. Numbers invariably speak louder than opinions.

While the democratic validity of a principle like threshold representation is obvious, inclusion by numbers is no guarantee of cultural accountability. No one, for example, can expect women artists to automatically represent the experience of their gender (or of women of different ethnicities and classes) any more than they can be assumed to lack the capacity to speak to male experience. As in other areas of social life, naturalizing the link between the identity of artists and the content of their work erodes the challenge of empathy across our cultural differences that is so crucial to a multiethnic society.

It's Even Worse in Europe

Unlike neoliberal market economics, which has penetrated societies all around the world, this model of group representation is not very exportable, and more often than not escapes comprehension as it crosses national boundaries. In most non-American contexts, the Guerrilla Girls' graphs and charts would be viewed as the perverse product of an alien culture. In the sphere of the arts this disparity is even more evident, given the vestigial appeal of aesthetic taste over and above all other principles of evaluation, given the successful importation, in many countries, of the backlash against "political correctness," and given the varying regional components of cultural politics, quite dissimilar in countries that do not share the colonial, slavery, and immigrant histories of nation-states in North America and Latin America. Insouciance is the more likely response to the Guerrilla Girls poster that proclaims, "It's Even Worse in Europe" (fig. 8).

Listen, for example, to the response of Jean Clair, the curator of the 1995 Venice Biennale, to a question posed by an *Artforum* interviewer

Figure 8   Guerrilla Girls poster.

about group representation as it pertains to the exclusively Euro-American composition of Clair's selections:

> The notion of art is strictly Western. It has no pertinence outside our culture. The issue of political correctness is thoroughly foreign to me. What strikes a European as more important are the ethnic wars dragging us back to the situation of 1914. That's why I'm tempted to evoke the refusal of representation in extra-Occidental cultures, especially Islam. You make an image and you're likely to have your throat cut. This is the kind of cultural problem that leads to religious wars, and it's happening right now.

How are you going to resolve this? asks the interviewer, bearing in mind that the 1995 Biennale was supposed to be a centennial celebration:

Figure 9   Gaëtan Gatian de Clérambault, photograph. Courtesy of Musée de l'Homme, Paris.

A sensational solution would be to invite the faculty at the Ecole des beaux arts in Algiers, where the director has already been assassinated, to teach in Venice. But they would probably all be killed.

Clair's ultimate solution, as he describes it, to the absence of non-Occidental representation was to show Helmut Newton's *Sie kommen*, "a diptych of five magnificent women, eugenic prototypes, nude in one photo, dressed as executives in the other—and photographs by Gaëtan Gatian de Clérambault, the 1930s French psychiatrist who was fascinated by the draped fabric worn by Muslim women" (see figs. 9 and 10).[18] There's no

Figure 10   Gaëtan Gatian de Clérambault, photograph. Courtesy of Musée de l'Homme, Paris.

doubt that this was a bold and inventive juxtaposition, or that it spoke, however indirectly, to current realities in European political culture.

Enviously recalling the Biennale's origins as an "enormous popular fair" with up to 500,000 visitors, Clair cites this particular exhibit in the context of his desire to expand the Biennale audience beyond the circle of the international artworld cognoscenti. In this respect, he is speaking the language of the contemporary curator, duty-bound to attract huge audiences, often through the mounting of much criticized but very popular blockbuster exhibitions. This prevailing trend covets the theme park audiences

that museums have always imagined they could attract, though traditionally this has been done through appeals to instruction and enlightenment
rather than to outright entertainment. Today, the seduction of the weekend tourist is urged at the very moment that neo-statist conceptions of
public culture as a medium for educating the popular classes have lost most
of their credence. So, too, it is important to see how Clair's timely nostalgia
for the popular fairs of yore emerges in direct opposition to what he means
by political correctness—the crusade on the part of advocates like the
Guerrilla Girls to make exhibition culture more fully representative of and
accountable to a broader range of individuals and communities.

Notwithstanding their daring juxtaposition, Clair's selections of Newton and Clérambault reaffirm the aesthetic classification of fine art just as
they confine the location of their interest to Orientalist Europe. Western
by Clair's definition, the select delineation of art is preserved here, rather
than expanded, as it had been in the popular turn-of-the-century Expositions universelles, where the criterion was inclusiveness—the display of a
worldwide spectrum of artifacts, technologies, and handicrafts, however
colonial in arrangement. In addition, the cultural practices that typify
non-Western societies—relating to custom, tradition, or heritage, and
lived daily rather than museumified—become potential objects of
voyeurism for Clérambault, the Orientalist Frenchman, as much a
national European "type" as Newton, the German aesthete. Ostensibly,
the veiled Moroccans and the eugenic nudes are intended to contrast the
non-Occidental "refusal of representation" with the utter visibility of
Western representation. Yet in both cases, images of women are chosen as
examples of effrontery to the masculine gaze. In the case of Clérambault,
the Muslim veil is not so much a refusal of representation as an exotic
obstacle in the path of the photographer's access to a colonized culture
(even if cited as ocular proof of his bizarre theories, advanced in his
courses at the Ecole des beaux arts from 1923 to 1926, that styles of clothing could yield insights into the essence of racial identities).[19] Perhaps
these photographs (numbering in the thousands and taken on trips to
Morocco during and directly after World War I) do recall the Muslim
taboo on figural depictions of the human body, but they equally remind
us that the veil also has the function, in this period of colonial history, of
defying the occupier who is intent on unveiling, violating, and possessing

Figure 11   Gaëtan Gatian de Clérambault, photograph. Courtesy of Musée de l'Homme, Paris.

a culture, illustrated most commonly by the female body (see fig. 11). Moreover, since all veiled women are the same, ultimately they have to be represented in a group setting, or serially shot and quantified, as if unresponsive to the individualizing portraiture of Western photography.[20]

As for Newton's women, these "magnificent" specimens of the race are corporate horsewomen of the apocalypse—inevitable, unstoppable, invincible. With nothing to conceal and everything to gain, they are a collective illustration, again, of some castrating superfemale order, too large, too much in charge, except of course in the iconographic repertoire of the masochist. Whether as Clérambault's exotic guardians of private space or Newton's monstrously perfect invaders of public space, neither of these sets of images are quite what the Guerrilla Girls have in mind when they stake their claim, based on the principle of group demographics, for the right to represent and be represented. The group imagery of the masked Girls can easily be distinguished from the principle of grouping among the women of Clérambault and Newton (see fig. 12). In addition, their use of gender imagery provides a different gloss on the iconographies of concealment and domination, transforming the exoticism of the former into a carnivalesque threat. Strength in numbers contrasts with the unnatural perfection of the clone.

Figure 12   Guerrilla Girls, © Teri Slotkin.

Bearing in mind Clair's comment about the history of the popular fair, I find it worth remarking that the products of women's labor were more widely exhibited in the great expositions of the late nineteenth and early twentieth centuries than in museums of the time. In order to justify the status of world fair, the fairs had to be inclusive enough to display the diversity of the imperial world's industrial and craft production. The principle of ethnic representation was acknowledged, but only if the conventions of representing ethnicity as a fixed identity in the colonial chain of being, running from civilization to barbarism, were respected. Take the story of Ota Benga, the first Central African forest hunter to take up residence in the United States. Before he shared a cage with a pet chimpanzee in the Bronx Zoo (he committed suicide thereafter), Benga was exhibited at the 1905 World's Fair in St. Louis. An accomplished mimic, he ran into serious trouble when he began to impersonate the marching bands and American Indians, thereby refusing to behave like a pygmy and upsetting the rules of display.[21] Then, as now, artists and performers charged with representing an ethnic group or community are often heavily constrained by conventions of authenticity. This often takes the form of complying with some expectation of "exotic" art that contrasts with Euro-American aesthetics. Sometimes this regulation is sanctioned directly by the state, in the case of the Indian Arts and Crafts Act of 1991, legislated with a particular view of recognizably "Indian art" in mind—quite removed, say, from the important critical work of Native artists who challenge the stereotypes of Indian authenticity, like Jimmie Durham, James Luna, or Edgar Heap Of Birds (all of whom are conspicuously absent from the National Museum of the American Indian). Non-Anglo artists are often under great pressure from curators to produce art that is recognizably *different* from, and unobservant of, the influence of Western art history.

In other cases, the regulation can be self-imposed on the part of communities themselves. The "Black Male" show, for example, which preceded the 1995 Whitney Biennial, was frequently charged by black commentators with failing to represent more "traditional" features of black masculinity. In response to the call for artworld diversity, the evolving community arts movement has produced its own commodity practitioners defined by the iconography and demands of ethnic authenticity, such as the "professional Chicano artist," so ruthlessly satirized by Guillermo Gómez-Peña and others. The struggle to produce transcultural art based on the experience of "border-crossing" has been the single most significant challenge, as Gómez-Peña puts it, to "the anachronistic myth that as 'artists of color' we are only meant to work within the boundaries of our 'ethnic communities.'"[22]

The Principles of Exhibition

If the nineteenth-century museum was intended as an agent of cultural administration for an emergent mass urban population, there's no evidence that its principles of exhibition acknowledged in any way the claims for group cultural rights that have become such a contested feature of cultural institutions in the last twenty-five years. The nineteenth-century museum had no such brief for cultural pluralism, and even less for the principle of demographic representation. After all, it evolved in an institutional climate where scientific racism prevailed—sanctioning a hierarchy of races and ethnic identities—and indeed was actively championed by the officers and curators of institutions like Chicago's Field Museum, the American Museum of Natural History, and the Smithsonian itself. Nonetheless, the museum's promise of a complete field of representation in its displays and its mandate to be universally accessible to the public provided the framework for later claims about cultural rights and equal representation. These claims became more and more visible in the climate of cultural politics that evolved in the wake of the civil rights movement.

The use of political arithmetic in government has not changed in the last century. Then as now, the federal system used census numbers as the proportional basis for distributing resources and political representation. What *is* new is the concept of using that same principle as a basis for claims to cultural rights and representation. Proportional entitlement and representation is now applied to the sphere of culture, not without much resistance, but nonetheless with considerable success. Why is this so? At least three reasons apply.

First is the democratic significance of numbers. Despite the fact that the culture of the arts is still governed by concepts of aesthetic *taste* and *quality*, and that the sphere of culture in general is supposed to be exempt from the numerical bottom line applied in most other sectors of society, the democratic connotation of numbers is too powerful to resist. Just as the arithmetic of the state was described by early statisticians like Adolphe Quételet as the creation of "moral statistics," so the principle of demographic representation is applied to cultural institutions today as a moral corrective in the direction of numerical equality. If, in the nineteenth century, the useful effects of art on the population could be quantified, then it is not such a great leap to suggest that the quantitative spread of the population be reflected in the selection and public display of art itself. What could be the moral basis, in a statistical democracy, for any other principle of representation?

The second reason relates to the history of cultural rights claims in the period since the Civil Rights Act. From the time of the passing of the Fourteenth Amendment in 1868 until the first affirmative action programs a century later, a dominant civil claim was the putative right of the individual to be treated apart from his or her race. This interpretation, while rarely observed in practice, is now nostalgically upheld by opponents of affirmative action as the true liberal basis of the so-called color-blind Constitution. Since the introduction of affirmative action programs designed to breach the walls of occupational racial exclusion, race- and gender-based interpretations of group rights have become more common. Consequently, proportional representation has been sanctioned either through affirmative action's appeal to the compensatory principle of remedial justice or, more radically, according to some principle of mirror representation whereby the distribution of opportunity and representation is seen to be proportionate to the existing racial and gender composition of society, and any deviation from that ratio is perceived as discriminatory. While these principles have been besieged in recent years, their appeal to the statistical ethos of representative government is a very powerful one. All institutions that depend on the public status of their activities have been obliged to respect this ethos in their attempts to create more diversity among their participants.

The third reason involves the claim of cultural institutions like the museum to represent the world, the nation, the community, or some surveyable field of the arts. In the case of the art museum, the claim to universal representation has always been shaky but intrinsic to its public function. In the last two decades, as critical anti-institutional art has flourished, the institutional authority of the museum has been rather successfully demystified, along with its curatorial powers to represent and exhibit art with unimpeachable taste. With the collapse of the claim to represent according to authoritative taste, pressure to acknowledge some principle of representative diversity, proportional or not, has been unceasing.

Most of the controversy that results from this pressure has been associated with temporary exhibits, or with the kind of periodic surveys presented by the various Biennales and by *documenta* at Kassel. At the Whitney, for example, much of the controversy was defused after the selection of its Biennial artists was entrusted to the singular, subjective taste of an individual staff curator, or in the case of the 1997 Biennial, to one insider—Lisa Phillips from the Whitney—and one outsider—Louise Neri from *Parkett* magazine. One result of the increased political significance of the temporary exhibit or survey has been that the role of the curator has been transformed from aesthetic arbiter to cultural mediator, brokering the interests of artists, dealers, collectors, and trustees. Ultimately, the curator can act as a broker for cultural ethnicity if he or she has ties to ethnic communities pushing for greater representation.[23] This is less likely to happen at the blue-chip museums than at minority museums operating under the wing of large institutions, like the Smithsonian's Anacostia Museum, or functioning autonomously as neighborhood or community museums, like New York's Museo del Barrio, the Studio Museum in Harlem, the Afro-American Historical and Cultural Museum in Philadelphia, the Museum of the National Center of Afro-American Artists in Boston, or the Rhode Island Heritage Society. While the growth of the latter has inspired the community arts movement and given legitimacy to the principle of community self-representation, it has also served the cause of diversity management all too well, relieving establishment institutions like MOMA and the Met of the obligation to confront cultural diversity more fully within their own walls.

Recent talk about the crisis of the museum has been tied to the crisis of the principle of institutional representation, urgently felt across the spectrum of education as in the arts. As I have argued, this crisis ought to be seen in the light of the modern history of representative democracy in the United States, with its vast statistical machinery. In modern times, that process has proven faithful to the precept of proportional demographics on the one hand, while exercising care, on the other, not to disturb the liberal credo of meritocratic entitlement with any suggestion of a system of opportunity tied to quotas—currently the dirtiest word in U.S. political culture. Just as important, however, the crisis over institutional representation has its roots in the museum's origins and its ambitious goal of universal coverage.

The Strange Death of Public Culture

The museum's predicament is also typical of the plight of public culture in the age of privatization. One of the most abused terms in our political lexicon, the concept of the public has long been associated with decline, depreciation, and loss—there always is a more expansive public that was enjoyed in days of yore. Many of the institutions perceived as guardians of public culture have often appealed cynically to evidence of cultural decline—usually by vilifying popular culture—in order to reinforce their access to subsidies, resources, and privileges. It's also true that if these institutions have cried wolf once too often in the past, there really is a new kind of wolf at the door today, as the race toward privatization quickens. While public culture in the United States has usually depended on a mix of government, nonprofit, and private funding, the market-driven tilt toward corporate sponsorship is now transforming the face of the arts and education. In response to the massive cuts in social services, nonprofit sponsors are increasingly inclined to encourage art that is community-oriented or that addresses social problems from which the state has withdrawn the aid of its depleted welfare service agencies. On the other hand, the pressure of corporate sponsorship has boosted the merchandizing of culture, even through cable shopping networks (now in the business of serving as museum stores), to a degree that public art may soon be seen as a series of branding opportunities.

In response, the defense of the *status quo ante bellum* in public arts funding has all too often rested on hackneyed appeals to the Romantic safe haven of "artistic freedom," eternally secure against philistines and barbarians. Whatever its worth as a measure of protection for artists against the interests of the state or the powerful and wealthy, the cult of artistic freedom has also nurtured the myth of the "artist in quarantine," regally immune to public accountability and accessible public dialogue. It has also sustained the arrogant gulf that separates fine arts communities from those who work in the cultural marketplace, in media, fashion, graphic arts, design, and journalism—that sphere of cultural labor that, in spite of its commercial overlordship, has released some of the most vital social and political energies of this century at the same time it has marginalized so many others.

With the evaporation of any substantial challenge to market civilization, economic elites have less and less need for public culture to serve as a cloak of respectability for their wealth and status. Nor does the transnational nature of their power require public culture to assume a national form in order to compete for prestige in the league of nations. So too, the reliance of anti-imperialist nationalists on their national cultures to resist the global flows of cultural product has often served as a way to suppress internal minorities or preserve the power balance between metropolitan and provincial culture. Such attempts to defend the national patrimony have been outflanked by the omnivorous appetite of the globalizing culture industries for incorporating local and regional differences.

In response, some versions of public culture have gone supranational—utilizing preexisting networks of communication, like the international art market/circuit, or new technologies, like the Internet. Within the nation-state itself, where the cynical use of the Culture Wars to villainize dissenters shows no sign of abating, the response cannot be single-minded. Even for those who decide to devote their energies exclusively to the preservation of public cultural institutions, public culture will never be the same, nor should it be. The current crisis of its institutions should not be regarded as an occasion for retrenchment, but as an opportunity for us to overhaul, modernize, redefine, and fully democratize their structures. You don't have to be a conspiracy theorist to see that the race to privatization is occurring at the very moment when genuine attempts are being made to democratize public culture and diversify its participants, its content, and its reach into a wide range of communities. Claims for diversity and cultural equity are less likely to be met by corporate sponsorship, unless they coincide with a particular multicultural profile suggested by the market research division.

Some elements of the older version of public culture have to remain in place. Without the appeal to universal representation, however impossible and incomplete in practice, we will lose the basis, in a statistical democracy, for demanding that exhibits, collections, and programs be inclusive and diverse. In this respect, the effective graphic impact of the Guerrilla Girls report cards are indispensable billboards for advertising the progress (or retrenchment) of claims for equity. Such notices are a public reminder of how much remains to be done to attain anything close to a critical mass of underrepresented artists and voices. Ultimately, however, these claims have a limited effect on the business structure of the artworld—the gallery system, the art market, the glorification of authorship, the control of access and participation, and the use of fine art values to police class divisions. From this angle, elevating women and minority artists into the pantheon of the masters may be a matter of fine-tuning rather than a structural overhaul. The fact that the memory, let alone the vestigial reality, of the alternative arts space movement has taken such a beating makes it all the more difficult to imagine and reconstruct alternatives. The perils of co-option—relentlessly cautioned by the alternative arts movement—are no longer even fit for discussion among younger artists whose formation postdates the early 1980s.

On the one hand, then, we must be conscious of the injustices involved in propping up institutions like museums that have a history of transforming cultural rights into social privileges and treating open access as a means of behavior control, and that are even now recruiting the voices of the socially marginalized to pretty up the statistics required by diversity managers. On the other hand, we must be opportunistic, as always, under conditions not of our own making, in making use of the resources that are available. This has to involve creative attempts to use the new patterns of sponsorship to change the frankly elitist relationship between institutions and their audiences, between artists and their publics, between art and popular culture. These new funding patterns offer a potential vehicle for democratizing those relationships at the same time as they threaten to deliver the artworld into exactly the kind of corporate overlordship that governs aesthetics in the culture and media industries. From the perspective of the state, public culture is no longer viable as an instrument of popular reform. The evolution of highly controlled and managed forms of popular entertainment, from Coney Island to pay-per-view televised sport, has resolved the problems of civic disorder posed by unsupervised free assembly. Having entered the field in the nineteenth century with a fierce reforming mission that has long since lost its zeal, government is retreating from the province of culture in a manner not unlike that of a colonial power withdrawing from its provincial possessions in the hope that regional market brokers will remain friendly to its will. The national patrimony will remain a concern—the legacy of the *Enola Gay* will not fade quickly. In the meantime, we will continue to lock horns over the politics of inclusion—who's in, who's out. We must also continue to ask whether the vast resources of museums might be better utilized than in authoritative presentations of exhibits to passive spectators. But the larger task will be to create and promote new versions of the "public" that are inclusive, that have popular appeal, and that are elastic enough to accommodate the vast energies of a strong democracy of opinion.

SEVEN

What the People Want from Art?

With the exception of the NEA witch-hunt of the late 1980s and early 1990s, no art event in years has garnered the kind of attention the U.S. media devoted to Vitaly Komar and Alexander Melamid's ongoing project "The People's Choice." Media coverage ranged from tabloid to highbrow and all across the artworld spectrum. For those willing to take the artists at their literal word, "The People's Choice" was a frank attempt to show how the relationship between artists and the broad public might be transformed. For those more skeptical of the artists' professed intentions but sympathetic nonetheless to the strategy, the project was a refreshing means of challenging elite uses of the fine arts and asking how artists might be more accountable to popular taste about art. For those who cared not a whit about the interrogation of taste, "The People's Choice" could be read as pungent commentary on the statistical machinery of the modern corporate state.

Investigating the topic ostensibly addressed in the NEA flap—artists' public accountability—"The People's Choice" consciously revived the holy specter of "people's art" by polling public attitudes to the visual arts in thirteen countries, beginning in the United States in 1994, continuing in France, Turkey, Russia, Holland, Iceland, China, Italy, Denmark, Ukraine, Kenya, Finland, and Portugal, and ending with the German poll in 1997. In effect, the opinions of close to two billion people—about one-third of the world's population—were sampled. Respondents in each country were asked a wide range of multiple-choice questions about such things as their consumer tastes and recreational activities, their politics and lifestyle habits, their knowledge of famous artists and historical personages, and their preferences for or against sharp angles, curves, brush-strokes, and particular colors, sizes, contents, and styles in painting. The surveys were conducted by professional pollsters; in China, it was the broadest such opinion poll ever conducted, extending to rural populations. The process of data gathering was received and dissected with a delicious solemnity unmatched by the most zealous of number crunchers, and the irony quotient soared as each detail of the poll was broken down into graphs and statistical spreadsheets.

Using this data, Komar and Melamid painted a pair of composite canvases, the *Most Wanted* and the *Least Wanted*, for each country. Most of the results are strikingly similar. All the *Most Wanted*s are tranquil landscapes around a lake, usually with a group of figures relaxing in the foreground and an animal or two wading around in the lake or on the foreshore; often a historical figure is in attendance—a heroic George Washington in the U.S. version, a contemplative Jesus in the Russian. Predominant in each is the overwhelmingly favorite color, blue. The majority of the *Least Wanted*s are garish abstractions featuring triangles and reds. The next to last poll, in Holland, produced a quite different result. The Dutch *Most Wanted* turned out to be abstract and paperback sized. The *Least Wanted* was a watercolor interior, looking out on a wintry urban scene. Other than the Dutch survey, the differences between the polls were not especially significant, except, I think, for the marked preference among the Russian and Chinese respondents for modern styles in their homes, as against a wholesale preference for traditional styles everywhere else. Wherever appropriate, respondents overwhelmingly agreed on the need for more funding of the arts and a public say in what kind of art should be publicly exhibited. The project spawned a host of exhibits, including ones at the Alternative Museum and at the Visual Arts Gallery in New York, where other artists interpreted the statistical results in forms and media quite different from the way Komar and Melamid chose to depict them. So, too, the artists produced customized versions for the municipalities of Richfield, Connecticut, and Ithaca, New York, after town hall meetings with citizens.

First and foremost, "The People's Choice" was not an attempt to produce populist art. Like the market-research apparatus that it utilizes, its first aim was to produce a public dialogue—or the appearance of one. In light of the poll's banal conclusions and the "bad" art that issued from it, the higher purpose might be seen as dialectical: to begin to imagine an outcome something like the opposite of the one actually achieved. What-ever a real people's art might be, it would not look like this. And yet, in a society where public communication and popular taste seem stage managed by a vast machinery of statistical smoke and mirrors, the *Most Wanted* is what you might end up with. Or would you?

Komar and Melamid are no Situationists cynically riding the spectacle monster to the gates of freedom, nor are they Pop mavens bathing in the antiaesthetic limelight. They have long been intimate with bureaucratic thought and practice, and their work feeds off a withering familiarity with the arts of the modern state: its procedures for manufacturing consent and its facility for squeezing every possible drop from the rhetorical fruits of communism and democracy while exhibiting little evidence of either ideal. In this respect, they have learned a thing or two from firsthand experience about the convergence theory of the U.S.-style capitalist state and Soviet-style state capitalism. The languages and roles of the old Soviet Union's "dissident artist" and its "artist in the service of the people" can just as easily be transposed to a system maintained by the statistical toolbox of corporate capitalism. Indeed, in the media flak generated by "The People's Choice" the artists cast themselves as ardent populists crusading on behalf of the American public, ventriloquizing the tabloids' vox populi contempt for the elitist artworld establishment. Evincing deadpan respect for the pollsters' quantitative science, they appeared as enthusiastic participants in a national exercise of statistical quality control. They even posed for the tabloid *Daily News* as over-the-top patriots, taking the Pledge of Allegiance with one hand and bearing Old Glory in the other, like anticommunist exiles zealously converted to the ways of the free world. One of the goals, of course, was to expose the knavery of a data-management system that delivers presidents and elections as fluently as it delivers customers for Honey Nut Cheerios. Diagnosing the poll's results for the readers of the *Daily News*, Komar and Melamid pointed out, "Maybe everyone is wrong in this country. We are not wrong because we are the artist. But we are wrong like the whole country is wrong. Products, politics, art created from polls is wrong. If using polls for art is wrong, then everyone is wrong. We are as wrong as Clinton is" (June 13, 1994).

Of course this kind of argument is print journalism's bread and butter. After all, the press is in one sense in competition with the pollsters. While its chief commodity—the circulation of opinion—is often shaped by market research, journalism nonetheless depends on the belief that market shares, demographics, and percentage points are not the whole story. In addition, the industries of public opinion are largely concerned with their own self-promotion. It's no surprise, for example, that those who talk most about the media's social dominance are media professionals themselves. How many times have you seen Ted Koppel or some other news anchor deliver a homily about the overweening power of television in our lives? The PR industry probably does sometimes deliver elections, and its awesome psychographic databases probably are responsible for much of the way public opinion is put together and disseminated as a done deal. It does no good, however, to allow pollsters' self-serving claims about their already powerful dominion to further reduce the complex life of civil society to the outcome of a framed questionnaire. How people respond to a slate of surgically prepped questions tells us virtually nothing about the opinions they might find they held in common if the conditions of a properly radical democracy permitted them to do so.

Their wicked humor aside, Komar and Melamid are nonetheless acute in making statistics the aesthetic medium of an intervention into "the national question." Statistics are a crucial technology of power in modern states everywhere (the word "statistics" derives from the German for "state," and the origins of this "science" are inseparable from the rise of nation-states), but the fetishism of numbers has above all played a crucial role in the development of U.S. society. Under the system of representative democracy mandated by the Constitution, census taking became an essential part of government, and census information is the basis for political uses of population demographics. Whether in government, industry, or civil society, the rule of numbers has generated a social logic of quantitative rationality that has come to touch every aspect of our daily lives. Figures that set the norms in the national inventory of facts, and therefore also in the diagnosis of deviancy, include the statistics of risk that underpin the insurance industry and the corporate-health state; the numbers games deployed in the mass-psychology calculations of the advertising industry; the Taylorization of labor processes; the standardization of weights and measures; market research and the concept of the average man, woman, and family; cost-benefit accounting; the statistical quality

Figure 1 Komar and Melamid, *America's Most Wanted*, 1994. Oil and acrylic on canvas (dishwasher size). Courtesy of Komar and Melamid.

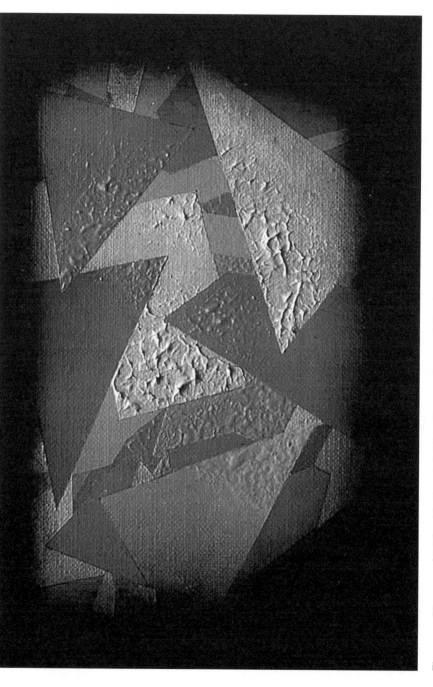

Figure 2   Komar and Melamid, *America's Most Unwanted*, 1994. Oil and canvas (paperback book size). Courtesy of Komar and Melamid.

Figure 3   Komar and Melamid, *China's Most Wanted*, 1996. Oil on canvas, 230 × 380 cm. Courtesy of Komar and Melamid.

Figure 4   Komar and Melamid, *China's Most Unwanted*, 1996. Mixed media on wood. Courtesy of Komar and Melamid.

Figure 5   Komar and Melamid, *Russia's Most Wanted*, 1994. Acrylic on canvas, 40 × 50 cm (TV size). Courtesy of Komar and Melamid.

Figure 6   Komar and Melamid, *Russia's Most Unwanted*, 1994. Oil on canvas, 134 × 60 cm (refrigerator door size). Courtesy of Komar and Melamid.

Figure 7 Komar and Melamid, *Kenya's Most Wanted*, 1996. Oil on canvas, 40.5 × 66 cm. Courtesy of Komar and Melamid.

Figure 8   Komar and Melamid, *Kenya's Most Unwanted*, 1996. Mixed media on wood, 14 × 22 cm. Courtesy of Komar and Melamid.

Figure 9   Komar and Melamid, *Holland's Most Wanted*, 1997. Mixed media on canvas, 26.95 × 34.3 cm. Courtesy of Komar and Melamid.

Figure 10 Komar and Melamid, *Holland's Most Unwanted*, 1997. Acrylic on canvas, 205.8 × 330.75 cm. Courtesy of Komar and Melamid.

control that defines minimum standards at minimum cost as the production principle of U.S. manufacturing; mental testing in educational and eugenic selection; TV ratings, baseball stats, and the supreme authority of the Gross National Product—virtually everything except, until Komar and Melamid, the making of art.[1] Though the sources of many of these revolutions in social and cultural behavior lie elsewhere, they are all historically related to a process of national self-definition that has come to be seen as distinctively American.

Many modern polling practices are an offshoot of Cold War computer war games developed to simulate battle scenarios in accordance with shifting variables. Just as advertising had been touted as a consumer society's bulwark against communist and fascist perversions of mass psychology, so the market probability research that emerged from anticommunist war gaming came to be seen as a way of keeping the free world one future ahead of the evil empire. The depth attitudinal polling that has led to today's virtually daily tracking of neighborhood psychographics is the very essence of Cold War democracy. News management, corporate symbolism, spin surgery, deep agenda setting—these are the PR tools that helped preserve our sacred liberties in the struggle against totalitarianism.[2]

If you want to take your ideas to the general (i.e., phantom) public, as Komar and Melamid have attempted to do with their project, then polling, as they say, is the way to go. In fact, the concept of the "general public" is inseparable from the demographics machine. As a result, the "general public" in the United States does not include a lot of people—all of the Left (and increasingly, many liberals), most of the intelligentsia, the underclass, gays and lesbians, prisoners, artists, immigrants, youth, all nonwhites, and, on the Right, Christian fundamentalists and white race supremacists. All in all, this adds up to the vast majority of the North American population of citizens and resident aliens over the age of thirteen, and constitutes, in their likely interpretation of public citizenship, the most active and the most inactive constituents of the state—in other words, the strongest and the weakest publics.

When addressing portions of the most active public, Komar and Melamid's project takes on a different light. In an interview for the left-liberal audience of the *Nation* magazine, Melamid presents "The People's Choice" as an inquiry into the means by which artists might reestablish communication with popular audiences. The connotations of his distaste for artworld elitism lie a little closer to home with readers of a magazine that can still honor elite value judgments in its culture pages, a legacy, in part, of the days when the *Nation* boasted anti-Stalinist culture pages and pro-Stalinist politics pages, and a strange epiphenomenon of the magazine today, which boasts writers with political views ranging from those who maintain that the Brezhnev era was the golden age of the Soviet proletariat to those who have long since rejected the viability of every one of the tenets of socialism. On the other hand, these are also readers who are familiar with some of the history of the quest for a people's art and who are cognizant, if not wholly skeptical, of the excesses committed in the name of both artistic freedom and the artist-in-the-service-of-ideology. Komar and Melamid's coy willingness to be seen as professionals commissioned by the people to execute their taste is a calculated commentary on the contradictions of this political art tradition.

Other than the pleasure derived from their horseplay, what are the consequences of Komar and Melamid's Swiftian modest proposal that art can be made Hollywood-style from the decision-making processes of focus groups and exit polls? The artists themselves claim an ancient lineage for the concept of artmaking by numbers:

> In a way it was a traditional idea, because a faith in numbers is fundamental to people, starting with Plato's idea of a world which is based on numbers. In ancient Greece, when sculptors wanted to create an ideal human body they measured the most beautiful men and women and then made an average measurement, and that's how they described the ideal of beauty and how the most beautiful sculpture was created. In a way, this is the same thing; in principle, it's nothing new. It's interesting: we believe in numbers, and numbers never lie. Numbers are innocent. It's absolutely true data. It doesn't say anything about personalities, but it says something more about ideals, and about how this world functions. That's really the truth, as much as we can get to the truth. Truth is a number.[3]

Pour épater les bourgeois today, Komar and Melamid approach aesthetic value as a matter of Western-style scientific truth rather than cultural taste. So perhaps the project's sharpest contradictions arise from a moment in which the bankruptcy of the avant-garde idea has been all but officially recognized, yet when vanguardism is reborn precisely in a knowing rejection of the privileges of the historical avant-garde. If polls tell the truth, or what passes for official truth in late capitalism, then polling is a more appropriate taste maker than the avant-garde artist—even if the result is not some progressive, proletkult chunk of the future but a schmaltzy return of art history's repressed. America's *Most Wanted*, a nineteenth-century-ish narrative landscape, carries much the same political meaning for progressive art today as did the picturesque Regionalism of '30s American Scene painters like Thomas Hart Benton, Grant Wood, and John Steuart Curry, all of them reviled as reactionaries by the people's artists of the day who were active in the Popular Front artist congresses against fascism.

Things were a little different in Moscow, which I visited in the fall of 1994 shortly after the Russian version of "The People's Choice" was exhibited there. In the Russian capital, the project helped reanimate the powerful legacy of the '70s conceptualist circle to which Komar and Melamid belonged before they emigrated to the United States. Ilya Kabakov's dusty, garretlike studio, informally bequeathed to the Moscow avant-garde, still hosted remnants of this circle. The space's allegorical centerpiece was an uneven pool table with pockets so tight that it was virtually impossible to pot a ball. The floors below were being renovated into million-dollar apartments for the "New Russians," those buccaneer beneficiaries of Boris Yeltsin's sacking of the state treasury. Now that Russia finally has a bourgeoisie for the avant-garde to shock, in-your-face body-based performance art was flourishing. In the meantime everyone, the artworld included, was learning the crude Western arts of individualism, from customized self-fashioning to blatant careerism. The stores, filled with expensive European goods, evince the current leaders' wisdom: let them eat cake. In this milieu, intellectual appeals to the people's will were pretty thin on the ground, barely passing muster as sick comedy the way they used to in Soviet times.

The dark wit of Russian conceptualism in its heyday was directed at the institutional symbolism of the state, just as its Western counterpart critiqued the institutions of the gallery and the art market. The relevant institutions today are media-oriented. Indeed, Komar and Melamid's Moscow show received media attention unprecedented for artists there, beginning when they brandished the results of "The People's Choice" to TV cameras on their arrival at the airport. This was seen as a parody of Alexander Solzhenitsyn's return to Moscow as Rip van Tolstoy, waving his notebook of conversations with people he had met on his long train journey and challenging the government to bend to the popular will contained therein. A press conference followed in Pushkin Square, Moscow's Fleet Street. Subsequently, national TV quizzed public personalities on their reactions to Komar and Melamid's *Most Wanted* painting. A regional commander in the army gave it the thumbs up. A nationalist leader said nyet.

In a time of anxiety in Russia over the national question, art critics were defensive, discerning more than a soupçon of antinational sentiment in Komar and Melamid's expatriate approach to the current crisis of taste. For the intelligentsia, "The People's Choice" evoked, among other things, the pledges of their nineteenth-century forebears to kneel before the wisdom of the *narod*, the people. This was bad enough; to wheel in capitalism's heavy statistical artillery on top of it was to rub their faces in a frightening future. Others saw a different nationalist specter in attendance: with the triumph over Socialist Realism and its iconography of workers and peasants still fresh in the cultural memory, the Russian *Most Wanted* suggested that a Bonapartist restoration of prerevolutionary *meshchanstvo* or kitsch taste may be a new force to contend with. In the meantime, in Moscow street locations where popular painting is habitually sold (in Izmaylovsky Park, outside the Central Artists House, and on the approach to the VDNKh), all the modern art styles except Socialist Realism could be found, but landscapes like *Most Wanted* were still in the majority. The joke, as always, was on "the people"—the people who buy these paintings.

Outside its local impact in the United States and Russia, the most flagrant outrage of "The People's Choice" lies in its resurrection of ideas about the universality of art. As Komar and Melamid conducted polls in each country, they came up with similar results and similar paintings. They are beginning to believe "experts" who say that there may be a genetic component to all this. In an age of multiculturalism and antiuniversalism, nothing could be more heretical.

Aside from the calculated effrontery, what emerges from this project are some equally shady theses about the state of citizenship today, in a climate where the very weakest forms of democracy are trumpeted as the heady fulfillment of the liberal political tradition. Polling is the strong arm of a feeble faith in citizens' capacity to have a competent opinion. A discussion of taste of the sort generated by "The People's Choice" may seem to have a limited bearing upon the future of citizenship, but it is by no means a foolish place to begin. Taste, in a consumer society, is a major instrument of enfranchisement and exclusion. Many people feel contests over cultural authority and power far more directly and intimately than they do contests over politics. How is this reflected in the artworld's organization of taste?

At some point in the early 1970s, it seemed that every British working-class home I knew boasted a reproduction of a particular oil painting on its living room walls. It was a head-and-shoulders portrait of an "exotic," olive-skinned Spanish woman, leaning coyly against a tree in a forest. Her look was inviting but not salacious, and if the coquette pose suggested the incursion of the pinup into domestic space, it is difficult to imagine that the woman of the house had not vouchsafed the bold presence of such a picture as part of the furniture. After all, this was in the period when sexual mores were being most dramatically expanded. It was also at the onset of the mass summer migrations of British working people to Spain on affordable vacations, and so perhaps some daily reminder of sensuous living in a foreign land would have been a welcome addition to the domestic environment of a northern country.

Whatever the reasons for its acceptance, the picture was a very popular item and thus a commonly shared object of class taste, at home in certain living rooms and not in others more socially upscale (in my own home, the place reserved for such pictures was occupied instead by the products of my father's own tapestry-sewing-by-numbers passion for reproducing Old Masters). The distinction accrued from purchasing and hanging this picture depended on possessing exactly what others—your friends, neighbors, or relatives—had on their walls. Exhibiting art, in this context, had very little to do with showing an *original* expression of taste. Quite the opposite.

For those, on the other hand, who seek out pictures that might be described as one-of-a-kind, hardly a week goes by in any large town without some crowded art fair spilling over the sidewalks and the parking lots. *These* are the places where the broad public shops for art, where people feel not only that their tastes are catered to but also that the art on offer includes them in some way. Every so often, perhaps in an obligatory tourist visit, they may go to the vast templed spaces of our public museums, where the codes of sanctimonious behavior are designed to encourage religious appreciation. They go to art church as if to the confessional box, seeking out interiority under the pressure of some class-induced guilt. For the most part, any further venture into the "artworld," as it is constituted by the gallery system, seems designed specifically to be alienating.

With few exceptions, art critics have shown about as much interest in the popular art circuit as nuclear physicists have. In other arts (literature, music), elite and popular forms to some extent share common institutional channels (distribution, reviewing, display, modes of consumption). In the visual arts, temporary aberrations aside, an ocean of indifference separates both the official and alternative artworlds from the street fair. There is no fine-arts equivalent of the detective novel, the TV sitcom, the twelve-bar blues, or the horror film, no fully evolved popular genres, unless you count comic books (claimed as much by literature as by the visual arts), or site-specific forms like graffiti, the street mural, or versions of community arts. Critics trying to cross the divide tend to end up playing the smirking game of kitsch-worship—reciting the rosary of the black-velvet Elvis, joining the sectarian order of Jeff Koons.

Like the *Star Trek* transporter, post-Pop art continues to beam up fragments of commercial culture, and every so often an event like Jim Shaw's famous *Thrift Store Show*—an exhibition of cheap found paintings— transplants a heavily edited slice of life from the discard pile of domestic art furniture. In addition, there is a growing curatorial interest in the category of "outsider art" produced by nonprofessionals in their homes, garages, and backyards. But few critics seem seriously interested in the role art plays in people's daily environments. For attention to the complex decoration of a teenage girl's bedroom—a curatorial task no less laborious than pulling together a gallery show and often, arguably, a more ingenious expression of taste—one turns to cultural studies scholars. How

people customize their own daily appearance and living environments—
these are the real public arts. But they have nothing much to do with
official conceptions of academic art, which, despite more or less well
intentioned goals of broad public access that date to the birth of the nineteenth-century museum, often still feel like an imposition of taste upon
the populace.[4]

The brouhaha in the United States over public funding of the arts that
began in the late 1980s might have provided an occasion to rethink this
elitist configuration. Never mind that this ruckus was the result of media
grandstanding by politicians in an age of rapidly hardening moral arteries,
or that its sensation-seeking targets were radical art practitioners like
Holly Hughes, Karen Finlay, Robert Mapplethorpe, Tim Miller, and
Andres Serrano. The principle, however hackneyed, of artists' public
accountability might have emerged as important enough to have generated some artworld self-scrutiny. In accord with the uneven economic
composition of artworld institutions, the reaction was predictably mixed.
Many artists' communities tended to close ranks, retreating behind the
veil of artistic freedom. The big artworld institutions appealed cynically to
evidence of the decline of public culture in order to reaffirm their own
privileges. And while the response from the vestigial alternative art
spaces—devoted, as ever, to expanding the range of what passes as acceptable public art—was gutsy and admirable, the overall outcome has been
to strengthen the feudal structure of the gallery system and the conservative tendencies of the museums.

The Great Depression saw an alleged golden age of publicly funded art
in the United States under various federal arts projects such as the Work
Projects Administration (WPA). In the ensuing dialogue, however naive,
between professional artists and the public, the artists who took to the
regional roads, armed with the good faith of documentary and agitprop,
did so in the belief that they were in a position to compete with William
Randolph Hearst in the battle for the nation's cultural soul. Today, as government is withdrawing from the province of arts funding, there is no
contest at all. Only the deluded believe that art can compete with advertising and commercial culture in the realm of public opinion, not to mention the popular ideology of nationalism. In the fifty years since the
demise of the WPA, the cultural marketplace has swept the field, monop-

olizing virtually all the important social energies and cultural resources that the vast majority of people use in their daily lives. The circulation and reception of cultural commodities, whether formal or informal, is really the only powerful aesthetic catalyst in advanced capitalist societies. You don't have to be an advocate of free marketeering to recognize this manifest fact. By contrast, the official arts have stuck close to their entrenched hierarchies of exclusion, jealously guarding their access to institutional protection and public subsidy. Many have donned the cloak of immunity provided by the safe haven of artistic freedom. The world of alternative art spaces subsists on the margins, contracting and expanding in response to a mutating social climate: since the early 1980s, it has been virtually squeezed out of the picture.

Given this legacy and the recent siege-like response to near extinction of state subsidies, what kind of debate about the accountability of artists is possible? One of the most unlikely responses came from Komar and Melamid, reared in a Soviet political culture where "artistic freedom" had a very different meaning, and where the idea of people's art became infused with a folie de grandeur unmatched since the days of courtly patronage. Their approach to this impasse was both satirical and sanguine. "The People's Choice" was clearly an onslaught on the stronghold of aesthetic "taste," once a heavily fortified milieu of the fine arts. At the same time, they seem serious about learning from people's opinions and prejudices: sitting in on focus groups and conducting polls have been part of what could be called their reeducation. Their claim that "the peoples choice" was a genuine collaboration—or co-authorship—with the people demanded serious attention.[5] Beyond their ever present spirit of mischief, they seem committed to finding channels of communication for artists beyond the gallery, the museum, the public art "site," and MTV. The public's interest in this artistic reeducation is another question altogether. One result of the NEA flap on Capitol Hill is a given wisdom that parodies the rallying cry of the American Revolution: no representation, no taxation. But the true vox populi on this matter as on others is likely to remain as elusive as ever, an ectoplasmic spirit of the night to conjure up whenever the need arises.

Komar and Melamid say they "were brought up with the idea that art belongs to the people," and they still "believe that the people's art is better than aristocratic art, whatever it is."[6] One could hardly say that such sentiments are alien to American culture, imbued with a fundamental antipathy to Old World airs and graces. On the political stage, however, we have perfected the arts of faux populism, where ventriloquists step to the microphones and deliver the most recent script, based on what the people do *not* want: taxation, welfare clients, ungodliness, central government, adult morality, social reciprocity. Public life is supposed to be more substantial than this charade, and yet everyone says that it is getting more and more difficult to tell the difference. But there's no point in mourning the good old days; we have to start, as Brecht said, from the bad new ones. Having lived beneath the dogma of History, Komar and Melamid know this all too well. In "The People's Choice" they issued a cunning invitation posed in the form of a direct challenge—if not this, then what? If this is not a satisfactory way for artists to establish communication with public communities, then what is? If this is not sincere enough, then what is? If this is not good public or populist art, then what is? If this is not how artists ought to be responding to our demographically driven consumer culture, then what is? If this is not beauty, then what is? If this is not the way art should be talked about in the popular media, then what is? If this is not un-American enough for you, then what is? If not this, then what?

EIGHT

The Lonely Hour of Scarcity

Recent reports in the press have brought to light a new kind of urban theft—the looting of newspapers from curbside recycling routes. Scavengers are pilfering up to a third of all collections in some cities and making a serious dent in municipal revenue by trading directly to recycling processors at prices that have skyrocketed in the last two years. Environmentalists have some reason to rejoice. (No one should shed a tear for haulage companies that have fiercely exploited recycling as a new "racket.") Unlike the relatively healthy market for plastics and aluminum, paper— the true staple of the landfill monster—has taken a long time to rise to a level of profitability, but is now trading at well over $150 a ton. It remains to be seen whether a black market in recyclable trash will come to flourish, and what effect it will have on the precarious moral attachment of the public to recycling. For the time being, we might reflect on the meaning of garbage theft in the United States in the age of resource scarcity.

Scavenging was widespread in Europe and North America until the early twentieth century, and the rag trade in particular serviced the paper industry before corporate access to the Northwest's forests established a timber base. Rampant during the Depression, it became a public spectacle again in the 1980s, when government policies created a vast urban class of homeless, many of whom became reluctant pioneers in the art of street-smart recycling at the same time (and largely because of the fact) that gentrification was producing yuppie "pioneers" on the real estate "frontier." Pop historians, nostalgic for cyclical theories about the decline and fall of civilizations, may see the new garbage scavenging as a symptom of the return of premodern scarcity. To the contrary, it is a highly developed form of market behavior, stimulated, like most boomlets, by a combination of state intervention, a significant sea change in middle-class habits, and durable speculation, based on reliable historical evidence, that the value of categories of waste is never fixed and that the dormant ones will eventually sustain a market, perhaps even a bonanza. (Gasoline, considered a useless waste product in the mid-nineteenth-century age of kerosene, is the most spectacular example of the latter.) These are market conditions quite different (in degree though not in kind) from the ones that prevail in many Third World countries, where high levels of resource utilization provide ingenious and efficient examples of salvaging waste, and where human life is often considered less valuable than the price paid for secondary use of waste. They are also a far cry from the high points of waste retrieval in the West—the patriotic scrap-collecting economies of wartime and the postwar reconstruction of devastated industrial countries like Germany and Japan—or the extraordinary periods of U.S. resource rationing like the rubber crisis of 1942 or the oil crisis of 1974.

Ever since the benchmark incident of the *Mobro 4000*, the itinerant garbage barge from Islip, it has been customary to work up stories about garbage into allegorical commentary on the apocalyptic state of American civilization. In the case of garbage piracy, the possibilities are rich indeed. After all, here is a scenario in which informal profiteering undermines a system whereby citizens actually volunteer to clean up corporate waste and enrich the state into the bargain. Individual guilt fuels the system, fed in turn by the well-known statistics of collective culpability. I hesitate to cite the numbers once again. With the United States' 5 percent share of the world's population still claiming up to 25 percent of the world's resources and generating almost 20 percent of the world's waste, only 1 percent of raw materials in use are being retrieved by resource recovery. Some of this guilt derives from acute Protestant shame over the spectacle of waste, but it is just as much a Protestant story about the spectacle of accumulation. New World stories about abundance, fecundity, and surplus, whether in nature or in technological productivity, have always elicited orgies of waste and destruction of wildlife and resources. Each new wave of abundance leaves its spent fuel in the trash can of history: the Atomic and Nuclear Age has bequeathed a garbage legacy for eternity, while the Age of Information has already accumulated mountains of cybernetic refuse, including a few reject languages (COBOL, RPG II, ALGOL, PROLOG), defunct operating systems

(CP/M), and extinct platforms (PT/DOS, SWTPC, MITS Altair) from Univac to PS/2.

Of course, no nation-state has a monopoly on the extravagant creation of waste, but no other state has fostered a polity in which the right to unlimited individual accumulation was granted so freely and fundamentally as a rational incentive to self-realization. This is an exceptional right in human history. It can be exercised in liberal societies only if the majority wills what C. B. MacPherson called a "net transfer of power" to the class of wealth as recompense for the opportunity to join this class.[1] More than in any other nation, white Americans succeeded in turning this contractual principle into common sense via the mythologies of exceptionalism, social mobility, self-help, racial superiority, and national destiny. It is also the case that the right to individual accumulation has been accepted only in modern societies where scarcity is perceived as a universal condition to be overcome in pursuit of abundance rather than simply tolerated as a temporary scourge.

Twentieth-century historians, from the ingenuous Simon Patten (*The New Basis for Civilization*) to the celebratory David Potter (*The People of Plenty*) to the skeptical Jackson Lears (*Fables of Abundance*), have exhaustively shown that the claim of abundance and cornucopia in nature and in market consumption has suffused the national characterology to a degree unmatched anywhere else. The concept of abundance still dominates modern American historiography, but its precondition—the creation of scarcity—is the more revealing story, and the one that I wish to follow here.

The assumption of scarcity is not simply an invention of modern affluent societies; it is the necessary premise for all social institutions and value systems that promote competitive individualism. That is why the U.S. case history of uneven development is so sustained and so obscured at one and the same time. From the perspective of MacPherson's net transfer of power, it could be said that the oligarchic economic system has been more instrumental in creating and organizing scarcity than in creating wealth. In periods like the present, when overdeveloped elites are experiencing weak, scattershot resistance to a coherent program of pro-scarcity politics, the evidence of organized scarcity is more apparent than usual. Punitive measures against poor, minority, and marginalized populations are sweeping away the humanitarian basis of the postwar liberal state. Now that moral competition with the Cold War socialist bloc has ceased, there is less need for the extensive PR campaigns advertising the superior humane profile of liberal capitalism. In the last decade of the Cold War, the sharp upward redistribution of wealth in the United States meant that these campaigns dwelled more on the comparative advantage in human rights than on levels of middle-class material achievement, as had been previously showcased, for example, in the "kitchen debate" between Nixon and Khrushchev in 1959. And yet the primary audience for these earlier campaigns was not the socialist bloc, nor its client Third World states, but the American electorate and its cognates in states that were economically allied or dependent. While the need for domestic consent has not evaporated, triumphalist morality has been tempered by a harsh round of austerity, introduced under the aegis of global competitiveness and deregulation. Accordingly, the famous American middle class, so solidly referential at its economic peak thirty years ago, has not exactly melted into air, but has nonetheless been struggling to keep itself out of the trash can of history.

More than any other social group, it was this notoriously wasteful consumer class that came to be identified with concerns about a global ecological crisis in the 1970s. Consequently, awareness about the "earth's natural limits" brought a new paradigm of scarcity into the world: a concept of scarcity that had hitherto not existed. This could be characterized as "this-time-we-really-mean-it" scarcity, and might be distinguished from the perennial social manufacture of scarcity through which elites have always sought to monopolize resources, control markets, and suppress the demographic majority. In short order, analysts from those traditions that had failed to account for the contradictions between economic development and natural sustainability—individuals as diverse as Marxists, technocrats, and neoclassical economists, among others—all acknowledged, albeit with different purposes, the existence of material limits in the biosphere.

For more than two decades now, public consciousness has sustained complex assumptions about both kinds of scarcity. In that same period, however, neoliberalism's austerity regime has ushered in what can only be described as a pro-scarcity climate, distinguished, economically, by deep concessions and cutbacks, and politically, by the rollback of "excessive" rights. As a result, the new concerns about natural scarcity have been paralleled, every step of the way, by a cruel imposition of socially generated scarcity. More often than not, then, the two kinds of scarcity have been confused, either deliberately, as a means of reinforcing austerity measures against the poor, or else inadvertently, through a lack of information and education about how natural resources are produced and distributed.

As someone who has criticized the revival of biologism and the concomitant "naturalization of the social" in recent years, I am well aware of how easily an argument against the pro-scarcity order is often misconstrued as an argument that the real ecological crisis somehow does not exist. Indeed, this is a familiar response wherever arguments influenced by social reasoning and pledged against biological determinism are confronted by appeals to "commonsense" materialism of the following sort: yes, we know that everything, including the experience of scarcity, is socially mediated, but nonetheless, there does exist a real world and it is hurting badly because of the onset of absolute scarcity in the form of eco-collapse. Indeed, the hothouse of ecological debate has presented the strongest version of this challenge to social critique because it includes the potential indictment that the critics, no less than the corporate elites, may be fiddling while Rome burns. If the lonely hour of scarcity's last instance ever does come around, then surely it will be here, where nature can no longer sustain life as a result of soil erosion, deforestation, desertification, biodiversity loss, marine degradation, ozone depletion, and advanced freshwater and airborne pollution.

I am entirely sympathetic to the political point being made here, but it helps no one to present it this way. At the very least, we have to figure out where one type of scarcity is related to the other and where it is not. Then we have to forge two different responses, in most respects related to one another, in some respects quite distinct. What we will find is that resource shortages and ecological degradation are *primarily* a result of the uneven social measures that manufacture scarcity all over the world for the economic and political gain of powerful interests. The systematic inequalities that block people's access to income, health, education, and democratic rights are *primarily* responsible for the geographical and sociological profile of the ecological crisis. In those instances where ecological scarcity appears to harbor no direct connection with socially generated scarcity, its character is defined by economic forces that are nonetheless fundamentally linked to the social and cultural tendencies that fuel pro-scarcity politics. Try as we might, there is no easy separation of the two kinds of scarcity.

Let us briefly review some of the history of this confusion about scarcity in the United States itself, in order to prevent us, as Santayana said, from reliving it. There is a tendency to refer to "the return of scarcity" in industrial societies in recent times, which invariably leads to speculation about a corresponding need to return to the state of liberal civil society before the emergence, in a time of relative abundance, of the welfare state, collective bargaining in the workplace, and civil rights.[2] The naked political agenda of this argument should be seen for what it is and opposed wherever it surfaces. Now that ecological damage is seen to have a properly global dimension, concerns about physical scarcity have returned to haunt the North. But this should not be confused with the use of such concerns to reinforce the domestic regime of austerity, exercised through the punitive regulation of target populations.

Recent statistics, for example, show poverty in the United States at much the same undercounted levels as in the early 1960s, when Michael Harrington's "discovery" of poverty in *The Other America* scandalized those who had swallowed the PR euphoria about "the best fed people in the world." Despite all the poisonous talk about welfare chiselers, the social composition of the poor is about the same as it was thirty years ago—while the majority are white working poor, a minority are periodically on (and off) the welfare rolls, and African Americans and Latinos are disproportionately poor. At that time, the state was condemned for excluding the poor from its programs; after all, the Cold War doctrine of the affluent consumer commonwealth had to put on an inclusive, democratic face. Today spiteful caricatures of client dependency are used to blame the state for creating poverty through its poor relief programs. Then as now, the politics of race played its role, first in the form of benevolence offered in exchange for compliance with white America's policies of assimilation and integration, and today in the form of race scapegoating aimed at uniting whites of different classes.

Similar shifts in social currency can be found today in the first major revival of anti-immigrant politics since the early 1920s. The 1920 census had revealed, for the first time in the United States, a majority urban population, many of whom were Southern and Eastern European immigrants with radical politics. The resulting crackdown against the influx of social-ist-minded labor was fomented by a fierce crusade against the "pollution" of the American Anglo-Saxon (and, by this time, Celtic, since it had finally been decided that the Irish were white) race, backed up by the sci-entific racism of leading eugenicists. The divisive use of race in today's assault on immigration reveals a political scenario in which it is right-wing, and not left-wing, radicalism that plays the pivotal role. Here, the prize is presented as the political loyalty of the white working poor, harshly stripped of 20 percent of their wages in the last two decades, and in a disposition to be swung to the hard right by racist appeals to immi-grant (and "preferred" domestic minority) usurpation of their jobs. In this scenario, a traditionally pollutant fraction, often referred to by the richly derogatory term of "white trash," is being salvaged from the realm of social rejection. Presumably, co-optation will prevent that fraction from joining a multiracial bloc of underclass discontent with insurgent poten-tial. Race, as always, is employed to divide those with common economic interests. The recent salvage job has been accompanied by a top-down glamorization of "white trash" culture, currently enjoying newfound pres-tige on the high-fashion runway, in advertising, and in the lavish glare of Hollywood attention.

For a related nineteenth-century example, one could look at the period of the labor movement studied by David Roediger in *Wages of Whiteness*, when white workers, infused with the patriotic, republican ideology of independence, were nonetheless reluctant to accept the self-image of industrial "wage slaves" (a favored term among labor organizing) primar-ily because of its proximity to the degraded status of unfree black labor. Uses of this and related terms by labor agitators, whether abolitionist or not, were highly volatile. In the pre–Civil War period, "white slavery" had pro-slavery connotations, "wage slavery" included a condemnation of slavery itself, while "slavery of wages" was a critique of capitalist disci-pline. Ultimately, the demeaning association of the slavery appellation for white workers severely weakened the free labor coalition that emerged after the war, fracturing its unity with racial divisions that have carried down to this day.[3]

Roediger's case history is instructive because it involves many of the classic ingredients of the U.S. recipe for uneven development: the debility of national working-class organization, the ready exploitation of racial divisions, the unstable labor market of an immigrant economy, the ideological appeals to free will, social mobility, and voluntarism. To complete this mix, one might add the weak mechanism of the federalist state, governed for so long by a coalition of southern Democrats, northern Republicans, and business lobbies, and the expansionist geography of new frontiers and markets, guaranteed most recently by the world trade agreements. The resulting character of this state formation leans toward the creation of scarcity to stimulate and protect markets and a chronic inability to put public interests above those of big business. In regard to poverty levels, Frances Fox Piven and Richard Cloward's classic study, *Regulating the Poor*, showed that poor relief programs have historically been used to regulate marginal labor and maintain social order. Far from a pattern of progressive liberalization, there is a periodic expanding and contracting in response to the demands that arise from political protest, whether in the form of militant grassroots organizing or civil disorder. In their analysis, the state initiated the direct relief of the Great Depression and the antipoverty programs of the Great Society in order to absorb only enough of the unemployed and placate enough of the discontented to restore order, at which point the programs appear to contract and are habitually directed, as in the case of urban renewal, *against* their clients. In the case of the 1960s, Cloward and Piven show how the mechanism of scarcity regulation and social containment broke down, and relief programs set in motion a welfare revolution in which participants gained direct access to local political empowerment. This occurred because of the unintended success of the programs in circumventing state and local managers and empowering neighborhood groups and storefront organizations in their opposition to the customary administering authorities.[4] The containment of this explosive expansion in the base of political participation was ensured only by the traumatic policies and austerity measures enacted as a result of the mid-1970s fiscal crisis at both the municipal and federal levels. As a result of that crisis, social programs were hit by round after round of cuts, the postwar social contract with labor was progressively eroded, the tax burden was shifted downward so that wealth could be created at the top, the poor, working and nonworking, were once again divided by racist persuasion in their competition for resources diminished by "planned shrinkage," and economic restructuring and disinvestment ushered in the low-wage revolution associated with the end of middle-class abundance. Business and government elites insist that austerity policies are simply a commonsense response to a *contraction* of the economy, unable any longer to support an overextended liberal state, or that they are part of an adjustment necessary for the economy to remain globally competitive. The massive upward redistribution of wealth and resources, the export of capital and jobs, and the bull market on Wall Street all tell quite a different story—that social scarcity is planned, organized, and legislated for the pursuit of investors' profit, and is not the result of some natural shortage or economic dearth. With the revival of concepts of self-help, local voluntarism, or market providence that eschew collective responsibility altogether, poverty is no longer a scandal, but once more a morally charged state of being, perceived as a sign of laziness and bad character; the poor, as a Rockefeller once put it, are people who simply don't have enough faith in capitalism.

The chief physical evidence of scarcity in human society is hunger, and it is to food production and distribution that we might look for confirmation of popular suspicions about planned scarcity. For this is the only accurate way of describing agricultural policy for most of this century, in which food production has been limited and regulated to guarantee profitable market prices. In the midst of the Depression, productive fields were still being plowed under, food surpluses were being bought and destroyed, and federal payments were being made for nonuse of land so that the farm lobby's precious markets would be appeased. Federal food aid was being fiercely resisted at a time when local charitable organizations—the by now traditional American mode of poor relief—had virtually exhausted their meager resources, and when the breadlines, trash picking, and starvation diets were at their height. Early republicanism's revolutionary codes of self-determination and self-reliance had come to be redefined by late nineteenth-century laissez-faire morality in the form of self-help and voluntary improvement. State subsidies for business and its infrastructural needs were a normative exception to the rule of self-help, while the state's abstinence from poor relief was the moral exemplification of the rule itself. Thus, apocryphal rumors about money being appropriated to feed starving cattle but not starving people were widespread, yet

Roosevelt breached the harsh Hoover taboo on federal intervention only after the food industry's crusade to maintain its markets resulted in the highly publicized slaughter of six million pigs. Even in the subsequent period of direct relief, it was the surplus rather than the basic foods that were touted by the Agriculture Department through its food stamp program, a principle that continues to this day through the programs that distribute vast federal purchases of surplus, usually highly processed, food.[5] The preferred industry ideal was a persuasive campaign to periodically change people's idea of a desirable diet in order to match market cycles of shortage and surplus. The new managerial science of nutrition was a crucial accomplice in this process, and the food lobbyists found that its cadres could easily be bought.

Let us not forget that the age of the Depression breadlines was also the age of crash diets for the well-off. Thinness and purgation were very much the rage in the sanitoriums, bolstered by decades of Victorian moralizing about overeaters' lack of self-control and the shameful effects of overindulgence on the American middle-class character. So while the poor had no choice but to eat less, the wealthy were eating less out of choice; the evidence of their social distinction was their moral abstinence from the abundance otherwise readily available to them (an equation revived in the 1980s decade of greed, when, in the immortal words of Babe Paley, you could never be too rich or too thin). Seasoned and spiced up by esoteric body philosophies, the wave of reducing diets was increasingly governed by science as the high-end quackery of the health gurus ceded to the technocratic sobriety of the academic expert. In his fine social history of eating, *Paradox of Plenty*, Harvey Levenstein shows that the authority of nutrition research, first put to the test in holistic, gourmet class circles, was quickly harnessed by the industry's powerful food associations, who funded nutritionists as legitimate academic scientists, all the better to enlist them as shills for the industry at the right price.[6] Thus was born the tawdry tradition of scientists fronting for the poison merchants in the food, alcohol, and tobacco industries. Nutrition science was used, wherever possible, to legitimate the massively profitable techniques favored by the giant processors, refiners, and canners. Its practitioners could be heard singing the praises of white bread and other bleached packaged products, and then celebrating the advent of vitamin-enriched foods, introduced to offset the vitamin pill market that had sprung up to compensate for nutrient-poor processed goods. Consequently, white bread became a wartime symbol of American affluence. David Potter could celebrate this fact without a trace of irony in *People of Plenty*: "Very few Americans, picking and choosing among the piles of white bread in a supermarket, have ever appreciated the social standing of white bread elsewhere in the world. To be able to afford white bread is a dream that awaits fulfillment for billions of the world's population."[7]

The explosive growth of the vitamin movement peaked in the wartime scare over thiamine deficiencies, when this "morale vitamin" was equated with the national defense and when thiamine deprivation was described as Hitler's secret weapon. With the onset of the flour millers' new "enriched" product, Levenstein notes another paradox of plenty: "that one could look well fed and actually be starving" through lack of essential nutrients. The federal announcement of the flour enrichment program was perceived as an attempt "to rescue some 45,000,000 Americans from hungerless vitamin famine." The period of the Great Depression had been marked initially by the wasting away of starving bodies. "It ended with the diffusion of completely different concepts of hunger and starvation: hunger that could not be felt, starvation that could not be seen."[8] Hidden hunger was a physicalist version of the psychic condition that Freudians have come to describe as "split subjectivity," in which two versions of the body and/or ego are actively engaged at one and the same time. Its implications for the unfolding of social identity in the postwar period were profound. Physical self-presentation would be perceived as distinct not just from the psychological "inner life" but also from the more quantitative, nutrition-conscious image of bodily health.

Institutional voices and scientific organizations sprang up to regulate and profit from this division between the two bodies. But the mobile nexus between diet, rates of consumption, health, and status was unevenly felt, as always. Obesity would become a sign of poverty (or the mark of a class that lived only in the present), while eating disorders generated by an induced mania for thinness became a widespread postmodern disease, afflicting millions of women for whom scarcity in any form was an alien condition. Nowhere was the paradox of plenty more conspicuous than in the North's aping of the visual iconography of the South's undernutrition. Most notoriously, Euro-American fashion advertising, ruled by an aesthetic that dictated pencil-thin body shapes, sought backdrops in the Third World that were populated with lean locals.

In the national health stakes, the nutrition experts and agencies like the FDA have walked a fine line between dietary reform and blatant industry protectionism. Progressive ideas about nutrition and food purity played an important role in this balancing act, fueling the fledgling consumer movement of Stuart Chase, Frederick Schlink, and Arthur Kallet in the 1930s and the revival of the anti–chemical additive campaign with Ralph Nader in the 1960s. The subsequent revolution in health food sparked by countercultural movements in the 1960s and 1970s appealed to environmentalist consciousness in pioneering a new kind of American diet—predominantly meatless—that took less of a toll on global food resources. But like the war on waste, the crusade for citizens to adopt a more ecologically sustainable diet has appealed primarily to American traditions of voluntary individualism. In the absence of significant government action on markets and conditions of production, the effect has been confined mostly to the gourmet and alternative consumer classes. The latters' economic capacity to respond has stimulated niche markets in sustainable consumerism, while the producers of scale have effortlessly incorporated the challenge of alternative diets in the form of "high-fiber," "low-cholesterol," "fat-free," and "enriched" product labeling.

When, after the end of World War II rationing, President Truman made an official call for U.S. voluntary conservation to ease worldwide hunger, popular response was limited (Hoover, the arch-opponent of Depression food relief, was appointed, appropriately, to head the Famine Emergency Committee). Levenstein attributes this mediocre response not just to the restoration of the national ideology of abundance but also to the still widespread popular suspicion of government accounts of shortages; folklore about official stockpiling, destruction, or shipping overseas of surplus food had been rife under the regime of rationing. Comparing the hoarding and cheating during American rationing with the achievements of national sacrifice and appeals for shared austerity during Britain's "finest hour," he suggests that the controls brought out the worst in Americans and the best in the British, who generally had "faith in their government."[9]

This comparison is a complex one, and certainly yields more conclusions than Levenstein provides. For one thing, the United States was discovering the virtues of military Keynesianism, the mainstay of its economy to this day. Since the voluntarism of the private sector is never enough to create and sustain markets and jobs, investors must always feed at the trough of public subsidies and tax incentives. The basic thesis of consumerism—expand demand by giving spending power to workers— had been proven shaky by the Depression years, and something more secure was needed. The troubled program of rationing reflected the traditional reluctance of federal authority to collude openly in any system of price controls, but it also underlined the unpopularity of attempts to organize scarcity officially on a mass basis. With its new "arsenal of democracy," the state could finally guarantee the constant demand requested by big business, in return for the granting of a limited welfare state. Organized consumption was more stable as a result.

Britain was in a quite different situation. With its home counties under direct siege, this imperial state with a strong tradition of paternalist rule, supported by a formidable, monarchist class structure, was able to command a vigorous response to the common call for austerity. But "national unity" with its myth of common sacrifice was an exceptional interlude between the acute conditions of British class conflict before the war and the sweeping challenge to class privilege launched by its postwar Labour government. Not surprisingly, the myth of "pulling through together" has become a favored conservative mechanism for creating consent for the austerity policies of the Thatcher-Major years. No such mythology has been available in the United States, where popular suspicion about maldistribution and corporate manipulation of markets has been persistent. Perhaps this suspicion was most egregious during the OPEC oil crisis, when allegations that storage tanks were full and that loaded tankers lay offshore in great numbers supported the belief (partially proven in congressional investigations) that oil and gas companies, with advance knowledge of the OPEC embargo, had contrived to create shortages.

Wartime Germany presents another case study altogether. Here was a national efficiency culture whose ingenuity in waste reclamation and resource utilization enabled its productive capacity to compete with the mighty Allied war machines while imposing relatively few restrictions on consumer production. Deprived of most of the resources enjoyed by the great industrial powers—oil, chrome, nickel, rubber, lead, copper—German industrial science (through the famous hydrogenation and gasification "processes" named after the likes of Haber, Linde-Frankl, Bergius, Pier-Farben, and Renn) succeeded in finding or synthesizing substitutes—primarily from air, coal, and water—for all war materials needed. Such was the efficiency of this effort that by the end of the war, plans were advanced for aircraft that would use no petroleum in production or operation. The invention of alternative fuels, nonferrous metals, and the harnessing of hydroelectricity, combined with an awesome voluntary retrieval program of waste collection and recycling, transformed wartime Germany (and its annexed *lebensraum*) into a model energy-efficient economy decades before the OPEC oil crisis forced industrialized nations to begin rethinking their energy dependence.[10] The legacy of waste avoidance has enabled Germany to initiate the world's most ambitious national solid waste policies.[11]

Are there lessons to be drawn from these three historical examples—the United States, Britain, and Germany—about the capacity of a population to respond to conditions of material scarcity? It appears, not surprisingly, that the strongest version of the national state enforces an austerity culture best, and that which appeals most to a language of voluntary individualism is least successful. Some ecologically minded commentators conclude that U.S. political culture cannot support broadly conceived limitations, least of all in the absence of a unifying cause like war, and that liberal societies in general cannot therefore preserve their generous concession to personal freedoms if they are to respond adequately to a world of shrinking resources. It does not help matters, they might say, when social anthropologists point out that every society has its own culturally bound way of defining scarcity and abundance, and that top-down austerity measures are often culturally insensitive and damaging. For example, when Margaret Mead and other anthropologists were recruited to the Committee for Food Habits as part of the wartime drive to improve dietary nutrition, their training in the "relativity" of values predisposed them against any overbearing intervention in cultural patterns or habits: Mead wrote that "the food patterns of the Southeast sharecropper, or the New England fisherman, the first generation Italian or the Mexican resident of Arizona, are all coherent parts of a cultural tradition. Changes made in these patterns without reference to the whole tradition may produce unanticipated dislocations of ways of life which are deeply entrenched."[12] So, too, the cause of cross-cultural sustainability loses out when Mary Douglas, for example, argues that each culture affirms the identity of its social order through prioritizing risks and categories of "pollution" in its own specific way. The Lele of Zaire focus on three chief risks—being struck by lightning, infertility, and bronchitis—while the chief risks in the United States are from smoking, alcohol, road accidents, and bad diets.[13] Social groups organize their power and resources against particular threats for reasons of cultural identity just as often as in response to evidence presented by empirical reasoning.

If the examples of Mead and Douglas are culturalist to a fault, it is easy to cite counterexamples to their arguments that are no less mediated by social interests. Despite the retention of food habits in ethnic and regional communities, the farm lobby and the food associations did succeed in establishing an "American" diet whose makeup and nutritional balance reflected their own interests and the markets they sustained at home and in their plantation empires in Caribbean and Latin American client states. As Sidney Mintz has pointed out, there can be no such thing as a "national cuisine" in the United States, but the pressure of Americanization on immigrant groups, combined with a hostility to foreign influences, helped shape the concept of national fare.[14] Above all, powerful industry blocs had a continuing stake in the national definition of the all-American square meal through each successive postwar culinary revolution: processed convenience food, the canned dinner, frozen foods, the TV dinner, the suburban barbecue, fast food franchising, the health-conscious diet, and the ethnic food boom. Of course, the interests of these corporate giants were not confined to domestic consumption; they penetrated overseas markets and intervened directly in other cultures, often as part of an official U.S. government package of food aid, and often with surplus foods that were locally inappropriate but that, under pressure, became part of the local diet, transforming ancient fish-rice-and-soy cultures into hamburger-and-wheatbread consumption zones, and creating the wasted landscapes that are the worldwide calling card of the livestock industry. The Foreign Agricultural Service of the U.S. Department of Agriculture functioned as the USIA did for U.S. culture in the Cold War period, promoting the export of American taste and dietary sensibilities, particularly among influential foreign elites. Political and strategic interests were also tied up in these exports; from the Marshall Plan onward, food aid was used explicitly to keep strategic nations from voting against neo-liberal capitalism.

The Green Revolution stands as a cautionary tale about the ultimate promotion of inequality by technocratic solutions based on productive efficiency rather than on agrarian reform. The subsequent explosion in high-yield grain production not only stunted protein production but also displaced millions of peasant farmers who could not afford the materials and technology needed for industrial agriculture. Fortified land monopolization by wealthy landowners and corporations resulted in an escalation of the paradox of plenty—a vast increase in hunger at a time of spiraling food output. But only the scale of the technological intervention distinguished the Green Revolution's impact from the general legacy of colonialism—massive hunger and malnutrition in countries where the majority of food production is controlled by large landholders for export to industrialized countries.

Just as the Green Revolution was getting under way, hunger was being "rediscovered" at home in the early 1960s, and U.S. citizens could be forgiven for reaching the same conclusions about domestic deprivation. While the scandal of hunger in a supposedly affluent nation revived the crusading liberal tradition among political elites like the Kennedys, it underscored to civil rights radicals the analogies between the continuing impoverishment of U.S. peoples of color and Third World colonial underdevelopment. Indeed, an influential analysis of black nationalism—the Black Nation thesis (an extension of a Communist Party position from the 1930s, dropped by the party in 1959)—came to see black America as an internal colony, retarded in its autonomous development, its wealth extracted and its human resources systematically exploited for the profit and advancement of core elites. Everywhere in U.S. history, white affluence and development have been directly dependent on black impoverishment and retardation.[15] The Latino case was little different, as summarized by Eduardo Galeano's bon mot, "Your wealth is our poverty."[16] As for Native America, the massive scale of land theft and mineral extraction from Indian lands presents an especially chilling case history.

With the repressive extirpation of Third Worldist nationalism and the onset of pro-scarcity politics in the mid-1970s, the War on Hunger and the antipoverty crusades were eroded by austerity measures redolent of World Bank and IMF policies of structural adjustment in the developing world. As class polarization deepened through the 1980s and 1990s, the features of an actively punitive campaign against the poor and lower middle class were fully exposed. Capital flight, massive social disinvestment, outsourcing practices, the decimation of labor unions' rights, and the revival of social Darwinist ideology in all its forms have weakened resistance to these campaigns, while tactics of racial division—Nixon's "southern strategy"—have won consent among significant sectors of the white electorate.

If there *has* been a return of scarcity and an erosion of middle class abundance in the United States, the causes are social, economic, and political from first to last. In this respect, the primary problem of our economic system is not the threat of material shortages but the threat of overproduction and the problem of disposing of the largest food surpluses in history. As Frances Moore Lappé and Joseph Collins at Food First have repeatedly pointed out, "There is scarcity, but it is not a scarcity of food. The scarcity is of people who have either access to the means to grow their own food or the money to buy it."[17] When it is routine trade policy for food production to be deliberately manipulated to raise the volume and lower the prices of export markets, we cannot talk piously about natural limits or obstacles to the feeding of populations; when the United States and the European Union are still permitted, under the Uruguay Round of GATT, to heavily subsidize the dumping of their surpluses onto increasingly food-dependent countries of the developing world, it is farcical to talk of a level playing field in free trading markets; when free trade liberalization is an opportunity for large agribusiness corporations to make vast peasant populations pay for imported food they had hitherto produced for themselves, it is immoral to blame "overpopulation" for the lack of food security.[18]

The market mechanisms deployed by the international food industry take their cruelest toll in developing countries, where fertile land is monopolized by wealthy elites, who withhold land use to boost their foreign exchange earnings and who displace peasant farmers onto erosion-prone soil. The resulting soil depletion accounts for most of the ecological degradation suffered through loss of topsoil, overgrazing, land exhaustion, or desertification. Related commodity cycles of glut and shortage are influenced by natural causes such as floods, pests, drought, and resource loss—but it would be misleading to portray them as *determined* by conditions of natural abundance or scarcity unaffected by social agency. For the most part, they are governed by patterns of short-term investment and profit maximization that respond to the market mechanism of the food industry, not to the structural needs of populations. When the economic marginalization of poor populations is also used as a medium for their political and social marginalization, then the full brunt of underdevelopment is felt.

This is the situation today in the United States, the world's breadbasket, where hunger is created by market conditions and political convictions similar to those in many an IMF client state. Whatever attempts were made in the postwar period to build a liberal state apparatus that would regulate and limit the tendencies of scarcity creation have been undermined by the massive maneuvering of transnational capitalism in its moment of global integration. In that same period—the last quarter of the century—concerns about the exhaustion of global resources have prompted speculation and policy making addressed to principles of sustainable development. Scarcity, in this "ultimate" form, where its global impact affects everyone, has come to figure as a fixed component of the political landscape. The global moment of ecological degradation has thus rendered unavoidable the contradiction between capitalist production and nature.

As for the relationship between socially generated scarcity and natural scarcity, this is less of a new development than a constituent part of modernity itself. When the eighteenth-century circulation of commodities in Europe first brought into being a (high) society governed by taste and fashionable consumption, the engine of social emulation and status buying was set in motion. The distinction between basic needs and the desire for rare items eroded as yesterday's luxury became today's necessity. There could no longer be enough by definition; scarcity was now a permanent condition because certain things would always be in short supply. Taste, style, and prestige consumption governed the world of unfulfilled desire. For some Enlightenment thinkers like Smith and Hume, this dynamic was essential to the creation of wealth and the advancement of civil society. For others, like Rousseau, it was a source of artifice, corruption, and inauthenticity. "Nature," now conceived as apart from and in large measure opposed to Society, was the realm of noncompetitive satisfaction of needs, unaffected by the market stimulation of demand.[19]

For a modernity tied to technological advance, expansion of trade, and capital accumulation, the unchanging appeal of Rousseau's stationary natural state would come to figure as the antithesis of social progress. For romantic utopians like William Morris, it became a pre-scarcity haven to get back to. For progressive utopians from Marx and Mill to Marcuse and Bookchin, post-scarcity was the preferred goal, to be achieved through political liberation or the power of technology. Two highly influential institutions of thought stood in the way. First were the economists of the marginal utility school, who sprang up to combat Marxist critiques of the labor theory of value. Marginalist theory regards scarcity as the natural outcome of the universal behavior of individuals rationally pursuing their interests and desires for goods. Stripped of any social, psychic, or historical characteristics, the rational, calculating individual, impossible to perceive as a creature of taste, always acts on a cost-benefit analysis of resources and desires. Scarcity is an integral, if not the underlying, component of the marginalists' world, where market demand determines the value of everything and explains the behavior of everyone.

The second obstacle to post-scarcity thought is the tradition, stemming from Malthus, that continues to offer statistical proofs of the falling ratio between population growth and food resources. The dismal science of the Malthusian equation is a thorn in the side of Rawlsian liberal theories that appeal to the just distribution of resources. Backed by the amoral authority of numbers, quantitative assessments of global energy or food budgets wield an immense power in a world ruled by the abstract gospel of GNP. Making the most of their rationalist appeal to value neutrality, the neo-Malthusian statistocrats can tailor their computer modeling to fit any occasion. Factors that don't compute—including social and environmental costs—are conveniently left out. High GNP rates in the United States conceal the growth of hunger in the land of plenty; low rates in the developing countries conceal vast internal inequalities. Global breakdowns, nation by nation, reinforce a sense of futility about the North-South divide. The number span is too great, the curves are too weak, the situation can only get worse. Inspired by the neo-Malthusian responses to the Club of Rome's 1974 report, the Ford and Rockefeller Foundations invested heavily in the resource-scarcity/population growth problem in the Third World, sponsoring the Green Revolution and population control policies. The result was global overproduction and a massive loss of food security in developing countries, deprived of the means to feed themselves. So, too, economic institutions like the World Bank and the IMF have used the equations to levy austerity policies friendly to transnational business, resulting in widespread civil disorders over inflated food prices in the mid-1980s that were termed the "IMF riots." Exporting nations like the United States entered into the business of food aid to advance their own strategic interests, to pretty up their humanitarian profiles, and to conceal their roles in the game of food politics. The most recent revival of Malthusian concern followed the response of population stabilization advocates at the Worldwatch Institute (*Who Will Feed China?*) to China's recent transformation into the world's second biggest grain importer.[20] It has been much debated whether this phenomenon, set against the backdrop of rising food prices on the international market, was the result of distortions generated by China's entry into the food market or by the accelerating exhaustion of its carrying capacity. At any rate, neo-Malthusian assumptions about overpopulation of the sort espoused by Worldwatch and others exert considerable influence over critical sectors of the environmentalist movement in the North, encouraging anti-immigrationist policies and diverting attention from the social justice of redistribution that governs the agenda in the South.

In these contexts and others, the admission of scarcity presents an opportunity to impose limits, cutbacks, concessions, and restrictions, usually in the name of conservation and waste reduction. There is nothing more wasteful than market economics, yet campaigns against capitalism's mismanagement are more often than not turned into opportunities to punish its victims. In periods like the Progressive era, for example, when the conservationist ethic was directed wholesale against corporate waste and inefficiency, it was accompanied by policies targeted at marginal populations. Conservationists of the prewar period directed a holy war against laissez-faire capitalism's exhaustion of nonrenewable resources, against the forces of urban industrialization and the growth of conspicuous consumption. It was a fierce Protestant crusade against waste in all its forms, including the degeneration of American Anglo-Saxon racial stock. This was the period, after all, that produced a literary epic of white male upper-class angst called "The Waste Land." The conservation of nature became a racial and sexual prescription, among other things, for Teddy Roosevelt's national campaign of "strenuous masculinity." Urbanization and immigration were an open threat to this version of "nature."[21]

The more progressive elements of the Progressive movement—the tradition of Veblen—supported efforts to rationalize productivity along scientific lines, heroizing engineers as the "practical" architects of a future ruled by reason and not capital. Their assault on corporate mismanagement would help to sanction the scientific management of Frederick Taylor and the totalizing policies of Henry Ford, neither of them labor-friendly. Ceding more power to management experts was a step toward waste avoidance, but it delivered workers up to harsher regimes of control over their labor and succeeded in establishing productivity—long hours, high wages—as the common goal of capital *and* labor during the boom years of the postwar social contract. Thus did the labor movement internalize the utilitarian discipline, routine punctuality, and habits of sacrifice that made up the "Puritan work ethic," distinguished above all for its abhorrence of waste. Even the partisans of the early consumer movement, like Chase and Lynd, held up the model of work-obsessed productivity at the expense of consumerism's wasteful indulgence. A leisure-oriented consumer democracy was not at odds with capitalist productivity, but rather the desired outcome of its rationalized managerial form of growth. If only capitalism's endemic problem of overproduction could be resolved and its patterns of distribution equalized, then society's masses would be free to realize their desires in the realm of stable consumption. An entire generation of Cold War liberal intellectuals expressed their disappointment with the results and turned on "mass culture" as the dehumanizing scourge of all public virtue, reviving, in the realm of consumption, the legacy of shame for wasteful activities that had once been reserved for production.

Most recently, Jackson Lears has depicted many of the historical components of the Puritan producer ethic: the plain speech, plain living traditions of republican virtue, the effeminizing of indolence and spendthrift tendencies, the suspicion of frivolity and luxury, and the fear of losing self-restraint in the face of abundance. With the onset of consumer society, these social neuroses began to be focused on a preoccupation with bodily perfection. The obsession with bodily waste runs steadily from anxieties about auto-intoxication and flawless bowel movements in the earlier part of the new century through the germophobia of the Cold War period to the most recent crop of eating disorders and fitness manias.[22] The capacity to summon up guilt around consumption is still unevenly distributed across social groups, tailing off among low-income groups. But its appeal is revived when government embarks on a moralistic crusade to dictate self-help and self-reliance to poor and marginal populations. The declaration that we are living beyond our means is the guilt-tripping disclosure with which economic elites commence each new round of pro-scarcity measures.

One major stimulus to the guilt industry, however, has been in the promotion of environmental voluntarism. Here, individual wastefulness is held accountable for mass deprivation around the globe. Americans are especially persuaded that their personal patterns of consumption and waste are directly responsible for hunger elsewhere. It is a widespread middle-class belief that a prudent lifestyle of self-restraint and personal waste management will alleviate misery in some benighted corner of the globe, and that enlightened actions on the part of individual Americans can affect thousands of Third Worlders. How can you waste food when half the world is starving? runs the dinner table refrain of our childhood. Yet none of these widely held myths comes close to accounting for either the economy of waste or the causes of world hunger. For the most part, they simply reinforce the chauvinistic illusion that the United States is the world's great provider, or that the more selfish and improvident its citizens are, the more the rest of the world suffers. Conversely, when America makes a sacrifice, there is an immediate relief from famine at the far ends of the earth. Lappé and Collins and others have demolished each of these myths in systematic assaults over the years on the global food system.[23] Far from being the charitable donor, the United States is one of the world's top food importers, while it is the hungry nations that are net food exporters; when the poor feed the rich who is the real dependent? Nor do U.S.

exports come cheap. The bulk are sold to industrialized nations at prices super-inflated in order to rescue the U.S. balance of payments, while aid to developing countries usually comes in the form of unwanted surplus foods, with high interest rates and the specter of dependency attached. Or else they are employed as political weapons in the strategic food-for-war struggle against forces opposed to economic liberalization.

In common with other industrial activities, food production has been moved overseas in the last two decades, as the agribusiness and processing giants like Unilever, General Foods, Nestlé, Cargill, United Brands, H. J. Heinz, Del Monte, Kraft, Jacobs Suchard, Consolidated Foods, CPC International, and Ralston Purina, in pursuit of a low-cost workforce, have swallowed up local firms all over the world. Taking advantage of the profitable conditions offered by feudal land tenure, Euro-American transnationals increasingly supply the national elites of the world from their Third World farms, ranches, and subsidiaries. Specialty items and grain-based livestock production take a massive toll on harvests, grazing ecosystems, and subsistence farming. Structural adjustment strictures often forbid national agricultural sectors in IMF client states to produce anything but export crops.[24] In a global market, food is treated like any other commodity whose value can be enhanced by making it scarce. Hence, land is underutilized, monocultural cash crops are promoted, and control of production is retained by neo-colonial, world-scale monopolies.[25] These are the conditions under which waste, scarcity, and ecological damage are prevalent, in a world where every country has the capacity to feed its citizens, and where, according to the UN World Food Program, total food output is one and a half times that required to feed the world's population.

In the last two decades, voluntarist dietary reform on the part of meat-dependent North American individuals has been highly motivational, not to mention healthy. Insofar as it feeds into the codes of personal redemption and self-reform, we would have to say that this kind of response is, at the very least, culturally appropriate—it's the "American way." As an act of moral faith it has generated a scientific revolution in health consciousness that has not entirely been co-opted by the industry's keen appetite to absorb and market its adversary. As a tangible example of reform, it shows that change can be achieved by people with no specific power or technical expertise, in this instance, in the specialty of nutrition. More to the point, it is an example of the kind of change that allegedly occurs only in response to authoritarian measures. On the other hand, these self-reforms have a mere symbolic impact when judged against the potential changes if the net citizen energy devoted to pursuing personal waste management were organized politically against the inefficiencies of the food market system and its wasteful packaging and advertising economy. In this respect, these personal actions are akin to the high-profile responses that wealthy governments (and rock stars) periodically make to the latest African famine crisis. In such cases, the emergency shipments of food provide temporary relief for the worst starvation but do nothing at all to address the structural causes of hunger and chronic undernutrition. Extreme outbreaks of famine may include among their causes local climatic conditions and are often shaped by the regional political economy of soil erosion, desertification, and pollution, but they are as endemic to the global food system as the habitual grain gluts, butter mountains, and milk lakes are to Western agribusiness. Underproduction is almost never the problem; distribution of income is always a major cause, augmented by the ecological damage wrought by the export and livestock production economy. In most cases, then, food aid is counterproductive, if only because it subverts the conditions for self-sufficiency that already exist in almost every country. Intervention can lead to dependence as surely as the system of food markets is designed to produce hunger and scarcity: "Why ask how people are to be fed, as if this had to be done by some external agent? Are people not motivated to feed themselves? . . . Who, when not deprived of the means, would not feed themselves?" writes George Kent.[26] In this respect, food is no different from any other aspect of North-South economic relations, where the outcome of intervention aimed in principle at wealth redistribution has been the net transfer of southern debtors to the North. Wherever food is exported and diverted from local needs, the rich are taking more than their already unfair share.

This is no less the rule in the United States itself, the land of high human consumption of pet food. That chronic malnutrition exists at all in an overproducing economy of scale testifies to the violence of domestic deprivation. That its existence is recognized and accepted as a permanent feature of the social, if not the natural, landscape shows that the mythology of perpetual scarcity is very deeply rooted in popular consciousness. Ever since the War on Hunger ran out of political patrons in the mid-1970s, public perceptions of the issue have been filtered through the muddy lens of poverty and welfare policy debates. In a short time, poverty and hunger were no longer a national scandal but were increasingly taken for granted. In the last ten years, a further shift has occurred: large sectors of America's poor have been redefined as immoral and selfish. The wedges driven in by the New Right created new moral distinctions: the "worthy" and the "nonworthy" poor, the "truly needy" and the "welfare chiselers," "latent poverty" (poverty that would exist without welfare) and "dependent poverty." The new divisions between the deserving and undeserving poor were a solid opportunity to promote paleo-conservative versions of the work ethic, family values, and race relations.[27] Shibboleths about welfare dependency are touted as fact and bolstered, if necessary, by tailor-made statistics. This is the low road that leads to neo-Malthusian conclusions about the overpopulation of the underproductive. When combined with homilies about the limits of the state's bounty and the erosion of available resources, it makes for a potent scarcity cocktail.

As I have argued here, however, the crucial shortage is in income and access, and the underdevelopment of both is political as well as economic. The persistence of poverty and hunger is not unlike the persistence of racism; its causes are structural, and its design is motivated. These issues of social injustice are often considered extraneous to the "real" ecological questions of biospheric degradation and species loss. The result, as we know, has debilitated sectors of the northern environmental movement and created a fractious relationship with the movement in the South. But socially generated scarcity is also often neglected by analysts on the economist left, invariably seen as a diversion from the unmediated ecological impact of capitalist modes of production. While no one can ignore the ongoing destruction of the nonrenewable world, the causes of degradation demand social and political analysis. Is there a way of addressing the material dimensions of the ecological crisis while ignoring the systematic social inequalities that create scarcity? Not on this planet. While natural and socially generated scarcity are not exactly the same thing, they share common underlying conditions. Is there then a lonely hour when biological scarcity is the "last instance" of determination in planetary life? No doubt there is such a moment, but our task is less to dwell on its advent than to try to make human societies where biological nature does not have to be the primary, let alone the final, determinant of our worldly relations. Such societies cannot be biologically sustainable if they continue to permit the use of social scarcity as a tool for the powerful to monopolize resources for their own ends.

NINE

Claims for Cultural Justice

Concepts like social justice, environmental justice, and racial justice spring readily to the lips of activists and reformers, and most of us could probably produce a thumbnail sketch or working definition of them. Some are even invoked by name in attempted legislation. For example, the Racial Justice Act, attached to Bill Clinton's first anticrime bill (and shot down in Congress in 1994), sought to address the scandalously disproportionate number of African American males on death row.

My intent here is to speculate about the concept of cultural justice and to examine some of the debates that have shed light on its meaning. One such discussion involves the formal treatment of cultural rights, which has achieved some level of recognition in national and international law. These rights, broadly applied to groups, appear to be a departure from the individualist basis of the liberal rights tradition, and yet they are increasingly seen as an integral element of citizenship in liberal societies. Another discussion arises from the recent imbroglio over affirmative action programs, against a backdrop in which the retreat from race-conscious legislation is in full swing. In this debate, the principle of recognizing cultural differences as a short-term compensatory response to historical injustice is at odds with the acceptance of cultural difference as a long term component of the quest for social justice.

In a backlash climate governed by appeals to "fair" or "neutral" treatment on a "level" playing field, claimants of cultural rights and affirmative action set-asides are habitually impugned as beneficiaries of "special" rights or privileges. Yet this objection is indefensible when the state itself is far from neutral, sanctioning normative values and practices that clearly reflect the history of its control by majoritarian interests. In addition, the state already plays a powerful administrative role in assigning identities, given the influence of its ethnoracial census categories and its system of apportionment on the basis of census demographics.

However attractive as a short-term medium of resource distribution, cultural politics cannot afford, in the long run, to take its cue from such census classifications. Within any group membership there are too many internal differences in values, beliefs, and practices—relating to gender, sexuality, religion, and subethnic groupings—for the state's bureaucratic categories or cultural nationalists' purist identities to satisfy the needs generated by a radical democracy. Group-differentiated rights will have to find a way to coexist with expansive libertarian protections and innovative forms of class politics. Strategic coexistence of this sort, I conclude, may be the key to forging a politics flexible enough to recognize that forms of cultural justice are integral to the sustainable pursuit of socioeconomic redistribution. Nothing is more crucial or more difficult, given the divisions that have unfolded between what is often termed the social Left and the cultural Left.[1]

The Approach to Cultural Rights

Cultural rights have attracted a good deal of attention in recent years. In a world increasingly beset by ethnocultural conflicts, it has become clear that the liberal focus on individual rights, generalized by international conventions after World War II through the concept of human rights, cannot do justice to the claims now being raised on the basis of cultural differences and minority rights. As Will Kymlicka has pointed out, human rights discourse has no way of responding to the heated debates over language rights, regional autonomy, minority representation, education curricula, land claims, national symbols, immigration policies, and so on.[2] These are issues that appear to demand treatment on the basis of group or collective rights, which may not always be congruent with the rights of individuals and which, in some cases, may suppress these rights.

Nor have socialist traditions been much more attentive to minority cultural rights, treating them as a divisive impediment in the path of the progressive socialization of centralized economies. Despite the efforts and achievements of almost thirty years of cultural activism, largely through the work of the new social movements, there remains in some sectors of the Left a lingering suspicion of cultural issues. This ranges from knee-jerk disdain for the "cretinizing" effect of popular culture to dogmatic repudiation of identity politics. According to this view, culture does not unite but divides people and, for the most part, is a diversion from *real* economic issues.

Cultural justice is not distinct from the transformation of socioeconomic conditions. Ideally, they are part and parcel of the same revolution, although some aspects of cultural justice are more easily abstracted from the economic environment than others. Increasingly, respect for people's cultural identities—conventionally associated with broad categories of gender, race, sexuality, nationality, and ethnicity—has come to be seen as a major condition of equal access to income, health, education, free association, religious freedom, housing, and employment. For some, this need for cultural respect is a necessary supplement to the basic human rights pertaining to freedom of speech, assembly, and conscience. The attainment of this respect is a consequence of the powerful petitions on behalf of what Charles Taylor has described as the "politics of recognition."[3]

As a result, much energetic debate has been devoted to the capacity of liberal democracies to accommodate respect for cultural particularity without renouncing their procedural guarantees of equal respect for all citizens. Ironically, this debate has occurred in the United States at a time when the legal arm of the liberal state is in wholesale retreat from affirmative programs and measures intended to remedy the socioeconomic consequences of centuries of cultural injustice. Many who have suffered socioeconomic injustice perceive their hardship as motivated by, or indistinguishable from, cultural disrespect, prejudice, and race hatred, and they are right to do so. A politics of recognition must take notice of these perceptions as well. Otherwise, it will be as culturally insensitive as the "blind" justice of liberal respect that it seeks to supplant.

Legal consideration of the cultural rights of social or ethnic groups is still in a rudimentary phase. Typically, such rights have been legally extended to national minorities whose traditional culture and material existence are threatened with extinction by majoritarian forces. Indigenous cultural rights—over language, religion, and traditional practices, including Native jurisprudence—have become a powerful instrument for negotiating with, and establishing moral authority over, the rule of majoritarian institutions. National minority rights can be a model for ethnic or immigrant groups seeking protection for their own distinct identities and traditions, but the latter are not aimed at self-government or differentiated citizenship. At the level of the nation-state, less powerful countries make similar kinds of appeals in the name of protecting their cultural sovereignty against the imperial sway of foreign influence, especially in the realm of the cultural marketplace, where Euro-American goods and values circulate most freely. Intellectual and cultural property rights are increasingly a feature of NGO consensus, in accord with the International Covenant on Economic, Social and Cultural Rights (ICESCR) and certain UN draft declarations. Such concepts of cultural equity have an extensive, if differentiated, appeal across the spectrum of minorities in the United States—from indigenous national minorities (Native Americans, Native Hawaiians) to commonwealth citizens (Puerto Ricans), and ethnic minorities who are either Anglophone (African Americans), bilingual (many Latinos and Asian Americans), or non-English-speaking immigrants. Cultural rights have even been claimed by white supremacist groups who submit that the survival of "white" cultural traditions is endangered by creeping multiculturalism.

In the case of (mostly indigenous) national minorities differentiated through citizenship laws in countries like the United States, Canada, Australia, and New Zealand, established cultural rights regarding language, land use, and the protection of traditional and religious practices are regarded as permanent and inherent rights, requisite to the self-government of cultural communities. For other ethnic (and not national) minorities, cultural justice may involve rights against discrimination and in support of cultural practices considered alien to the majoritarian mainstream and thus a hard sell in the marketplace. These may also be regarded as rights related to more or less permanent cultural differences, since the liberal state, in its post-assimilationist phase, no longer has an interest in eradicating such differences. The categories of rights described above can be invoked to protect minorities from the socioeconomic power of the majority. Opportunities accorded under affirmative action programs go further in helping minorities and women attain representation within the mainstream of national life in positions of institutional power. But neither the rights nor the opportunities can require such institutions to redistribute resources more radically.

Nancy Fraser has argued that there are some forms of symbolic redress, such as establishing respect for marginalized identities, that might be viewed as the cultural equivalent of the liberal welfare state. They promote superficial, onetime compensation for recognized groups that eases liberal guilt, but accomplishes little in the way of restructuring the underlying principles that generate injustices, economic and cultural. Fraser's "transformative" justice involves a deep restructuring of the relations of production, in the economic sphere, and the relations of recognition, in the cultural sphere. "Affirmative" justice, by contrast, merely involves the strengthening of group identities in their claims on resources and respect. As Fraser notes, however, the transformative option is the more remote for most people, because it is the more destabilizing and radical alternative.[4] It is also the most distant horizon in our current political environment because it involves explicitly socialist and utopian measures.

At a time when state programs of affirmative action are being decimated, minorities feel they are being punished and further disadvantaged. In this respect, it is important to remember that affirmative action policies were conceived as a first step, not the last, toward solving the problems of cultural and social injustice. As such, they established an important break with the occupational caste system, breaching the walls of socioeconomic segregation. With the liberal retreat from race-conscious legislation in full swing, it is important to stand firm in support of these policies and their achievements, while searching for ways to plant the seeds of what Fraser calls transformative justice.

Proponents of affirmative action have been at pains to show that the arguments for specific cultural rights are inseparable from the conditions of economic and social inequality, and yet there is no simple legal basis in a liberal democracy for recognizing this relationship. If we are at all interested in the larger social transformations that redistributive justice can effect, we must be committed to believing that cultural justice is not simply a temporary, expedient vehicle for remedial legislation, to be dispensed with on some false consensus about the attainment of a level playing field. As long as there is every reason to believe that racism is a permanent feature of U.S. society, its political antitoxin must be just as durable, and just as normative. It would be better, then, if we were to view cultural justice as in for the long haul, as an integral part of a long revolution in social justice. The alternative is weak forms of redress that service majoritarian self-esteem—an integral component of new liberal forms of racism. Malcolm X once compared racism in America to a Cadillac—they come out with a new model every few years. With the auto industry ever in the doldrums, and the legacy of slavery and segregation sure to endure well into the next millenium, it's high time we had a better comparison, more suited perhaps to the dizzy age of electronic chip speed. In the meantime, senior politicians offer a couple of strange footnotes in the summer of 1997. President Clinton convened a new commission on race, hoping for a "national conversation" that will address "the unfinished work of our times" and "redeem the promise of America" through racial healing. And Congress gave much consideration to a proposal to issue an official apology for the long wound of slavery. Both of these initiatives were received with vigorous cynicism on each end of the political spectrum. African Americans, in particular, have every reason to recall that similar earnest rhetoric in the past was at least backed up by real economic initiatives—the Emancipation promise of forty acres and a mule, during General Sherman's march through the rebel South, and the pledge during the Civil Rights era to use federal power to vanquish residential and occupational segregation. As it happens, Sherman's promise was never kept, and the post–Civil Rights period has seen a long, slow retreat from the liberal commitment to racial justice. By contrast, the Clinton rhetoric comes unaccompanied. With affirmative action programs likely to be in tatters soon, there are no new plans in Washington to break the holding patterns of prejudice, no new policies to stem the racialization of poverty, nothing to write home about. So watchers of America will see nothing more than the familiar flag-waving, emotional symbolism, and warm watery talk about moving toward a more just society.

Yet such gestures are already part of a far-flung political style. Following Australia's official apology to Aborigines delivered by Paul Keating, Clinton made amends to Native Hawaiians, ex-PM Murayama apologized for Japanese war crimes, Tony Blair expiated on behalf of the Irish potato famine, and Swiss bankers have been trying their best to repent, just to name a few. An outbreak of *apologitis* is afoot in the world's centers of power. The symptoms are empathy without mourning, and atonement without liability. On the one hand, this condition is easy to ridicule as just another version of Clinton's stock-in-trade "I feel your pain" management style. But it can also be seen as a weak form of the "politics of recognition," whereby respect for the rights and identities of aggrieved or marginalized groups is formally acknowledged by the state. In this instance, however, the new political style bids for respect in a way that too closely courts resentment.

Extensive Justice

While formal entitlement is the ultimate goal of many claims for cultural rights, and while the nature of protection sought for such rights ranges from civil tolerance to institutional empowerment at the top levels of representative government, the components of cultural justice are often informal in nature. Legal formalism, in the practical grip of the powerful, and in a system so devoted to negative forms of liberal individualism, is not always well equipped to deliver the appropriate quotient of justice. Justice cannot fully be accomplished through the formal work of legal process; it also involves transforming cultural and social behavior in ways that lie beyond the customary reach of legislation. Even in the courtroom, which is only one of the sites where the law is enacted, justice often means something quite different from legality. Thus we have "jury nullification" (whereby jurors vote according to their conscience and not in strict obedience to a judge's instructions about evidence or laws they may find unjust) and, more generally, a long tradition of civil disobedience that sanctions dissent in the face of unjust or inadequate legislation.

Similarly, formal legal processes are often seen to be too mechanistic in their attention to procedural rules and not sensitive enough to the cultural security and social needs of citizens. Worries even arise, for example, when a Supreme Court appointee is perceived to have led a sheltered, bookish existence, too removed from the busy throng of the nation's complex cultural life—as was the case in the confirmation hearings for David Souter's appointment to the Court. Can legislators from a socially and ethnically limited background do justice to claims infused with challenging assumptions about social and cultural differences? Is it their explicit task to abstract the claims from all ties to the busy, social world, insofar as this is possible to do? Public and legal debate about American liberal jurisprudence is beset by such contradictions.

The national fixation on origins, foundations, and constitutionalism has always been fiercely at odds with the spirit of innovation that infuses new narratives, "outsider" experience, and contemporary interpretations into the legal canon. In the case of rights claims, the contradictions have sharpened; attention to group rights has increased at a time when the separation of state and ethnicity is most vigorously being promoted. Depending on how history has treated your kind, the restriction of natural rights proclamations to the population that first defined and then enjoyed them—those eighteenth-century white males who alone were recognized as free, property-bearing citizens—can be viewed as a foundational guarantee of hypocrisy or a recipe for some future state of justice, always incomplete, and therefore indispensable to those excluded from the initial menu. As a result, the subsequent struggle between majoritarian interests and minority rights has been relentless; in the wake of the "ethnic revival" of the 1960s and 1970s, it remains one of the central tensions governing the national system of distributive justice.

If the state were already neutral in its treatment of cultural differences, then the liberal preference for regarding cultural and ethnic identity as a private matter—like religious affiliation—would have some justifiable basis. Nondiscrimination, as a blanket policy of liberal justice, would meet more of the requirements for guaranteeing equal treatment. Far from being neutral, the state is the historical product of centuries of majoritarian decision making, governed by the interests of dominant social and ethnic groups. Its national symbols, public holidays, Christian workweek, heteronormative morality, and Anglo-conformity in civic values all reflect that ethnocentric history. So, too, the state has been especially active in the business of defining racial identities. The current census groupings—African American, Asian American, Hispanic (or Latino), Indigenous (or Native American), and European American, to be joined perhaps in the 2000 census by a "biracial" category—are only the latest in the long evolution of the state's management of ethnoracial identity. In sum, the state already intervenes heavily in the domain of cultural recognition, so it is indefensible to argue on those grounds that it should never take an affirmative stance toward recognition claims.[5]

Take the rallying cry of "No Justice, No Peace" that arose in response to the first Rodney King verdict. This was not simply a demand for a retrial that would fairly allocate culpability to members of the Los Angeles Police Department who administered the beatings. It was an implicit challenge to the idea that African Americans have ever expected, and can ever expect, full protection under the legal system of the state, given (a) the solid legacy of legal and civic denial, (b) the growth of an extensive criminal court and penitentiary apparatus that has been almost as effective in its de facto racial demarcation as Jim Crow, (c) the persistence of segregation in housing, income, education, health, and the occupational division of labor, and (d) the aborted commitment to race-conscious legislation ushered in after the Civil Rights Act (CRA). There is no question that the latter development signals the collapse and retreat of liberalism from its post-CRA agenda for a racially just society. While "No Justice, No Peace" resonates, rhetorically, with the anticolonial spirit of "No Taxation without Representation," its broad challenge stands in historical judgment over the failures not only of liberal rights discourse, but also of the state form of representative democracy ushered in by American republicanism.

Just as the demand for popular representation did not end with, but was partially foreclosed by, the Constitutional Convention, the call for minority justice has been managed by the limited legislation that majoritarian elites grant under pressure from mass movements, only to retreat as soon as possible from the race-based agenda through which they were fostered.[6] The most notable moments have occurred in the brief period of Reconstruction, and in the postwar civil rights period, driven as much by a Cold War climate that required civil rights legislation to save face in the international game of public relations as by the desire to respond to civil pressure. The history of civil rights has shown that the attainment of formal equality, though a crucial symbolic victory, has a limited long-term effect on the materially disadvantaged (if unaccompanied by structural change), even while it encourages the popular bromide that "racism no longer exists."

Doing justice to cultural *and* economic rights involves a protracted revolution in which people's social identities as well as their economic circumstances are seen to be transformed. Ultimately, of course, this means transforming the identities associated with white heterosexual males *along with* the identities associated with women, lesbians and gays, and ethnic and racial groups.[7] This is why so much of the work of social movements has been aimed at changing daily habits of mind, behavior, and modes of social integration. Formal equality is only one component of that revolution, although, given the strong historical link between rights discourse and American institutions, it is impossible to sustain a public debate about the shape of the national culture without raising foundational questions about rights and citizenship. We hardly need to be reminded that the U.S. legal system has displayed its most spectacular failures in the protection of the rights of minority populations. Even at the level of formal equality, as Patricia Williams has argued, it will be necessary to expand our understanding of what rights entail: "(t)he task is to expand property rights into a conception of civil rights, into the right to expect civility from others."[8] This latter task entails translating civility into a genuine respect for different cultural practices and modes of being, where respect is normalized in the daily life not only of institutions but also of public and popular culture.

But deep civility and respect demand more than simply majoritarian concessions to the cultural distinctions of others. Psychologically, such concessions often serve merely to boost majoritarian self-esteem. It also requires an overhaul of those distinctive forms of cultural identity that arise from white skin privilege, empowered masculinity, and the heteronormative presumption. Without this overhaul, when the V-8 engines of our dominant cultural identities are stripped down and retrofitted for a more sustainable social ecology, we will still be traveling at different speeds on the same highway.

The intractability of this sphere of cultural relations might be measured by the ugly reaction to the informal proscription of racist, sexist, and homophobic jokes, cast in recent years as the "imposition" of political correctness. Such humor is not exactly illegal (although its contextualization in the workplace and elsewhere can count as harassment), but its degree of prevalence speaks volumes about the current progress of cultural justice in any society. No one wants a humorless culture—a plague too long associated with leftists—but the freedom to utter speech like this is informally perceived as a cultural right, or wrong, on the speaker's part.

Comics, professional and amateur, who joke about Jewish or African American mothers or who use recognizably ethnic speech patterns usually have supporting ethnic credentials, while those who cross ethnic boundaries, in the tradition of Lenny Bruce, have a clear political point to make. Black speech and Yiddish locutions are unconsciously used in daily life by most Americans, indeed most English-speakers, and yet people feel defamed if and when these speakers draw inappropriate attention to their use of this speech. There is often a subtle link between these speech acts and more overt hate speech, which has been on the rise in public discourse for some time, much of it directed, again, at single African American mothers, proverbially always on welfare. There is a much greater gulf between the tolerance, say, for vernacular black usage by whites, most notably in sports and music cultures, and the contempt for official language claims for Black Speech, as exemplified by the recent furor over the Ebonics proposals on the part of Oakland educators seeking to instill cultural self-esteem among underprivileged black students.

Any such considerations of self-esteem disappear entirely when American language use passes beyond English. The constitutional battle over making English the official language of the United States (English Only laws have been passed in over two dozen states in the last decade) has been one of the many ugly elements of the anti-immigrant backlash, directed mostly at Spanish-speakers. Public discussion of Spanish-language use habitually avoids reference to the language rights granted to Mexicans under the 1848 Treaty of Guadalupe Hidalgo—rights subsequently rescinded by Anglophone settlers. Is there a continuum that links the constitutionality of English Only—an issue consistently evaded by the current Supreme Court—with the demeaning impact of daily speech acts? If so, it is part of an extensive realm of cultural justice, in which respect for cultural difference might be viewed as a durable principle of civility rather than a temporary, bureaucratic form of historical restitution.

Fairness

Compare the notion of extensive justice with the conservative legal use of "fairness" as currently applied to race-conscious programs such as affirmative action. The backlash against such programs and legislation, led by Antonin Scalia, William Rehnquist, and Clarence Thomas, is based on the premise that they are "unfair" to minorities and majorities alike. In recent cases concerning affirmative action and set-asides, the Supreme Court has decided that "benign" preferential treatment on the basis of race and in the name of equality is morally and constitutionally equivalent to laws designed to subjugate a race. For Thomas (in *Adarand Constructors v. Peña*), "government cannot make us equal: it can only recognize, respect and protect us as equal before the law." For Scalia, in the same decision, there "can be no such thing as either a creditor or debtor race. To pursue the concept of racial entitlement even for the most admirable and benign of purposes is to reinforce and preserve for future mischief the way of thinking that produced race slavery, race privilege, and race hatred. In the eyes of Government, we are just one race here. It is American."

This is the worst kind of analytic jurisprudence in action, flaunting its blindness to every last shred of cultural justice. On the other hand, we can expect that the willful retreat from race-conscious legislation as a medium for redistributive justice will only go so far. The self-esteem of the white majority depends on a show of benevolence in allocating a limited share of the resources under its control to minorities. As Girardeau Spann has argued, the good cop–bad cop routine staged between congressional legislation and Supreme Court judicial review has proved effective in managing the process by which the bare minimum of redistributive justice is permitted. Because programs like affirmative action tend to be centralized and are supported primarily at the federal level, minorities are obliged to compete for resources on a national scale rather than a local one, where regional power and political self-determination are easier to achieve. Majoritarian preferences and assumptions are more easily enacted and absorbed into the formal writing of decisions in the highly centralized forum of the Supreme Court.[9]

The Clinton administration's policy of "mend it, don't end it" is a classically mindful expression of the prohibitive costs to the white majority when it is seen to renounce all responsibility for remedying those racial inequities it created. Any abdication of political will that is too visible is likely to incite civil disorder and urban revolt. Nonetheless, the plurality decisions of the Supreme Court and state legislation like the California

Civil Rights Initiative have accelerated the tendency to forbid any race-conscious remedial acts and to recognize only overtly intentional discrimination as a constitutional violation. Demonstrating racial disparities or institutional racism is no longer recognized as proof of unequal protection under the Fourteenth Amendment. Legal conservatives would have us believe that twenty-five years of remedial legislation have eradicated or compensated for all such constitutional violations, and that it is time to return to business as usual: in Scalia's words, "we must soon revert to the ordinary principles of our law, of our democratic heritage, and of our educational tradition."[10] For Scalia and his sympathizers, the period of temporary unfairness is almost over. The Constitution will once again be "color-blind." The legal landscape of rights will be returned to its assumed default condition of neutrality, uniformity, and universality; the ground rules will be back in effect. Fair play will resume.

The invocation of fairness in this context is a simple but effective code word for ignoring the historical roles that slavery and segregation have played in creating the modern legacy of racial subordination. Fairness, as applied here, stands in stark contrast to any principle of justice that involves taking race into account on more than simply a remedial basis, en route to improving the lives of all citizens. Effective principles of justice must confront the present and future legacy of the racial formation of a state in which African Americans in particular were included as nonparticipants (not excluded), and where their chattel labor was a condition of freedom for the white majority to assert its natural rights and its monopoly of wealth and property. Only in this historical light can we rightfully understand Scalia's "ordinary principles of our law" to be nothing ordinary at all, but rather the result of the economic and social history of a nation-state, and therefore an embodiment of majoritarian interests in their very ground rules. As for Scalia's disingenuous reference to "our educational tradition," he is referring to precisely the sector of social opportunity where African Americans, Latinos, and Native Americans are most disadvantaged, since they tend to fare worse than others when placed in a "meritocratic" system of standardized testing. In the face, moreover, of today's heated debates about multicultural education, anyone who knows the least thing about the historical record of religious battles over school curricula, much more fractious in periods of the nineteenth century than today, will recognize Scalia's appeals to some common educational tradition as a ludicrous fiction.

The principles of affirmative action—designed primarily to bring minorities into the mainstream of public life—have always inspired some ambivalence, even among their advocates, but the 1994 congressional election that brought Republicans to power was the event that elevated opposition to racial preference into a solid political "wedge." Suddenly affirmative action was proclaimed by pundits to be a leading cause of injustice in the nation (Aid to Families with Dependent Children [AFDC] ran a close second), and popular sentiment was held to be running against it. Statistical revelations about the existence of a glass ceiling for women and minorities were brushed aside in the Republican stampede to embrace the rights of economically depressed white males, newly victimized by the preferential treatment of less qualified blacks and by the crushing financial burden of assisting welfare mothers. Within a few months, affirmative action and AFDC had been catapulted into the gladiators' ring reserved for the two or three issues that the pundits designate, at any one time, as eligible for the public spectacle of political debate.

How did this come about? Was it the sour culmination of Richard Nixon's wily Southern Strategy? Perhaps, although voting patterns in the 1996 elections did not support the expectation that affirmative action would work as an effective wedge. Was it a reflection of the desperate resentment of white workers, beaten down by the cruel advance of the low-wage revolution? Probably, although as always, the worst-hit by economic depression have been men and women of color. Besides, low economic status is hardly ever divorced from racial sentiment, given that white workers continue to enjoy the psychological "wages of whiteness" that David Roediger has described as the birthright of poor whites in the United States.[11] Was it a symptom of the collapse of liberal morality, which once held the plight of African Americans to be the immoral core of national injustice, and which increasingly is complicit with neoconservative ideas (including those of black conservatives) about the intractable "pathology" of the "culture of poverty" among urban blacks? No doubt, although this has been complicated by new liberal calls for affirmative action based on class.

Whatever the favored explanation, the backlash against affirmative action was not concocted overnight. Making a political idea into shared common sense, even among a relatively homogeneous group, is a complex process in which legislation does not simply emerge as a final outcome, elevated above the fray and exuding an air of neutral commonality that makes all other claims seem, by comparison, exceptional and interested. But there were also other factors at work in the sphere of public opinion, no less committed to paying lip service to the creed of fairness and neutrality, no less bent on trampling on cultural justice.

Cultural Politics and the Culture Wars

One of these factors was the Culture Wars—a fractious public debate about cultural values, or more specifically, the values of an assumed common culture in a nation-state whose history has been marked by an extraordinary degree of multilingualism, a plurality of religious traditions, and a variety of diverse regional and ethnic subcultures. Indeed, it is more accurate to observe that this debate has been over the shape of the dominant culture in the United States rather than over a patently false consensus about common culture. The prosecutor's case against multicultural challenges to the dominance of white, Christian, Anglo-European values might be summarized in a way that echoes Scalia's comments about constitutional law. *It is time to revert to the ordinary principles of our culture*, which in peacetime (as opposed to the extraordinary conditions of the Culture Wars) are free from political conflict of the sort aroused by petitions for a successor multicultural curriculum. Neutral principles of excellence, as embodied in the ground rules of the common cultural heritage, must once again prevail. Whether it is the ground rules of a culture or those of the law, a neutral environment is one in which dominant interests are able to masquerade informally as a background, default condition. Dominant cultural groups always fare best under the rule of the gender-free, color-blind, heteronormative "common culture." As many have pointed out, it is such a common culture that traditionally operates as affirmative action for privileged white males. In the same way, the rules of property, contract, and tort law make the vast inequalities in our society seem like part of nature, or at least like factory settings. Attempts to change the settings are thus seen as aggressively unfair alterations of a commonly recognized norm in order to meet the needs of those with "special interests."

It is not my purpose here to take issue with what is fair and what is not—the proverbial "level field of play" is much too corrupt to honor such a discussion. If nothing else, the Culture Wars have proven that cultural politics matters, and that it is not a mere diversion from the struggle for improvements in the material conditions of people's lives. Indeed, proprietary struggles over culture have proven to be one of the fiercest sites of entrenched resistance to change in the post-CRA era. The vast amounts of funding and media persuasion devoted to the Culture Wars by conservatives are evidence of the high stakes and passions invested in monoculturalism. Right-wing foundations and their mouthpieces have made speech-for-hire into the dominant public force in these debates, reinforcing the belief that powerful white males have proprietary rights over the history and culture of the country. Nor is there any evidence that these conflicts are subsiding. The avalanche of official political attention to cultural issues has only swelled in recent years, barely missing a beat after Clinton's accession in 1992, when neoconservatives like Irving Kristol declared that the Culture Wars were over, and that his side had lost.

At the time of writing, the stage set aside for public controversy is occupied by the debate over Ebonics, the National History Standards, the future of the NEA and the NEH, same-sex marriage, the Science Wars, and the regulation of Internet speech. The vestiges of previous conflicts are still active, like smoking volcanoes: political correctness, bilingualism, hate speech, multiculturalism (and its more radical strains: multiracialism, cross-culturalism, and interculturalism), educational testing, the "unassimilable" cultures of new immigrant communities, family values, gays in the military, gangsta rap, and sexually explicit and violent imagery. Interspersed between these battlefields are the megastadiums hosting the trials of the month, where many of the great cultural pathologies of national civil life are dissected for mass media consumption. Timothy McVeigh, O. J. Simpson, Colin Ferguson, and Sheik Abdel Rahman, and offstage, the memories of Lorena Bobbitt, Rodney King, Howard Beach, the Menendez brothers, Amy Fisher, Woody Allen, Mike Tyson, Baby M, Charles Stuart, William Kennedy Smith, Glen Ridge, and Central Park, not to mention the large, televised pseudotrials on Capitol Hill like the

Supreme Court judge confirmations, Clarence Thomas–Anita Hill, hearings on Iran-Contra, and the like. On Capitol Hill, the Republican class of 1994 adopted a prosecutive posture toward the alleged "cultural elite," intent on wringing out every last drop of liberal guilt from the hyperemoting anchormen and women of the TV nation. And in higher education, where the Left has gained its strongest foothold in the last two decades, the sustained attack on tenured radicals continues unabated. This campaign is only the most visible feature of the drive to corporatize colleges and universities, where the low-wage revolution has penetrated so deeply that the de facto erosion of tenure has long preceded attempts, now on the horizon, to abolish this principle that is so vital to the freedom of academic speech.[12]

With this example of academic labor in mind, we may be tempted to consider that the furor over Great Books, cultural studies, multiculturalism, and political correctness in the academy is simply a diversionary smokescreen for advancing the economic interests of managerial elites and trustees. This is a callous misrecognition of the powerful attempts to fuel the race fires in education that began in the battles over school integration after *Brown v. Board of Education* and that continue today in curricular moves to teach the history of women and people of color. It also ignores the fact that education and cultural products in general are a vast economic sphere in their own right. North American graduate credentials are one of the most valued sources of cultural capital in the world, and the research activities conducted through the arm of higher education account for a huge portion of the information sector of the national and transnational economy. The debate about cultural values not only affects these economic sectors directly, it is part of the content of the information itself. These are much more than simply contests over national cultural symbolism; they have immense economic value within sectors of the culture and information industries.

This becomes clearer if we move beyond the Great Books debate— should T. S. Eliot make room for Toni Morrison?—to the realm of raunchy popular culture, the other preferred target of conservative morality brokers. Here the traditional contradiction between free market conservatism and cultural conservativism is all the more apparent, and the lords of Hollywood and the moguls of multimedia are foreordained to take the heat. Culture trading is a vast economy of transnational scale, and its dependence on spectacular products puts it in direct conflict with the national moral campaigns of cultural conservatives, whether Christian, Islamic, Hindu, or Jewish, whether in France, Algeria, India, or Israel. Indeed, the new transnational trading zones are often defined by the willingness of their national clients to liberalize the circulation and reception of cultural and information products. Legislation that favors the global reach of the transnational media Goliaths still vies with judicial attempts on the part of national bodies to regulate the flow of culture across their sovereign borders, attempts that themselves often appeal to a selective, moralizing definition of national, regional, or local cultures. In this global context, local cultural justice, embodied in older reformist agendas like UNESCO's New International Information Order, has long been part of the response to the perceived imperialism of Western culture industries, in a climate where the "free flow" of neoliberal markets results in a one-way flow of cultural products. Nothing appeals more powerfully to the nation-state system of world politics than the concept of a country's right to self-representation in the global field. More often than not, however, it is this "frontier justice" of nationalism that facilitates the domestic repression of minority cultures.

The new patterns of economic integration are not fully global. They have been culturally marked by regional, supranational agreements like NAFTA, G3 (Mexico, Venezuela, and Colombia), the Andean Pact, ASEAN, the EEC, and the Southern Cone (Brazil, Argentina, and Chile). Cultural brokering within and between these entities is performed on behalf of powerful producer states or industrial blocs like Hollywood. A more critical form of brokering accepts that the new public spheres and funded networks emerging along with supranational economic integration are potential sites of visibility for groups and communities socially or politically denied at the level of individual states. These new sites are real opportunities for cultural justice, hitherto available only in forums like the United Nations, to indigenous groups constituted as nations or to international movements (women, environmentalists, political prisoners) through NGOs with access to the United Nations. Like organized labor, pushing now for a living wage for workers in offshore factories and free trade zones, cultural activism increasingly crosses borders.[13]

It is important to imagine these new supranational cultural formations in provisionally utopian ways, despite their bureaucratic underpinnings. This habit has a long precedent in the syncretic traditions of music, dance, and religion of the African diaspora, for which mixing and fusing cultural influences is the core principle of survival and innovation. The latest exemplars are champions of the *mestizo* aesthetic of the American borderlands, for whom the history and experience of cultural and racial mingling offers a model for postnational cultural life: the future is *mestizo*. One result is a hysterical medley of syntheses, where there is no evidence of cultural purity and no expectation of a stable or authentic identity. Guillermo Gómez-Peña, border performance artist and court jester of hybridity, offers the "taco-surrealist" picture of a dechauvinized culture in his mock prophetic vision of "the New World Border" after the Gringostroika of "the Free Raid Agreement":

The monocultural territories of the disbanded United States, commonly known as Gringolandia, have become drastically impoverished, leading to massive migration of unemployed *wasp-backs* to the South. All major metropolises have been fully borderized. . . . They all look like downtown Tijuana on a Saturday night. . . . The legendary U.S.-Mexico borderline, affectionately known as "The Tortilla Curtain," no longer exists. Pieces of the great Tortilla are now sentimental souvenirs hanging on the bedroom walls of idiotic tourists like you. . . . The twin cities of San Dollariego and Tijuana have united to form the Maquiladora Republic of San Diejuana. Hong Kong relocates to Baja California to constitute the powerful Baja-Kong, the world's greatest producer of porn and tourist kitsch. The cities of Lost Angeles and Tokyo share a corporate government called Japangeles, in charge of all the financial operations of the Pacific Rim. The Republik of Berkeley is the only Marxist-Leninist nation left on the globe. . . . The CIA joined forces with the DEA and moved to Hollywood to create a movie studio that specializes in producing and distributing multicultural utopias. . . . Ageing pop star Madonna has reincarnated as Saint Frida Kahlo. She roams around nasty streets in search of people who suffer from identity blisters and heals them. . . . Nearly every important city in the FUSR has a Museum of Cultimultural Art. They all feature classical shows from the '80s and before as a reminder of what culture used to be before Gringostroika destroyed all traditional borders and categories. Among the most popular travelling exhibits are "1,000 Ex-Minority Artists."[14]

It is not by happenstance that this macaronic image of a hybrid near-future has emerged at the same moment as a fierce rekindling of nativist sentiment in the United States. Long-standing North American settler fears about the displacement of native-born labor and the nonassimilability of cultural traits have been reawakened. But what does anti-immigrationism mean in a nation that exports culture more successfully than its heavy manufacturing products these days? (Aside from weapons and civilian aircraft, software and culture are the leading U.S. exports.) This latest nativist revival is set against the perceived waning of the modern nation-state, triggered by the vast economic restructuring that is shifting the exercise of fiscal power away from the centralized national bureaucracies into the quasi-sovereign fiefdoms of the corporate trans-state. As its presumed cohesive authority fades, the state's faltering capacity to function as a consistent expression of national cultural purpose provides an added sense of moral panic to fears about the loss of national identity. There seems no doubt that globalization is an important context for the heated debate about multiculturalism, framed on the right by race phobias about the advent of anything approaching cultural equity, in the center by fears about the centrifugal tendency of cultural "fragmentation," and on the left by concerns about the corporate management of cultural diversity or the hidebound essentialism of identity politics.

Unlike in other postcolonial settler states like Australia and Canada, multiculturalism is not official, top-down, national policy in the United States. Critical multiculturalism in the United States arises directly from the legacy of the racial formation of the state—bound up with Native genocide, African chattel slavery, Asian exclusion, and Mexican criminalization—and is quite distinct from the assimilationist tensions between cultural identity and national citizenship that applied to European immigrant groups. Those tensions had been managed by the social engineering programs of Americanization, explicitly intended to purge pre-industrial cultural traits and labor habits among immigrant workers, and by the national celebration of ethnic pluralism that came to incorporate the unofficial persistence of their distinctive cultural identities. Among non-Euro populations, the persistence of racial stratification and prejudice—in labor, income, health, housing, and civic respect—appears to be more fundamental in its structural hold on the nation's political economy. The deep racialization of these inequities is not likely to be remedied by prettying up corporate diversity statistics (while corporate capitalism is left unaltered) or by injecting some color into school curricula. But deep respect for the cultural identities and histories of others to the point of self-transformation may prove to be a necessary, daily precondition of any significant change.

The Numbers Game

Struggles for cultural equity may begin and end with these deep alterations of civil society and daily life, but they cannot afford to ignore numerical assessments of recognition and redistribution—not in a nation-state so devoted to statistical forms of expression in government and in economic life. The representative nature of North American democracy and the quantitative nature of its evolved bureaucratic state have had considerable impact on the shape of these struggles. Consequently, the quest for cultural justice has been aimed at not only the securing of inviolable rights, but also the visible attainment of representation in public service and professional life. A typical outcome can be summed up by Bill Clinton's promise to make his 1992 administration "look more like America" by deferring to ethnic and gender demographics in making government appointments, a procedure adopted, before and since, by many nonfederal and private institutions and encouraged by some affirmative action policies.

These policies have been largely successful, even in blue collar and public employment, but have arguably worked best at the managerial and (pre)professional levels, beyond which the notorious glass ceiling is in effect. The successes have also been accompanied by new kinds of class polarization within minority communities because the racial division of labor has remained relatively untouched, relegating workers of color to the least desirable jobs or excluding them from legitimate job markets that carry health benefits and social security. So, too, the habitual price of representation in the middle-class professions is acceptance of the culture-bound, behavioral codes of middle-class Anglo-conformity: precisely those ground rules of civility that in the past have guaranteed racial exclusivity through their characteristic blend of race and class prejudice. The result is a growing divide between the sufficiently empowered, in a position to broker the redistribution of resources, and the disadvantaged and impoverished, from whom the former are culturally detached. This divide complicates a system of distributive justice that requires strong representatives or brokers to back up claims for the disadvantaged caught in the poverty trap.

When the establishment of congressional representation by population entailed the first rigorous census taking in a modern nation-state, the extensive uses of census data in the United States increasingly came to pervade the administration of national demographic life at all levels. Employing data, primarily organized around family units, to motivate and explain policy making has long since become the rule of government. Majority and minority are more than just a numbers game, but they are also precisely that, and all the more so since the Office of Management and Budget issued its Statistical Directive 15 of 1977, which created what David Hollinger has called the "ethno-racial pentagon" of national bureaucratic life: African American, Asian American, Hispanic (or Latino), Indigenous (or Native American), and European American.[15] While these categories are highly contingent, they are impressively resilient once put in place, and very quickly attain the air of natural, normalized facts, creating expectations in others' minds about how to treat members of each category. They make very little sense as categories linked by some common culture—what does such a culture mean, for example, to those of Vietnamese, Chinese, Korean, Japanese, Thai, Filipino, Samoan, and South Asian descent who are all identified as Asian/Pacific Americans? Over time, however, these categories exert a cohesive cultural influence on those obliged to share group membership.

With the bureaucratic creation of such broad, multiethnic categories, census classification has continued to boost numbers of whites. Most Mexican Americans, for example, are primarily from Native stock, and yet many are now classed as whites; Hispanics have therefore "lost" millions of Native Americans. The blood quantum that quantifies the category of race for Native Americans had long been used as a means of depleting Indian numbers, given the rates of intermarriage that were encouraged during periods of intense assimilation. Here was an example of the "statistical extermination" of Indian populations: the continuation of genocide by statistical means. This bureaucratic sleight of hand was part of a legal history that runs from the Doctrine of Discovery and Rights of Conquest to the restriction of trading rights, the breakup of traditional land tenure and federal incorporation of land into domestic assets, the destruction of traditional jurisprudence and religious observance, the brutal policy of the Indian Wars, the termination of sovereign nations (109 nations were terminated between 1953 and 1958), the massive urban relocation of half the Native population under the Relocation Act of 1956, the murderous counterinsurgency against indigenous leaders in the American Indian Movement, and the radioactive colonialism of military policy around the tribal lands of the West and Southwest. While statistical assessments of demography have played a pernicious role in this history, they have also become an important tool for legal opposition to the expropriation of Native lands and resources. Revised numerical estimates of pre-contact urban Indian populations have been used (a) to contest the "legality" of Conquest and Discovery, based, as these doctrines were, on the thesis of "vacant lands," (b) to strengthen the case for remedial legislation and for reclaiming the land base, and (c) to generally challenge the cultural mythology of the vanishing Indian. Accordingly, census numbers of those declaring themselves Native American have risen dramatically.

A different form of demographic mentality has governed the modern color line in North America, most notably in the administration of the one-drop rule and its legacy—the persistence of bichromatic public consciousness about two nations, black and white, to the exclusion of all other perceptions of American culture. This color line, which once separated what neoconservatives used to call "unmeltable ethnics" in the black nation from assimilable ethnics in the white nation, remains very much in effect, primarily on account of institutionalized racism. In a fiscal climate where limited resources are made available to competing minorities, there is considerable pressure on empowered African Americans to use the bichromatic mentality to advance their interests over those of other non-white minorities. In an age of social austerity, or more accurately, pro-scarcity politics, targeted at the working poor and unemployed, this competition for resources and low-wage jobs is sharpened. The contest is not just among minorities, but also between native-born and immigrants. Lobbying for a demographic share of shrinking resources is difficult enough, campaigning for resources on the basis of restitution or ancestral reparations is even harder.

These are the circumstances under which the politics of ethnoracial tradition come to be appraised in transactional terms. Not surprisingly, a cultural calculus comes into play. Purist appeals to blood identity and undiluted heritage are important cards to be played in the game of dis-tributive politics. Claims for cultural justice are reduced to fiscal assess-ments, where authenticity and racial essence figure as blue-chip collateral. Such conditions of enforced scarcity discourage any recognition of cul-tural mixing; acknowledgment of mixed-race hybridity tends to weaken and undermine the legitimacy of entitlement claims. Under these condi-tions, then, cultural essentialism assumes a commodity value that is diffi-cult to renounce in hard times.

At some level, minority demographics, however undercounted from census to census, get their share of recognition from the system of state apportionment. Given the history of denial and exclusion and the abdica-tion of any political will to confront racism, cultural justice is unlikely to be served any other way soon. But there is a high price for any society to pay in accepting a cultural politics that takes its cue from such census clas-sifications. Culturally, it closes off the often vast differences in values, beliefs, and practices espoused by members within these group identifica-tions. Sometimes these differences are the result of multiple ethnic tradi-tions—Cuban, Mexican, Iberian, Puerto Rican, Dominican, among others, in the case of Latinos. Sometimes they are the result of divergent social identities, relating to sexuality, gender, and religion, within these subethnic groupings themselves. Ultimately, the language of collective identity, whether encouraged by the state's bureaucratic categories or by cultural nationalism, cannot fully satisfy the need for autonomous action and self-organization that radical democracy lives by.[16] People do not divide up into neat cultures, bound by homogeneous or coherent ingredients. Whatever authority might be attached to group rights on the basis of ethnocultural identity, it is also unjust when these rights are used to repressively impose internal conformity on members in order to preserve group solidarity or cultural purity.

Lowering the Tone

The emergent phenomenon of conservative, even racist, multiculturalism suggests some additional hazards. Consider the version proposed by welfare-basher Charles Murray and the late IQ quack Richard Herrnstein, best known as authors of *The Bell Curve*. They call it "wise ethnocentrism," and it appeals cynically to the alleged virtues of cultural difference. Minority groups, Murray and Herrnstein argue, should be released from the injunction to assimilate, and should be encouraged to protect and sustain their "clannish" self-esteem. Cultural groups are different; they should remain so. There is no need to compare one with another, and even less need to encourage any mixing between them. In this version, a straightforward prescription for segregationism masquerades as tolerance for human variation.[17] Behind this appeal to "clanism" lurks Murray's hankering after a Jeffersonian natural aristocracy and a caste order where everyone knows their place, and where everyone will cheerfully accept their point of distribution on the bell curves—the gene pool, presumably, taking the place of the safety net.

Etienne Balibar has most forcefully argued that the new racism proceeds not from older myths of superiority about biological heredity, but rather from nominally antiracist beliefs about the harmfulness of abolishing cultural differences. (In the affirmative action debates, the Right has similarly seized the moral high ground of antidiscrimination.) Culturalism, Balibar argues, has come to replace biologism as the basis for a racism without race.[18] It may be that this is more true of the insurgent European racism Balibar is describing than of the situation in North America, but at the very least it seems to me that Balibar is a little premature in declaring the death of biological racism. To see why, one need look no further than *The Bell Curve* itself, which used discredited ideas and data about the alleged link between genes and intelligence to buttress its policy claims and to fuel the war against welfare programs.

Murray and Herrnstein's barnacled appeals to genetic determinism were no more novel than their obsession with race-based public policy. What *is* new about the context for circulating these bromides is an emergent industrial environment driven, in large part, by biotechnology and genetic medicine. Despite *The Bell Curve*'s alleged connection between genes and intelligence, the book makes no mention of "hard" science, least of all the kind of molecular biology that has reinvented our thinking about genetics in recent decades. In the splice-and-dice biotech labs, genetic material no longer has the fixed, immutable status it used to occupy in the theory books of destiny. If anything, industry boosters have reveled in the claim to be able to intervene in and modify the alleged connection between genes-and-anything, thereby opening up a whole new chapter in the history of eugenics. Murray and Herrnstein had good reasons for avoiding hard science—their soft science was soft enough. But their widely publicized theses about the genetic basis of cognitive strata in society helped reinforce the racist perceptions already in the public mind that inequalities related to genetic endowment can never be overcome, least of all by spreading tax dollars around.

The Bell Curve has had lots of company. Policy-oriented books that argue a genetic or Darwinist basis for social, moral, and cultural behavior are a booming genre.[19] Cultural racism may have lost some of its official backing, but some form of hereditarianism is always at the ready with trumped-up statistics and pseudoscience to prove that redistributive politics is being wasted on the "cognitively disabled" or "genetically inferior" poor. If nothing else, the appeal of these arguments shows that science, not cultural values, is the common language in liberal democracies. By this I do not mean to suggest that science is not shaped by cultural values, nor that everyone has equal access to the authority that science confers on truth claims. On the contrary, any movement for cultural justice has to address the way science both meets social and cultural demands and fashions these demands in turn. With the new eugenics waiting in the wings, or stealing in the back door, and with the legacy of nineteenth-century scientific racism still dormant and festering in the public mind, there is no defensible alternative.

The regard for cultural justice, insofar as it goes beyond the limited domain of claims for representation or reallocations of recognition and respect, must ultimately be tied to criteria that the actually existing state does not satisfy. Why? Because, unlike so much of the state's legal framework, which derives its authority from appeals to precedent, substantive justice derives its moral authority from what is radically lacking in the state. There is a liberal version of this called "the promise of America" in which the eternally young nation (despite being much older than most of the world's sovereign states) serves justice on all her children in some future, ideal state of the union. Liberation politics, in the form of the civil rights movement (followed by women's and gay liberation), appealed in part to such a narrative; the state, once transformed, will be coterminous with the transformation of its citizens. Sadly, the commitment to advancing beyond the initial stages of this transformation has been blocked.

Identity politics is in many respects the successor to the liberation politics of the civil rights generation. It assumes that its constituents are already transformed, and demands not only their recognition as women, or lesbians, or Latinas, but also their right to representation and empowerment within the state and public institutions on the basis of these identities. A third generation of movement politics seeks to expose the state's protection of dominant interests under the guise of neutrality. For example, it challenges the heteronormative assumptions made by the state about the sexuality of its citizens.[20] This initiative, associated with queer theory, can be aligned with a race politics that aims to challenge the ethnicity-free assumptions behind normative white identity, and whose watchword is the "abolition of whiteness." The equivalent for gender politics challenges the state's division of the public and private spheres insofar as the division rests traditionally on masculine, proprietary privileges. As long as whiteness, masculinity, and heterosexuality are actively promoted by the state (through government spending, for example, that subsidizes suburbia, heterosexual families, and male breadwinning), this preferential treatment should be revealed and challenged. Last, we must recognize the profound anti-essentialist sentiments with which people decide to exclude themselves, in certain times and places and for a variety of reasons, from group membership. A group, after all, is defined as those who identify, partially or wholly, with some dominant notion of the unique qualities associated with group membership. In this context, the values and expectations associated with the politics of group identity may be perceived as a "trap" or a limitation on individual freedoms. Related to these sentiments, but less negative in its source impulse, is the recognition that we all have multiple identities at different times and places, and that the potential fullness of social and cultural life can be pursued only through this range of identities.

In my opinion, we cannot afford to abandon any of these forms of politics; claims for cultural justice must be able to draw strategically at various times on liberation politics, identity politics, anti-essentialism, and a politics that challenges state neutrality. Flexible communication between generations and communities demands it, no less than the long overdue rapprochement between the cultural and social justice wings of left-liberal thought. For too long, there has been a division between those concerned with justice claims relating primarily to gender, race, and sexuality and those concerned with economic issues. Group-differentiated rights will have to coexist along with innovative forms of class politics and libertarian protections. Among other things, such a coalition is the only way to prevent white male interests from dominating class politics and middle-class interests from dominating cultural politics. The managers of the United States' representative institutions have often been more willing to grant political than economic democracy, since symbolic reform is less of a concession than the redistribution of material wealth. On the other hand, many people increasingly feel their right to recognition of their cultural identities almost as strongly as they seek the benefits of the social wage. In many cases, such recognition is a prerequisite to the economic and social benefits that result from redistribution. Cultural recognition, as Iris Marion Young has pointed out, plays a visible role in the division of labor and the decisions that are made about the geography of investment and the organization of production. Material inequalities are as much the primary target of identity politics as of class politics. Identity recognition, even when it purports to be an end in and of itself, is usually always a means to a material end.[21] It takes a great deal of effort to separate the one from the other—effort that is surely better spent in the common pursuit of goals.

Notes to Chapter 1

1. In March 1997, name.space, owned by pgMedia, Inc. of New York, sued Network Solutions, Inc. in U.S. Federal District Court for antitrust and conspiracy to commit antitrust (http://namespace.xs2.net/ns./legal.html). The case sought inclusion of the nearly four hundred new top-level names served by name.space, and proclaimed to be in the public domain, in the ROOT.ZONE file controlled by NSI.

2. The widespread tendency to demonize Internet activities as a breeding ground for inaccurate information, rumor, and heady conspiracy theory of all stripes was compounded in May 1997 by the *San Jose Mercury News* editor's retraction of support for Gary Webb's infamous articles and documentation, posted for all to see on the newspaper's Web site, about the CIA's alleged smuggling and distribution of crack cocaine into poor Los Angeles neighborhoods. For details on the stories and the backlash against the *Mercury News*, see Alexander Cockburn and Jeffrey St. Clair, *White-Out: The CIA, Drugs and the Press* (New York: Verso, 1997).

3. Coopers and Lybrand, *New York New Media Industry Survey: Opportunities and Challenges of New York's Emerging Cyber-Industry* (New York: New Media Association, 1996).

4. Juliet Schor, *The Overworked American: The Unexpected Decline of Leisure* (New York: Basic Books, 1991).

5. Doug Henwood, "Info Fetishism," in James Brook and Iain Boale, eds., *Resisting the Virtual Life: The Culture and Politics of Information* (San Francisco: City Lights, 1996), 168.

6. AnnaLee Saxenian, *Regional Advantage: Culture and Competition in Silicon Valley and Route 128* (Cambridge, Mass: Harvard University Press, 1996).

7. Barbara Garson, *The Electronic Sweatshop* (New York: Simon and Schuster, 1988).

8. Ivan Illich, *Energy and Equity* (New York: Harper and Row, 1974), 30.

9. Ibid., 39.

10. See Andrew Ross, "Getting Out of the Gernsback Continuum," in *Strange Weather: Culture, Science, and Technology in the Age of Limits* (London: Verso, 1991), 101–36.

11. Wolfgang Sachs, "Wasting Time Is an Ecological Virtue," *New Perspectives Quarterly* 14, 1 (winter 1997): 8.

12. Al Gore, *Earth in the Balance: Ecology and the Human Spirit* (New York: Houghton Mifflin, 1992), 358–89 (hereafter cited as *EB*).

13. See Dennis Hayes, "Digital Palsy: RSI and Restructuring Capital," in Brooke and Boale, *Resisting the Virtual Life*, 173–80: and idem, *Behind the Silicon Curtain: The Seductions of Work in a Lonely Era* (Boston: South End Press, 1989).

Notes to Chapter 2

1. Michael Manley, introduction to Stephen Davis and Peter Simon, *Reggae International* (New York: Rogner and Bernhard, 1982), 13.

2. Dick Hebdige, *Cut 'n' Mix: Culture, Identity, and Caribbean Music* (London: Methuen, 1987), 110.

3. Other signatories included Tony Rebel, Beres Hammond, Sly Dunbar, Mikey General, Gussie Clarke, Lloyd Stanbury, Scotty, Richie Daley, Ibo Cooper, and Jessie Jendeu.

4. Famous rivalries have included Prince Buster vs. Derrick Morgan, Jazzbo vs. I Roy, and Beenie Man vs. Bounti Killer, to choose three different periods.

5. *Vibe* 74 (December 1995).

6. Elsie Le Franc, *Consequences of Structural Adjustment: A Review of the Jamaican Experience* (Kingston: Canoe Press, 1994); Tom Barry, Beth Wood, and Deb Preusch, *The Darker Side of Paradise: Foreign Control in the Caribbean* (New York: Grove, 1984); Norman Girvan and Richard Bernal, "The IMF and the Foreclosure of Development Options: The Case of Jamaica," *Monthly Review* 33, 9 (1982): 34–48.

7. See Belinda Edmondson, "Trinidad Romance: The Invention of Jamaican Carnival," in Belinda Edmondson, ed., *Caribbean Romances: The Politics of Regional Representation* (Charlottesville: University Press of Virginia, 1998). Edmondson describes how two rival processions contested the direction of Jamaican carnival from the beginning—one confined to Uptown, the other incorporating more Jamaican music and snaking down Half Way Tree Road.

8. Anita Waters, *Race, Class, and Political Symbols: Rastafari and Reggae in Jamaican Politics* (New Brunswick: Transaction, 1985).

9. Michael Manley gives an engrossing account of these years in his own political memoir, *Jamaica: Struggle in the Periphery* (London: Third World Media/ Writers and Readers, 1982).

10. Paul Gilroy, *There Ain't No Black in the Union Jack: The Cultural Politics of Race and Nation* (London: Century Hutchinson, 1987), 188.

11. Carolyn Cooper, *Noises in the Blood: Orality, Gender, and the "Vulgar" Body of Jamaican Popular Culture* (Durham: Duke University Press, 1995), 136–73.

12. Just when Uptown residents had gotten used to the sound of reggae in the night air, dancehall's more cacophonous style rose above the cicada chorus, reviving the conflict initiated by Marley himself when he moved into his Hope Street residence and sang, "I want to disturb my neighbors." See Cooper's comments in *Noises in the Blood*, 5.

13. Frank Owen, "In Praise of Slackness," *Village Voice*, June 13, 1995, 63.

14. Most incongruous was the infamous New York Police Department report on "Rasta Crime" published in the *Caribbean Review* 14, 1 (1985).

15. Laurie Gunst, *Born Fi' Dead: A Journey through the Jamaican Posse Underworld* (New York: Henry Holt, 1995), 161.

16. There is virtually no literature on homosexuality in Jamaica. Two reports by Barry Chevannes contain relevant comments and information: *Sexual Practices and Behavior in Jamaica* (Washington, DC: Academy for Educational Development, 1992), a report linked to AIDS prevention and control: and *Jamaican Men* (Kingston, Jamaica: N.P., 1985), a report to the National Family Planning Board on Jamaican male sexual behavior.

17. Isaac Julien's film *Black to the Future* (1994) presents an incisive commentary on the cultural politics of the dancehall scene, most notably on the issue of homophobia. Also see Inge Blackman's film about dancehall girls, *Ragga Gal D'bout!*

18. Peter Noel, "Batty Boys in Babylon," *Village Voice*, January 12, 1993.

19. Carolyn Cooper, "'Lyrical Gun': Metaphor and Role Play in Jamaican Dancehall Culture," *Massachusetts Review* 35 (autumn-winter 1994): 429–47.

20. The Fugees have produced a body of songs that speak more or less directly to the transnational experience of Caribbean migrants, or "refugees" in their Haitian context. Their version of the Wailers' "No Women No Cry," set in Brooklyn, and their version of "Killing Me Softly with Your Song," which riffs on the "soundboy killing" of rival DJs, are brilliant examples of the transcultural exchange and superimposition of U.S./Caribbean meanings.

21. See George Lipsitz, *Dangerous Crossings* (London: Verso, 1995).

22. See Philip Kasinitz, *Caribbean New York: Black Immigrants and the Politics of Race* (Ithaca: Cornell University Press, 1992); Constance Sutton and Elsa

Chaney, eds., *Caribbean Life in New York City: Sociocultural Dimensions* (New York: Center of Migration Studies, 1987); and Nancy Foner, ed., *New Immigrants in New York* (New York: Columbia University Press, 1987).

23. Nancy Foner, *Jamaican Migrants; A Comparative Analysis of the New York/London Experience* (New York: Center for Latin American and Caribbean Studies, New York University, 1983).

24. A. Lynn Bolles, "Kitchens Hit by Priorities: Employed Working-Class Jamaican Women Confront the IMF," in June Nash and Maria-Patricia Fernandez-Kelly, eds., *Women, Men and the International Division of Labor* (Albany: SUNY Press, 1983), 138–60. Peggy Antrobus, "Employment of Women Workers in the Caribbean" (Barbados: Women and Development, University of West Indies, 1979).

25. Kathy McAfee gives an exhaustive account of these developments in *Storm Signals: Structural Adjustment and Development Alternatives in the Caribbean* (Boston: South End Press, 1991). See also Cynthia Enloe, *The Morning After: Sexual Politics at the End of the Cold War* (Berkeley: University of California Press, 1993), 102–43; and Peggy Antrobus, *Structural Adjustment: Curse or Cure? Implications for Caribbean Development* (Barbados: University of West Indies, 1989).

26. Linda Y. C. Lim, "Capitalism, Imperialism and Patriarchy: The Dilemma of Third World Women Workers in Multinational Factories," in Nash and Fernandez-Kelly, *Women, Men, and the International Division of Labor*, 70–91.

27. Faye Harrison, "Women in Jamaica's Urban Informal Economy: Insights from a Kingston Slum," in Chandra Talpade Mohanty, Ann Russo, and Lourdes Torres, eds., *Third World Women and the Politics of Feminism* (Bloomington: Indiana University Press, 1991), 173–96.

28. Le Franc, *Consequences of Structural Adjustment*, 52.

29. Jacqui Alexander, "Not Just (Any)Body Can Be a Citizen: The Politics of Law, Sexuality and Postcoloniality in Trinidad and Tobago and the Bahamas," *Feminist Review* 48 (autumn 1994): 5–23; and idem, "Redrafting Morality: The Postcolonial State and the Sexual Offenses Bill of Trinidad and Tobago," in Mohanty, Russo, and Torres, *Third World Women*, 133–96.

30. Barry Chevannes, *Rastafari: Roots and Ideology* (Syracuse: Syracuse University Press, 1994); Horace Campbell, *Rasta and Resistance: From Marcus Garvey to Walter Rodney* (Trenton: Africa World Press, 1987); M. G. Smith, F. R. Augier, and Rex Nettleford, *The Rastafari Movement in Kingston, Jamaica* (Mona: ISER, University of West Indies, 1960); Rex Nettleford, "African Redemption: The Rastafari and the Wider Society 1959–1969," in *Mirror Mirror: Identity, Race, and Protest in Jamaica* (Kingston, Jamaica: William Collins and Sangster, 1970); Dennis Forsythe, *Rastafari: For the Healing of the Nation* (Kingston: Zaika, 1983).

Notes to Chapter 5

1. The California Appellate Court had issued conflicting rulings about the admissibility of the techniques, but was still adhering to the vague criteria of the *Frye* test for its rulings. The 1923 Washington, DC, case of *Frye v. United States* (293 F.2d 1013 [D.C. Cir.]) had established a precedent for adjudicating the line between "the experimental and the demonstrable stages" of a science, whereby a conservative duration must have lapsed between discovery of a scientific procedure and its forensic application. While the newer techniques of the PCR (polymerase chain reaction) amplification method were at issue, concerns related to the older techniques of RFLP (restriction fragment length polymorphism) analysis were also presented by the O.J. defense team. Evidence based on both techniques was eventually admitted in the trial.

By the time of the O.J. trial, some states, but not California, had adopted the approach favored by the decision in *Daubert v. Merrell Dow Pharmaceuticals, Inc.* (113 S. Ct. 2786, [1993]), which called for a more sophisticated and informed analysis of scientific evidence than *Frye* had done. The *Daubert* decision was against *Frye*'s traditional bias toward peer review and general scientific acceptance, and it reaffirmed the discretionary power of judges to assess the relevance of the scientific evidence to the case in reviewing its admissibility.

2. See Dorothy Nelkin and Susan Lindee, *The DNA Mystique: The Gene as a Cultural Icon* (New York: Freeman and Co., 1996).

3. Troy Duster, *Backdoor to Eugenics* (New York: Routledge, 1990), 99–100.

4. 545 N.Y.S. 2d 985 (Sup. Ct. 1989).

5. National Research Council, *The Evaluation of DNA Forensic Evidence* (Washington, DC: National Academy Press, 1996), Overview, 28.

6. R. C. Lewontin, *Biology as Ideology: The Doctrine of DNA* (New York: HarperCollins, 1992), 79–82.

7. William F. Buckley, "O.J. on Our Mind," *National Review* 47, 12 (June 26, 1995): 71.

8. Cited in an editorial, *Atlanta Journal and Constitution* October 4, 1995, 13A.

9. *Madam Foreman: A Rush to Judgement?* featuring Armanda Cooley, Carrie Bess, and Marsha Rubin-Jackson (Beverly Hills, CA: Dove Books, 1995), 75 (cited hereafter in the text as *MF*).

10. Barry Scheck, "DNA and *Daubert*," *Cardozo Law Review* 15 (1994): 1959–97.

11. Lawrence Tribe, "Trial by Mathematics: Precision and Ritual in the Legal Process," *Harvard Law Review* 84 (1971): 1329.

12. Marjorie Maguire Schultz, "Reasons for Doubt: Legal Issues in the Use of DNA Identification," in Paul R. Billings, ed., *DNA on Trial: Genetic Identification and Criminal Justice* (Plainview, NY: Cold Spring Harbor Laboratory Press, 1992), 20.

13. Sheila Jasanoff, *Science at the Bar: Law, Science, and Technology in America* (Cambridge: Harvard University Press, 1995).

14. Rochelle Cooper Dreyfuss and Dorothy Nelkin, "The Jurisprudence of Genetics," *Vanderbilt Law Review* 45, 2 (March 1992): 313–48.

15. Ian Haney Lopez, *White by Law* (New York: New York University Press, 1996).

16. R. C. Lewontin and D. C. Hartl, "Population Genetics Problems in the Forensic Use of DNA Profiles," *Science* 254 (1991): 1745.

17. See Ranajit Chakraborty and Kenneth Kidd, "The Utility of DNA Typing in Forensic Work," *Science* 254 (1991): 1735; Bruce Weir, "Population Genetics in the Forensic DNA Debate," 89 *Proceedings of the National Academy of Sciences* 11,654 (1992); William Thompson, "Evaluating the Admissibility of New Genetic Identification Tests: Lessons from the DNA Wars," 84 *Journal of Criminal Law and Criminology* 22 (1993), 42–61.

18. National Research Council, *DNA Technology in Forensic Science* (Washington, DC: National Academy Press, 1992). Scheck points out that "since the NRC report was published, the overwhelming number of appellate decisions in Fyre jurisdictions have rejected methods used by the major forensic laboratories for making statistical estimates, and along with it, the DNA evidence." Scheck, "DNA and *Daubert*," 1965.

19. Ruth Hubbard and Elijah Wald, *Exploding the Gene Myth* (Boston: Beacon Press, 1993), 151.

20. Eric Lander and Bruce Budowle, "DNA Fingerprinting Dispute Laid to Rest," *Nature* 371 (1994): 735; and letters from R. C. Lewontin and Daniel Hartl, *Nature* 372 (1994): 398–99.

21. In fact, the 1996 report concludes that while "virtually all populations will show some statistically significant departures from random mating proportions . . . many of the differences will be small enough to be practically unimportant." NRC, *Evaluation of DNA*, 1–11. The U.S. group that showed the most marked internal variation—a "statistically significant departure"—is American Indian; there do not yet exist adequate databases for many Native peoples.

22. Paul Rabinow, "Galton's Regret: Of Types and Individuals," in Billings, *DNA on Trial*, 6. See also idem, *Making PCR: A Story of Biotechnology* (Chicago: University of Chicago Press, 1996), in which Rabinow analyzes the commercial development of the polymerase-chain reaction process.

23. The Council for Responsible Genetics and the ACLU have filed an amicus brief in the lawsuit challenging the building of Defense Department databanks.

24. Philip Bereano, "The Impact of DNA-Based Identification Systems on Civil Liberties," in Billings, *DNA on Trial*, 121.

25. Federal Bureau of Investigation, *VNTR Population Data: A Worldwide Survey* (1993); and numerous studies published by Bruce Budowle et al., in the *American Journal of Human Genetics* and the *Journal of Forensic Science* from 1992 to 1995. Even more extensive efforts to classify the genetic range of race have been initiated in the Human Genome Diversity Project, under the auspices of Stanford University.

26. Rabinow, "Galton's Regret," 17.

27. For all of the advances in DNA databasing, the degree of human genetic diversity assignable to racial difference has not changed much since Lewontin provided the estimate of 6.3 percent in 1972. He ended his study with the following proposal: "Human racial classification is of no social value and is positively destructive of social and human relations. Since such racial classification is now seen to be of virtually no genetic or taxonomic significance either, no justification can be offered for its continuance." "The Apportionment of Human Diversity," *Evolutionary Biology* 6 (1972): 397. In his letter in *Nature*, he points out that the FBI's research efforts in the field of DNA typing would be better devoted to producing "idiotypes," or unique genetic identifications, rather than the system it has developed, which requires reference to racial groupings.

Notes to Chapter 6

1. Some of this history is recounted in Lucy Lippard's books, especially *Get the Message? A Decade of Art for Social Change* (New York: Dutton, 1984) and *The Pink Glass Swan: Selected Feminist Essays on Art* (New York: New Press, 1995).

2. For a documentary of alternative arts spaces in New York City, see the catalog for *Cultural Economies: Histories from the Alternative Arts Movement, NYC*, organized by Julie Ault, at the Drawing Center, 1996.

3. Elizabeth Hess, "Guerrilla Girl Power: Why the Art World Needs a Conscience," in Nina Felshin, ed., *But Is It Art? The Spirit of Art as Activism* (Seattle: Bay Press, 1995), 327.

4. Tony Bennett, *The Birth of the Museum: History, Theory, and Politics* (London: Routledge, 1996); and Carol Duncan, *Civilizing Rituals: Inside Public Art Museums* (London: Routledge, 1995). My descriptive account of the nineteenth-century museum draws liberally on their work.

5. Bennett, *Birth of the Museum*, 91ff.

6. Duncan, *Civilizing Rituals*, 48–71.

7. Ibid., 63.

8. Michael Fitzgerald, *Making Modernism: Picasso and the Creation of the Market for Twentieth-Century Art* (New York: Farrar, Straus and Giroux, 1995).

9. Until recently, security guards have been the only people of color, aside from school groups, likely to be seen in museums. Notable among the artists who have focused on security components of the museum institution are Julia Scher and Fred Wilson.

10. Reesa Greenberg, "The Exhibition Redistributed," in Reesa Greenberg, Bruce Ferguson, Sandy Nairne, eds., *Thinking about Exhibitions* (New York: Routledge, 1995), 362.

11. Neil Harris, "A Historical Perspective on Museum Advocacy," in *Cultural Excursions: Marketing Appetites and Cultural Tastes in Modern America* (Chicago: University of Chicago Press, 1990), 82–95.

12. Neil Harris, "Museums, Merchandising, and Popular Taste," in *Cultural Excursions*, 56–81.

13. Bennett, *Birth of the Museum*, 59–87. George Brown Goode's classic volume is *The Principles of Museum Administration* (York: Coultas and Volans, 1895).

14. Quoted in Faye Levine, *The Culture Barons: An Analysis of Power and Money in the Arts* (New York: Thomas Crowell, 1976), 150.

15. Faith Davis Ruffins, "Mythos, Memory, and History," in Ivan Karp, Christine Mullen Kreamer, and Stephen Lavine, eds., *Museums and Communities* (Washington, DC: Smithsonian Institution Press, 1992), 574.

16. David Finn, *How to Visit a Museum* (New York: Harry Abrams, 1985), 10.

17. The different kinds of social access experienced in museum going by disparate groups is examined in Pierre Bourdieu, Alain Darbel, et al., *The Love of Art: European Art Museums and Their Public* (Palo Alto: Stanford University Press, 1969).

18. Jean Clair, interview by Lauren Sedosky, *Artforum*, April 1995, 26, 106.

19. Leslie Camhi, "Stealing Femininity: Department Store Kleptomania as Sexual Disorder," *Differences* 5, 1 (1993): 26–50.

20. See Malek Alloula, *The Colonial Harem*, trans. Myrna Godzich and Wlad Godzich (Minneapolis: University of Minnesota Press, 1986), 7–15, and introduction by Barbara Harlow.

21. Philips Verner Bradford and Harvey Blume, *Ota Benga: The Pygmy in the Zoo* (New York: Dell/Delta, 1992). Thanks to Steve Feld for this example. See his "Pygmy POP: A Genealogy of Schizophrenic Mimesis," *Yearbook for Traditional Music*, vol. 28 (New York: International Council for Traditional Music, 1996), 1–35.

22. Guillermo Gómez-Peña, *Warrior for Gringostroika* (Saint Paul: Graywolf Press, 1993), 33.

23. Maria Ramirez, "Brokering Identities: Art Curators and the Politics of Cultural Representation," in Greenberg, Ferguson, and Nairne, *Thinking About Exhibitions*, 21–38.

Notes to Chapter 7

1. Daniel Boorstin, "Statistical Communities," in *The Americans: The Democratic Experience* (New York: Vintage, 1973), 165–244.

2. Joyce Nelson, *Sultans of Sleaze: Public Relations and the Media* (Toronto: Between the Lines Press, 1989), 74; and Roland Perry, *Hidden Power* (New York: Beaufort Books, 1984).

3. See the project layout at the Dia Center for the Arts Web site (http://www.diacenter.org/km/project/).

4. See Paul Willis, *Common Culture: Symbolic Work at Play in the Everyday Cultures of the Young* (Boulder: Westview Press, 1990).

5. See Joanne Wypijewski, ed., *Painting by Numbers: Komar and Melamid's Scientific Guide to Art* (New York: Farrar, Straus and Giroux, 1997), 9.

6. "The Search for a People's Art," *Nation*, March 14, 1994, 334.

Notes to Chapter 8

1. C. B. MacPherson, *Democratic Theory: Essays in Retrieval* (Oxford: Clarendon Press, 1973), 16–19.

2. See William Ophuls, *Ecology and the Politics of Scarcity* (San Francisco: Freeman, 1977). Other writers drawing on the neo-Malthusian tradition have emphasized the link between natural limits and the concomitant need for social limitations. Garret Hardin, *The Limits to Altruism: An Ecologist's View of Survival* (Bloomington: Indiana University Press, 1977); Donald Worster and Paul Ehrlich, *The Population Bomb* (London: Pan/Ballantine, 1972); William Catton, *Overshoot: The Ecological Basis of Revolutionary Change* (Urbana: University of Illinois Press, 1980); George Bergstrom, *The Hungry Planet: The Modern World at the Edge of Famine* (New York: Macmillan, 1965).

3. David Roediger, *The Wages of Whiteness: Race and the Making of the American Working Class* (London: Verso, 1991), 43–94.

4. Frances Fox Piven and Richard Cloward, *Regulating the Poor: The Functions of Public Welfare* (New York: Vintage, 1971, updated 1993).

5. See Jim Hightower's exposé of the state-corporate nexus in food, *Eat Your Heart Out: Food Profiteering in America* (New York: Crown, 1975).

6. Harvey Levenstein, *Paradox of Plenty: A Social History of Eating in Modern America* (New York: Oxford University Press, 1993).

7. David Potter, *People of Plenty* (Chicago: University of Chicago Press, 1954), 136.

8. Levenstein, *Paradox of Plenty*, 22–23.

9. Ibid., 98–100, 81.

10. Martin Pawley, *Building for Tomorrow: Putting Waste to Work* (San Francisco: Sierra Club Books, 1982).

11. With manufacturers required to build into their products full life-cycle responsibility for waste management, Germany's wholesale adoption of the polluter-pays model stands in stark contrast to the EPA's weak voluntary standards. See Bette Fishbein, *Germany, Garbage, and the Green Dot: Challenging the Throwaway Society* (New York: Inform, 1994).

12. Mead, cited in Levenstein, *Paradox of Plenty*, 72.

13. See Mary Douglas, *Purity and Danger: An Analysis of Concepts of Pollution and Taboo* (London: Routledge and Kegan Paul, 1966); and Mary Douglas and Aaron Wildavsky, *Risk and Culture* (Berkeley: University of California Press, 1982).

14. Sidney Mintz, "Eating American," in *Tasting Food, Tasting Freedom: Excursions into Eating, Culture, and the Past* (Boston: Beacon Press, 1996), 106–24.

15. See Manning Marable, *How Capitalism Underdeveloped Black America* (Boston: South End Press, 1983).

16. Eduardo Galeano, *The Open Veins of Latin America: Five Centuries of the Pillage of a Continent* (New York: Monthly Review Press, 1973), 53.

17. Francis Moore Lappé and Joseph Collins, *Food First: Beyond the Myth of Scarcity* (Boston: Houghton Mifflin, 1977), 22.

18. See Kevin Watkins, "Free Trade and Farm Fallacies: From the Uruguay Round to the World Food Summit," and Nicholas Hildyard and Sarah Sexton, "Too Many for What? The Social Generation of Food 'Scarcity' and 'Overpopulation,'" *Ecologist* 26, 6 (November–December 1996): 244–55 and 282–89.

19. Nicholas Xenos, *Scarcity and Modernity* (London: Routledge, 1989).

20. Lester Brown, *Who Will Feed China?* (Washington, DC: Worldwatch Institute, 1995).

21. See Donna Haraway, "Teddy Bear Patriarchy," in *Simians, Cyborgs and Women* (New York: Routledge, 1991).

22. T. Jackson Lears, *Fables of Abundance: A Cultural History of Advertising in America* (New York: Basic Books, 1994), 166–200.

23. Frances Moore Lappé and Joseph Collins, *World Hunger: Twelve Myths* (New York: Grove Weidenfeld, 1986); idem, *Aid as Obstacle: Twenty Questions about Our Foreign Aid and the Hungry* (San Francisco: Institute for Food and Development Policy, 1980).

24. See Kathy McAfee, *Storm Signals: Structural Adjustment and Development Alternatives in the Caribbean* (Boston: South End Press, 1991); Walden Bello, *Dark Victory: The United States, Structural Adjustment, and Global Poverty* (London: Pluto Press, 1994).

25. See Michael Watts, *Silent Violence: Food, Famine, and Peasantry in Northern Nigeria* (Berkeley: University of California Press, 1983); Amartya Sen, *Poverty and Famines: An Essay on Entitlement and Deprivation* (New York: Oxford University Press, 1981); Catherine Lezra and Michael Jacobson, *Food for People, Not for Profit* (New York: Ballantine, 1975).

26. George Kent, *The Political Economy of Hunger: The Silent Holocaust* (New York: Praeger, 1984), 148.

27. See Sanford Schram's discourse analysis of these categories in *Words of Welfare: The Poverty of Social Science and the Social Science of Poverty* (Minneapolis: University of Minnesota Press, 1995).

Notes to Chapter 9

1. See, for example, the exchange between Nancy Fraser and Iris Marion Young in *New Left Review*, nos. 222 (March–April 1997) and 223 (May–June 1997).

2. See Will Kymlicka, *Multicultural Citizenship* (Oxford: Oxford University Press, 1995); and Will Kymlicka, ed., *The Rights of Minority Cultures* (Oxford: Oxford University Press, 1995). Generally speaking, Kymlicka's concern is to show how liberal theory *can*, in fact, accommodate certain kinds of group rights in response to the challenge of minority claims.

3. Amy Gutman, ed., *Multiculturalism: Examining the Politics of Recognition* (Princeton: Princeton University Press, 1994).

4. Nancy Fraser, "From Redistribution to Recognition: Dilemmas of Justice in a 'Postsocialist' Age," in *Justice Interruptus: Critical Reflections on the "Postsocialist" Condition* (New York: Routledge, 1997), 11–40.

5. Kymlicka, *Multicultural Citizenship*, 108.

6. Stephen Steinberg, *Turning Back: The Retreat from Racial Justice in American Thought and Policy* (Boston: Beacon Press, 1995).

7. The growing scholarship on "whiteness," some calling for its "abolition," is a relevant body of literature: Toni Morrison, *Playing in the Dark: Whiteness and*

the Literary Imagination (Cambridge: Harvard University Press, 1992); David Roediger, *Towards the Abolition of Whiteness* (New York: Verso, 1994); John Harvey and Noel Ignatiev, eds. *Race Traitor* (New York: Routledge, 1996); Theodore Allen, *The Invention of the White Race* (New York: Verso, 1994); Ruth Frankenberg, *White Women, Race Matters; The Social Construction of Whiteness* (Minneapolis: University of Minnesota Press, 1993); Shelley Fisher Fishkin, *Was Huck Black? Mark Twain and African-American Voices* (New York: Oxford University Press, 1993); Alexander Saxton, *The Rise and Fall of the White Republic* (New York: Verso, 1992); Michael Rogin, *Blackface, White Noise: Jewish Immigrants in the Hollywood Melting Pot* (Berkeley: University of California Press, 1996); Melvin Oliver and Thomas Shapiro, *Black Wealth/White Wealth: A New Perspective on Racial Inequality* (New York: Routledge, 1995); Cheryl Harris, "Whiteness as Property," *Harvard Law Review* 106 (June 1993); George Lipsitz, "The Possessive Investment in Whiteness" (and other essays in the same issue), *American Quarterly* 47, 3 (September 1995): 369–87.

8. Patricia Williams, *The Alchemy of Race and Rights* (Cambridge: Harvard University Press, 1991), 165.

9. Girardeau Spann, *Race against the Court: The Supreme Court and Minorities in Contemporary America* (New York: New York University Press, 1993), chap. 8.

10. *Freeman v. Pitts*, 112 S. Ct. 1430 (1992).

11. David Roediger, *The Wages of Whiteness: Race and the Making of the American Working Class* (London: Verso, 1991).

12. See Cary Nelson, ed., *Will Teach for Food* (Minneapolis: University of Minnesota Press, 1997): and idem, *Manifesto of a Tenured Radical* (New York: New York University Press, 1997); and the special *Social Text* issue on academic labor, summer 1997.

13. Andrew Ross, ed., *No Sweat: Fashion, Free Trade and the Rights of Garment Workers* (New York: Verso, 1997).

14. Guillermo Gómez-Peña, "The New World Border: Prophecies for the End of the Century," *Drama Review* 38 (spring 1994): 119–42.

15. David Hollinger. *Postethnic America: Beyond Multiculturalism* (New York: Basic Books, 1995).

16. See Anthony Appiah, "Identity, Authenticity, Survival: Multicultural Societies and Social Reproduction," in Gutman, *Multiculturalism*, 149–64.

17. The most succinct formulation can be found in Charles Murray and Richard Herrnstein, "Race, Genes and I.Q.—An Apologia," *New Republic*, October 31, 1994, 27–37.

18. Etienne Balibar, "Is There a 'Neo-Racism'? in Etienne Balibar and Immanuel Wallerstein, *Race, Nation, Class* (London: Verso, 1993).

19. Much of the genre (and much more respectable than *The Bell Curve*) is channeled through the new field of evolutionary psychology. See Robert Wright, *The Moral Animal: Why We Are the Way We Are: The New Science of Evolutionary Psychology* (New York: Pantheon, 1994); or Matt Ridley, *The Origins of Virtue: Human Instincts and the Evolution of Cooperation* (New York: Viking, 1997).

20. See Lisa Duggan, "Queering the State," *Social Text* 39 (summer 1994): 1–14.

21. See Iris Marion Young, "Unruly Categories: A Critique of Nancy Fraser's Dual Systems Theory," *New Left Review* 222 (March–April 1997): 147–60.

About the Author

Andrew Ross is professor and director of the graduate program in American studies at New York University. His books include *The Chicago Gangster Theory of Life* (1994), *Strange Weather* (1991), and *No Respect* (1989). He has also edited/coedited *No Sweat: Fashion, Free Trade, and the Rights of Garment Workers* (1997), *Science Wars* (1996), *Microphone Fiends* (1994), *Techno-Culture* (1991), and *Universal Abandon?* (1988). His cultural and political journalism has been widely published.